Over the years, humanity has nurtured a camouflaged, ever-growing beast that keeps devouring the life forces of many through the world's acceptance of destructive competitions, soul-sucking expectations, and a dubious promise of a perfect future at the cost of appreciation for the present. The result is a collective waste of years and an endless supply of pain and suffering. Coming from Geoff Keall who has persevered through Celiac's disease, a family crisis arising from the actions of a pedophile, and a serious injury, The Semantics of I AM delivers a guide to ending suffering. Geoff Keall shares his insights about capitalism, moving from New Zealand to Australia, managing the long-term effects of multi-generational sexual abuse, living and working with forestry employees from different backgrounds, and arriving at a liberating realization.

Wow! What a book! With the magnitude of the revelations and the eloquence and artfulness of the delivery in his book, it is evident that Geoff Keall practices his preaching of creating beauty out of abundance as opposed to lack and desperation. The Semantics of I AM is so deep and packed with knowledge that I would love to read it over and over again. Geoff Keall's book is for those who have tried different self-help books and several other things and still feel they are not where they need to be. It proposes a new way of thinking, which has challenged the foundations of my beliefs.

Approach The Semantics of I AM with an open mind, rapt attention, and a readiness to question your life values.

The Semantics
of i AM

LEAVING YOUR PAST—LOVING YOUR FUTURE

GEOFF KEALL

BALBOA.PRESS
A DIVISION OF HAY HOUSE

Balboa Press books may be ordered through booksellers or by contacting:

Balboa Press
A Division of Hay House
1663 Liberty Drive
Bloomington, IN 47403
www.balboapress.com.au
AU TFN: 1 800 844 925 (Toll Free inside Australia)
AU Local: 0283 107 086 (+61 2 8310 7086 from outside Australia)

Print information available on the last page.

ISBN: 978-1-9822-9006-1 (sc)
ISBN: 978-1-9822-9007-8 (e)

Balboa Press rev. date: 04/16/2021

I dedicate this book to Cheryl, who not only suffered all those years ago but also endured the journey with me while I searched for justice where none existed. To my daughter Sarah, who has grown steadily stronger since that fateful day when she was nine and told it was all a dream. I'm sorry you're there in New Zealand, while we're here; you're so brave. And to our three sons, Jason, Brendon and Aaron, forgive me for changing your lives immeasurably fourteen years ago. Dragging you from your childhood in New Zealand to another land because I needed to escape what seemed an impossible situation. You don't get to choose your parents or your childhood, but through it all you chose to build a solid foundation from which to grow. Thanks for the encouragement to write a book, I hope you all enjoy the snippets of your family history and discover insights useful to your own journeys through life. All that went before was necessary to bring me to this point of peace with my past. I hope this book helps you to find your own peace; after all, we are the thoughts we love. Without you along for the ride, it would've been a wasted journey. I am proud of you. With love always, Dad.

Like learning to walk, our ego is a habit learned unconsciously. In childhood, we choose our egos' relative value by interpreting feedback. Easily achieve calm by consciously changing this value.

CONTENTS

PREFACE

I WROTE THIS STORY FOR ANYONE WHO HAS UNSUCCESSFULLY TRIED to escape a maze of intolerable suffering and who feels he or she lacks what it takes to live in the modern world.

A search for meaning regarding repetitive, disruptive events in my life revealed that a change in perspective is the key to freeing us of the endless confusing pathways that all lead back to the same little house of horrors. Those pathways mercilessly mock us with memories of the moments in our life that confirm our deficiencies. The Semantics of i AM reveals an adaptive, holistic view of the world and our relationship with it, allowing us to approach life with effortless grace and gratitude.

I have broken the book in to three parts. Each part can be read in isolation, but the book flow is designed to be continuous. Part 1 is a subjective explanation of the constructed ego we know as our Christian name. Part 2 is the story of I Am Geoff, it covers the challenges during my life that led me to believe that to live is to be a victim, experiencing a never-ending struggle. I only include it to show that the approach discussed in part 3, has the power to lift you out of your own rut. I wrote part 3 first, in the summer of 2017/18. It is the central motivator for writing this book. It reveals the revelation that led to a new understanding, beginning a new and better view of what it is to be alive on this amazing planet we call Earth.

DEFINITIONS

Semantics: The study of meaning in language. (Language is a translation of sensory data into words.)

Semantics of i AM: Life experience arises from our use and understanding of language.

Servomechanism: an automatic device that uses error-sensing feedback to correct its actions.

INTRODUCTION

M Y MOTHER GAVE BIRTH TO ME—THE THIRD OF FIVE BOYS—IN 1958 in Pahiatua, a rural town in the North Island of New Zealand with a population of less than 3000 people. At the time Dad was a nurseryman and, unsurprisingly, Mum a full-time mother. Joyful times engaging in physical activities fill my early childhood memories. Like most boys growing up in NZ, I had a passion for sport, hero worshipping many rugby and cricket players like Chris Laidlaw and Glenn Turner, both prominent sportsmen during my childhood.

I signed up to play rugby, the national winter game, as soon as the rules allowed and played every winter until I suffered a serious knee injury when I was nineteen. Despite my enthusiasm for the game, being a thin and sickly child with chronic asthma, my only recognition was 'tries hard'. As a teen I suffered from intense stomach pain that was blamed on the stitch, but which turns out was a symptom of celiac disease, an autoimmune disease explaining why I was a pathologically thin, slow developer.

My brothers and I regularly got into mischief, whether setting Dad's garden shed alight, jumping off the rooftop water tank or shooting each other with spud guns, the technological wonder of the day. Occasionally, our wayward behaviour even led to a visit from the local police officer or other emergency service.

When I wasn't climbing roofs and setting fire to things, I loved to lose myself in the pages of a war comic or book—a popular genre of children's literature back in the 1960s. I read for enjoyment and loved action and adventure, science fiction books and sports biographies. *The Adventures of Tom Sawyer, The Wooden Horse, Lord of the Rings* and *Dune* were among my favourites.

But this carefree happiness didn't last. By the time I started high school, my outlook on life had transformed. The failure of my parents' marriage seemed to provide conclusive evidence that we live in a hostile world conspiring to trip us up, hell bent on making our life miserable. Now I was a fearful teenager, deciding that I was ill-equipped to survive—let alone thrive—on this unforgiving planet. Seeing myself as a victim through my own thoughts guaranteed that the negative in which I believed manifested in my life.

Years of schooling leaves no doubt in students' minds that we assess self-worth by comparing ourselves to our peers. In my estimation—the only one that really counts—I fell short on this assessment. So I started searching for the information that would close the gap, the elusive key unlocking the door to success. In the process I lost my habit of recreational reading. Being was no longer good enough, success required doing and forcing until becoming.

In our modern society, learning to read isn't about pleasure; our education is a social investment, provided in the hope that one day we'll contribute to the economy as employees. I became a voracious devourer of self-help books, combing every page for the secret formula that would empower me in all situations—a formula that would make me untouchable and stifle my deep feelings of inferiority and shame. Seduced by the hype of the eleven-billion-dollar self-development industry promising to make me better, I became convinced that success depended on learning what they taught—techniques and methods on how to fake it until you make it, be more competitive, successful and rich. 'More' was the mind virus of my generation.

Then, after a succession of unwelcome experiences, ten years ago I realised that my belief that self-improvement is a prerequisite to success is an oxymoron. A change to my childhood-formed beliefs that shaped my unquestioned foundational view of the world was all that was needed. The idea that we are failing because we need fixing reveals that our earliest seeded core beliefs result from wrong thought. Unsurprisingly, adding new techniques on top of faulty beliefs rarely achieves lasting improvement—a skyscraper built atop a faulty foundation eventually fails. No amount of meditation, affirmation programming or acting as if to form new and better beliefs can help displace the deeply rooted beliefs about who we think we are. Those beliefs will continue to define us, because we are unaware of them.

We are living according to a limited system we designed in response to a child's view of the world. These ingrained thoughts are the heart of us. Any new thoughts we form about ourselves are always subconsciously compared to the child I's beliefs about who we are, and if they are incongruent with the views we formed in childhood, they are ruthlessly rejected. I didn't believe I was worthy of success and happiness, and no self-help guru was going to convince me otherwise since as Samuel Butler said, 'A man convinced against his will is of the same opinion still.'

PART 1

I AM A CONSTRUCT

CHAPTER ONE

IN THE BEGINNING

MY LATE FATHER WAS THE FIRSTBORN IN A FOURTH-GENERATION family of six from Carterton, New Zealand. By the 1950s he'd moved to Pahiatua, where his own father had established a successful clothing store. After graduating from Wairarapa College in Masterton, he worked for a plant nursery, selling gardening supplies. Motivated by his Protestant religious ancestry, he soon became restless and left to train as a Methodist minister. His first posting was in Paeroa, a small town in the Coromandel where my second youngest brother was born, after which we moved to Northcote, a suburb of NZ's largest city, Auckland, where my youngest brother was born.

In 1962 Dad held the inaugural service at the new Northcote Central Methodist Church, which is still in active service. But his sympathies lay with the controversial views of Lloyd Geering, now Sir Lloyd George Geering, (ONZ, GNZM, CBE) leading to his irreconcilable falling out with church elders and our return to Pahiatua. Geering faced charges of heresy in 1967 for his views denying the immortality of the soul and the physical resurrection of Jesus. After a televised hearing in front of the Presbyterian General Assembly, they withdrew all charges. He later became Professor Emeritus at Victoria University of Wellington, where he still lives. He was knighted in 2001. Now aged 102, he has some twenty books to his name.

I fondly recall travelling by steam train from Auckland to Palmerston North as Dad's special companion (Mum and the rest of the family followed later.) Back then trains steamed down the middle of the main street, making for an impressive-but-sooty arrival. On his return to Pahiatua, Dad planned to open a gardening store, but Grandad initially employed him in his recently completed, purpose-built clothing store. He soon achieved his ambition; Sure-Gro Garden Supplies opened its doors in 1964. Mum and Dad operated this weather-dependent business throughout the 1960s, so after school my brothers and I called the shop home.

Opening another gardening supply store in town created some controversy with another operator. I overheard a conversation between Dad and his established opposition who threatened he'd eventually force Dad into bankruptcy.

Six years later, a major drought in the summer of '69 forced Dad to close Sure-Gro permanently, beginning a chain of events that would forever change our family's future. I recall being in the deserted store while Dad and Mr J, who'd made the threat several years before, negotiated a price for the saleable stock—stock once part of a dream he'd realised but now a symbol of a devastating failure from which he never recovered. Children aren't immune to the sense of gloom that descends with the death of a parent's dream. The accompanying feelings of grief are as real as those experienced with the passing of a loved one.

Major tangible and intangible change accompanied the business failure. Our family home, lovingly planned and built seven years earlier, was sold to cover debts, and so we became renters again. Rental accommodation for families in NZ is not a stable, long-term living solution, so shifting homes at least once a year became our new normal. Considering these events occurred in a modern, capitalist economy, unsurprisingly we joined the ranks of the poor. Dad immediately left for Auckland to find work and urgently needed income—and maybe to escape the shame he felt. Because of his menswear experience, he tried his luck at Hugh Wright Ltd, a popular menswear store founded in 1904. Wrights had no vacancies, but he persisted, and although Hugh Jr was a tough nut to crack, he somehow secured full-time employment.

In April 1970, during my second-to-last year of primary school, Mum, Dad, three of my four brothers and I travelled the 600km by overnight train to Auckland. By now the steam train had given way to diesel and the track moved from the town centre to its outskirts, signalling an end to the heydays of rail. My eldest brother (sixteen) had finished college and chose to stay behind, boarding with friends. We rented a house at 10 Seine Road, Forrest Hill—a growing suburb, northeast of Northcote—though our new life was anything but sane. I attended the recently opened Takapuna Intermediate School, where classes were collegiate style with an unfamiliar system of rotating classes and teachers. I was used to one room, one teacher for an entire year. After school I was in for another surprise. I knew I'd have to catch a bus home, but which one? It seemed as if there were more buses to choose from than children! Inevitably, panicked in the confusion, I got on the wrong one. After travelling for what seemed like forever, I finally realised this wasn't the way home and decided I'd better get off. Having no idea where I was and becoming more and more distressed, I retraced the route as well as I could. Then, when I'd all but given up on finding my way back home, I saw my elder brother's welcome face walking toward me. I'd never been so happy to see him!

The Milford rental house was small, having only two bedrooms, so my brothers and I slept in the same room. Every night while falling asleep, we heard Mum and Dad squabbling, dredging up past issues and making accusations, leaving us feeling sad and anxious. Six months later, Dad convinced Hugh Wright to open a branch store in Palmerston North, making him manager. It thrilled us to hear that we'd be moving south again, back to more familiar surroundings, hoping it would make our parents happy again. In August 1970, rather than catching the train again for the long ride back to Palmy, Dad hired a new Holden Kingswood car—so exciting. We drove for the first time on State Highway One, New Zealand's main road, which traversed some of the most remarkable landscapes in the world. The winding nine-hour trip from Auckland took us past the majestic snow-capped Mt Ruapehu (2797m) to Palmerston North (or Palmy; Maori, Te Papa-i-Oea), where we would start the third and last term at our third school of the year.

Palmy is cold, wet, but fortunately flat. We didn't own a car or have access to an urban school-bus service, so every day I'd ride three kilometres to and from school in one of the world's windiest climates. Most days I wore a cheap, grey, thin plastic windbreaker that doubled as a raincoat; it was all we could afford. One especially cold, wet day, while walking my bike to the school gate, a senior pupil tapped me on the shoulder and pulled me aside in a random uniform blitz. Apparently my lousy, barely effective grey coat broke the school uniform code—black coats only. He forced me to join a several-deep line up of other miscreants in front of the administration block. Though under-developed and slight of build in my first year at the boy's high school, I still defiantly defended my parents against this ridiculous, discriminatory rule. They were sacrificing to afford even this cheap protection against the elements, yet these administrative bullies were arbitrarily discarding perfectly good clothing, and worse, parading us, soaking wet, for being poor. However, rules are rules. They rubbished our coats, leaving us to ride home looking like wet rats. I didn't bother with a coat again, thinking that Mum didn't need additional financial stress.

My parents' relationship continued to deteriorate, and we saw less and less of Dad. Sometime later, he explained this was his way of getting us used to his absence. In April 1974, four years after his business failure, he left home for good, negatively affecting my view of the world and future expectations. When I hear Dad's favourite album, Neil Diamond's *Hot August Night (Live at the Greek Theatre)*, I'm instantly transported back to that summer of 1974 when happiness and hope turned to grief, illustrating the power of subconscious memory to bring past feelings into the present, given the right cue.

I always tried my best in school; it was a way of giving back to my parents, to acknowledge the hardships they were enduring on my behalf. Every school lunch break I ate all the soggy sandwiches in my lunchbox, regardless of whether I was hungry. I knew the love, effort and financial sacrifice Mum put into making them. That changed with Dad's departure; my motivation to achieve left with him—after all, nothing breaks like a heart! I'd managed above-average results in high school, now, though, because of my anger at what the world was doing to me and the shame of losing one of the two people I most loved, my results tumbled.

Their separation occurred at a critical point in my education. In the 1970s, third-year secondary school students had to sit a national exam to achieve the School Certificate, which gave employers a nationally consistent, relative measure of the next batch of school leavers or prospective employees. Students were examined under strict supervision on five core subjects considered crucial to the country's continued economic growth. For the average student with no aspirations to attend university, these examinations were advertised as the culmination of their education. Exam performance would determine future employability and success. The pressure to perform was unrelenting. Until Dad's departure, I graded in the upper quartile in all school subjects; afterwards, I lost interest and barely passed three of the five core subjects. Not the best finish to my educational climax!

Psychologists say that children benefit when unhappy couples separate. Apparently, separation removes their major source of stress—constant anxiety generated by the disruption to their core beliefs surrounding their family identity. I disagree; the effects of my parents' separation were significant. Children in their early to mid-teens suffer lasting damage that a younger child, having more time to reconstruct a happy family history, may not feel. Teenagers are naturally self-conscious and strive to fit in with their peer group. I had a lot of perceived shame that came with poverty magnified by being part of a broken home. I believed these events were personally significant, and they haunted my life for decades. Through the ignorant application of thought, without conscious intervention, past decisions continue to influence our quality of life in the present.

To pay the bills, Mum got a job at a nearby nursery, a business she'd learned in the happier days of Sure-Gro back in Pahiatua. Mum remained in the nursery business until she retired, and even now at eighty-six, we pick her brain for gardening tips. With help from my nearby brothers, she still maintains a manicured, colourful summer garden. Out of necessity, she took on additional work Saturday evenings, catering at a renowned wedding venue, and every Sunday Mum treated us to the renowned leftovers. Despite her pioneering-family work ethic, Mum didn't earn enough to meet the rental payments on our house, forcing us to move for the fifth time in five years.

We shifted into a government or 'state' house, which for me confirmed our total fall from grace. In my teens we'd always rented, but this was different. Private rentals looked like any other house in the street; there was no stigma attached to them. Living in a state house was, to me, like wearing a scarlet letter that made me the equivalent to the children's home 'maggot'. Now a senior at high school, I saw this as the ultimate shame. As it was, I had few friends and definitely no girlfriend. This move meant that wasn't about to change. I wouldn't be bringing anyone home to this place! I should've been thankful to have a roof over my head, but when I learned where we'd be living, I turned red with rage, lashing out at the wall in frustration, leaving a hole, and worse, upsetting Mum. Life descended to a new low; my ego was well and truly ground to a dust.

Fortunately, I scraped through with enough marks to qualify me for my penultimate year of high school when I would hopefully redeem myself. I lifted my game for fear of having to leave school to join the adult world of work, deciding university was an easier option. At least living the hermit lifestyle at home gave me plenty of time for revision, and I managed accreditation in all five core subjects, which meant that my internal exam results excused me from having to sit national University Entrance exams. I passed again in my last year, achieving a nationally recognised 'B Bursary', a financial award to assist with tertiary education costs. Finally, I was shot of secondary school.

CHAPTER TWO

CONCEPTION:
WELCOME TO THE JUNGLE

W E ARE BORN INTO A COLLECTIVE, ALLEGEDLY EVIDENCE-BASED, objective belief system that has as its central premise the concept of Darwinian evolution where only the fittest among us survive and thrive, ensuring the continuation of our species. Except for our DNA and RNA transferred to us from our parents, we begin with an essentially blank canvas. From our first day, unlike the rest of the animal kingdom, Homo sapiens must learn everything from scratch to ensure their survival, developing skills enabling them to achieve independence in this new and foreign environment. At first, interpersonal communication skills are clumsy and limited. When upset by something, we immediately seek a remedy. For example, hunger drives us to seek attention by crying—a non-specific macro attention-seeking approach. These cries are met with a swift and mostly successful response that improves over time as our inexperienced caregivers become more efficient at interpreting our cries.

As new-borns we experiment with these cause-and-effect responses, experiencing hit and miss results in an iterative improvement process. We progressively achieve better and better outcomes and add our own interpreted meaning to each response until we're maintaining emotional stability and minimising personal inconvenience. Being totally dependent, though our needs are immediately satisfied, sets us up for a future emotional fall. New parents, experiencing the feeling of unconditional love for the first time, will do anything to keep us safe and sound. From a practical perspective, they search for a return to stability through their own trial-and-error process. Speak to a few parents accustomed to this new normal and they'll tell you stories of sleep deprivation while learning how to keep their baby satisfied.

Before long we learn to crawl and start eagerly exploring our surroundings. At this stage we're bought back to earth with a thud with well-meaning disciplinary feedback that teaches us acceptable behavioural boundaries. Parents likely subconsciously use their own upbringing as their disciplinary guide, complicating the situation because each parent was raised with a different set of behavioural rules. This introduces an additional source of potential conflict and confusion within the relationship, which can be difficult to resolve. Not to mention third-party childcare and its disciplinary practices. With experience and experimentation, we realise that different behaviour elicits a particular response, some positive, some not. These responses may be physical, verbal or visual.

Exploration of our environment helps us learn new skills; we form boundaries around what makes us feel good compared to what makes us feel bad. Naturally, to avoid pain we attempt to maximise behaviour that receives good reactions. However, this assumption is only valid if we receive consistent, objective feedback—an unrealistic expectation. Parenting doesn't come with a prescriptive manual. Behavioural parameters are subjective; today we're scolded for our actions, and tomorrow we aren't. Parenting feedback is confusing for children unable to logically link consistent behavioural cause and effect. In the beginning children are unable to question their caregivers, so inconsistent discipline seems to them to be personalised to their shortcomings, rather than specific to a particular behavioural cause.

Continuous streams of subjective feedback from caregivers, along with exposure to a rapidly expanding range of experiences, leads to us developing increasingly refined complex responses. Information input from our senses is unquestioningly added to our tiny, but continually expanding, database of memories in a self-adjusting loop. This feedback process establishes lifelong subconscious habits, becoming the foundational core beliefs forming our ego or sense of identity.

Transitioning from the insulated, protective home environment to preschool, our first brush with Darwin's theory in action is traumatic for all involved. We need to develop increasingly sophisticated communication skills, because the techniques that worked with immediate family aren't as effective in our expanding community. Forced out of our comfort zone, we must compete and negotiate with relative strangers. This places us in a vulnerable position, activating various forms of fear response—fear of ridicule, failure, abandonment—and all number of emotional traps, which test our ability to stay engaged with the present moment. In this new environment, our natural feedback learning process can work against us. Some find the transition to be an ongoing challenge, constantly battling overwhelming negative feelings, including anxiety, unhappiness, self-consciousness and anger. Naturally, we try to escape these feelings, but we have to attend school, so our only option is avoiding the situations causing our anxiety.

We focus on closing down the experience of life, rather than letting it happen without judgement. If only we focussed on the abundance that is available to us, a state exceeding our awareness, rather than on perceived shortcomings. For example, continually perceiving feedback as negative, painting ourselves as victims with little or no control over outcomes and at the mercy of others who we rate as more able, results in an avoidant behaviour habit. Flawed thinking casts us in the role of victim, mentally checking out of the system. For example, in the fourth grade, I was afraid to ask questions in case my peers ridiculed me. My teacher raised this at the parent-teacher meetings, so my parents told me to speak up. It was important to express my views because they added to class discussions. Their encouragement fell on deaf ears because I never accepted praise unless it fit with my assessment. This avoidant mind-set focuses our attention on the wrong goal; we're using our amazing self-correcting, learning servomechanism to resist the lessons life continually sends us designed to free us from limiting thought. Spiritual growth depends on us being open to experiencing the emotional pain we fear. This makes us resilient to the inevitable storms we're destined to encounter.

We are raised on an education model that leaves students with the impression that life revolves around learning facts and objective skills.

The level of mastery achieved ultimately decides our value to society. From our first day, we bear the cross of comparison in everything we do, soon realising that our relative value is derived from standardised tests, grading us from best to worst. Our concept of life is limited within a tightly regulated programme, dependent on the beliefs valued within the current social and economic system. Future prosperity is inextricably linked to our ability to progressively master prescribed competencies across twelve or thirteen years. Students are moved through this cookie-cutter system regardless of whether they achieve benchmarks within the allotted time. We come to believe that success and happiness live out there in a future 'you' who is dependent on the assimilation of a continuous stream of expert knowledge, a sure-fire recipe for anxiety—what will be my fate if I miss out on key information? Being future focused to achieve prescribed 'important' benchmarks places boundaries on creativity, dumbing us down, moulded into little people all the same. Instead of exploring our unique capacity to create a satisfying life from our creative thoughts, we're herded toward a common goal. Many students are left floundering, reducing their future earning potential because the system isn't designed to wait for them. This is our introduction to the idea that we are born incomplete, our completion being dependent on others, the oracles or gurus of our time.

The education system is set up to maximise economic production, which is expedient from a financial-system standpoint. However, it fails when it comes to enlightening every child of their innate power of free will to create a personally resonating reality. Rather, it trains us robotically, raising us to enrich the establishment. While we need to teach and motivate our children pragmatically so they can eventually provide for themselves, we also need to introduce them to their capacity for free will and critical thinking. This will enhance well-being and help repair the deterioration in our collective mental health.

An education system emphasising lack produces adults with little faith in their innate ability. They believe that the answer to success lies out there in the ever-expanding knowledge base. We try to find the magic 'self-improvement' pill that will make us invincible in every situation, so we never have to experience the pain of failure again. Eventually, because life continually delivers lemons, we become lost and confused. There is no pill. Trying to master or control events before they happen through learned techniques is both futile and energy sapping. Achieving life mastery by simply accumulating knowledge is a flawed concept, an ideology biased learning habit, popularised by the public education system, that promotes the belief that knowledge is all that stands between success and failure. This belief leaves us with the impression that mastering government-sanctioned curricula is the path to adult validation. It teaches us a habit of 'expert' dependency, rather than self-reliance and independent thought, and creates a society of outward-focused victims searching for the secret to quiet our anxious, searching minds. Being needy becomes our unconscious response to life; we blame everything but ourselves if we don't get what we want. Sadly, what we want so badly is often just an uncritical rehash of the popular view of the society in which we were raised. If we belligerently struggle with an uncooperative world and refuse to comply with our self-created model of 'this is how it must be for me to be happy', we set ourselves up for failure. The 'out there' is how it is despite us, not because of us; it is always perfect; it cannot be any other way.

Peace of mind is achieved when we realise we can only affect meaningful change in our lives by dealing with what we're encountering right NOW. Living a thriving, joyful life requires us to be mindful of the feedback we get from our physical senses, mixed with faith in our universal power. Deprecating self-talk sentences many of us to go through life thinking the world doesn't understand us, that we just don't fit in. The truth is we're perfect; it's our life model that's wrong. Adjusting the model through which we're interpreting our world transforms our life. Our mental servomechanism is a miracle under our command, always at the ready to develop a new model, effectively allowing us to change our spots to whatever we choose. In contrast, children have no choice but to absorb everything told to them in good faith, unquestioningly, no room for critical thought, like sponges, passively absorbing the lessons received from their immediate environment. Only in this sense are we victims of our upbringing. After all, the quality of our nurturing and education isn't perfect because our teachers are human (for now).

The ideas presented here show how self-doubt and excuses, which leave us feeling comparatively powerless, are learned, and how, armed with new understanding, we can unlearn them and give ourselves a second chance to consciously control the process of building our personalised life model. Even with this information, we can still choose to remain a victim or, more accurately, a martyr, but at least it's with our conscious permission, under our terms. (Collins English Dictionary: A victim is oblivious to their condition while the martyr is aware but continues to revel in their suffering.) A victim is anyone who uses excuses to justify and explain their current situation, however absurd and irrelevant their explanation

CHAPTER THREE

WHAT'S IN A NAME?

U NLIKE OTHERS WITHIN THE ANIMAL KINGDOM, AT BIRTH OUR vacuous yet pliant brain has limited instinctive capability, compromising our immediate survival. To comprehend our relationship to all we encounter in this foreign environment, we must learn to translate every stimulus and piece of feedback until, through trial and error, we achieve independence. This real-time ability to adapt by building our own unique, environmentally specific survival model, gives us a significant long-term advantage over other animals. We know this model or ego by our Christian name.

Months before our birth, expectant parents pour over culturally appropriate names in search of the 'one' that will distinguish us from the tribe. Once given, it's the constant anchor in our relationships. When spoken, it's a hot button, our call to attention, bringing us instantly into the present. Our parents hope their chosen name thrives, eventually growing into a robust and congruent identity. In time, our name becomes a unique, tangible avatar of our learned beliefs, formed from interpretation of emotionally significant events—a self-constructed model that gives the world unique meaning. Because we build it with blind faith in our primary influencers, model accuracy is limited. It can only be as accurate a representation of reality as the models it has access to through luck of birth. Prefaced by our persistent name, we are fashioned by our immature interpretation of what others do to us and what reaction we get when we do stuff to others. The meaning we attach to these events becomes our enduring truth, although it's unlikely the literal truth.

At first, we lack the critical evaluation skills to accurately make sense of what's happening around us. Oblivious to its objective accuracy, we accept sensual information like a sponge, passing it directly into the database of 'me'. This is how we build our reference of enduring core beliefs, which form the model of who we think we are and against which we compare all future feedback. We become adept at translating simple actions, like physical gestures and voice tones and touch, in a way that confirms approval or disapproval of the unique model embodied in our name. This model is the 'who' that turns up when we respond to our name. Both the model and our name, being one and the same (integral), form the objectified i AM; in my case i AM Geoff. Geoff begins as the central core belief to which we attach additional beliefs, building our multidimensional self-image. It's a preface, loaded with interpretations of how we see the world and how we think it sees us. This is the source of our limitation and neurosis.

This assisted self-design process is the beginning of the end for many of us. The moment our 'I' is labelled with our parent's handpicked Christian name, we become separated from the concept of 'i AM That'. What started as pure potential is now limited to our evolving view of the label, attributed to the reflection we see in the mirror each morning. The moment we are named, we become I am Joe, or I am Mary—where Joe and Mary substitute for 'That' in 'i AM That'. Our self-view, determined by the comprehension of our childhood upbringing and the inter and intra-cultural models we experienced, becomes our cognitive bias, making us unique regarding our values and emotional triggers. This is our schema (c.f. schema therapy), a construct of parents, grandparents, wider society and, not least, government influence that manifests in adult life as subconscious reactions to identifiable stimulus. When I say, 'Hi Joe,' or, 'Hi Mary', my opinion of them is limited to the finite concept I have formed and memorised from our previous encounters. This is my mental token or avatar of what I think and feel when acknowledging their name, which, because of interpretive bias, is likely different to another.

We dynamically adjust to our physical environment by translating the input received through our senses via our nervous system, a complex electrochemical servomechanism. Reliable, objective feedback allows us to refine our approach, so that with persistence we eventually learn how to confidently and successfully repeat a task so that we consistently achieve the same result. Trial and error are essential to attaining proficiency and, if desired, mastery over physical tasks. This iterative approach to physical skill training isn't as effective when applied to ego-mind development, where sensory input is a confusing mix of both subjective and objective information received from other sentient beings. A child's nervous system can't differentiate between subjective and objective feedback; everything is accepted as objective truth. Our nervous system does its best to find patterns within this contradictory, interpersonal feedback. However, the trial-and-error process that works well in helping us master the physical environment ends in frustration, rather than habitual proficiency.

Ego construction happens in this environment of mixed messages where our self-developed and rapidly growing comprehension system filters imperfect information that leads us to believe that individual survival and success depends on others' failure. We're continuously comparing our past and present experience, aiming for progressively better results. Like the learning outcome of putting our hand on a hot stove, the lesson is unambiguous, swift and permanent. In contrast, interpersonal feedback is often ambiguous, its intended meaning lost in translation because of conflicting belief systems.

Well-meaning feedback, rather than being interpreted as helpful, corrective advice, is seen as a personal attack on our ability or potential. For example, take email or SMS when a message to an associate or friend receives an unexpectedly blunt response. Based on their personal experience, the recipient places their interpretation on our words and grammar, interpreting a meaning we neither intended nor considered. They're reading our words but superimposing their voice, emphasis and ego, activating their own cognitive bias, which leads to misunderstanding. While adults may quickly resolve such disagreements, children haven't learned to clarify meaning by asking questions. They naturally and naively accept things at face value. As adults, it's irrelevant whether the intent is malicious; it's always our choice how we interpret it. We can influence our emotions consciously rather than unconsciously. It's the difference between being fragile or resilient to seeming hardship. Our learned beliefs determine the meaning we attribute to all sensual input. Until we realise this, we remain victims to those beliefs.

Our adult subconscious life responses arise from the comprehension database system developed by our infant/child mind. This database, our library of operating schemas, comprises interpretations of experiences and teachings passed on by our parents and other significant influencers, whether these be religious, political, media or corporate, and they manifest as authoritative, inner-voice instructions. The subconscious spontaneously and seamlessly accesses this database, retrieving what it considers is the appropriate response to any external stimulus. Even as adults, our response is identical to our parents in terms of voice intonation and mannerisms—scary! While many of these subconscious schemas benefit us, others are glass ceilings limiting our potential. Continued dependency on these lack-focused, archaic, habitual-response patterns, hinders development of faith in our ability to overcome obstacles. Collectively these schemas form our constructed ego, which I call the 'little i (lie)'. Failure to perceive this construct condemns us to live our life in a dream-like state, while it acts for us, pulling our levers as if it were the Wizard of Oz.

An anonymous quote states, 'The definition of insanity is continually repeating the *same thing* and expecting a different result.' Yet while we remain clueless to the ego construct, this is our inevitable destiny, our karma. Through repetition of instruction across the years, our reaction (the *same thing*) is hard-wired into the subconscious. In this state, when faced with similar stimuli, our life experience becomes no more than a series of predictable, spontaneous conditioned responses. These stimuli are virtually buttons others can press, giving them control, able to lead us without our conscious awareness or permission. Our children have this down to a fine art; we know from experience how skilled they are at achieving a specific response by pushing certain emotional buttons. Adding insult to injury, we condemn ourselves for being persistently triggered, a flaw we're evidently powerless to change. Truth is, our triggered response is the real flaw; it is merely the impersonal expression of obsolete, habitual behaviour relics, controlling our response. While under their spell, we remain resistant to change, set in our ways.

Meanwhile, despite what we think, our dynamic world moves on. Eventually, after years of being buffeted, bullied and worn down like rocks in a stream, we encounter a world out there that bears no resemblance to the model we accidently formed all those years ago as a child. Failing to transcend our ego destines us to become grumpy, unengaged or worse. Yet hidden in plain sight is a universal gift that allows us to remain soft like water, rather than resistant like stone:

> 'Water is fluid, soft, and yielding. But water will wear away rock, which is rigid and cannot yield. As a rule, whatever is fluid, soft, and yielding will overcome whatever is rigid and hard. This is another paradox: what is soft is strong.'

> – Lao Tzu

C H A P T E R   F O U R

LIMITED BY LEARNING

I N HIS BOOK *THINK AND GROW RICH*, CONCERNING THE ATTAINMENT of personal success, Napoleon Hill predicts that 'somewhere, as you read, the secret to which I refer will jump from the page and stand boldly before you, IF YOU ARE READY FOR IT! When it appears, you will recognize it. Whether you receive the sign in the first or the last chapter, stop for a moment when it presents itself, and turn down a glass, for that occasion will mark the most important turning-point of your life.'

For most of my life, the secret escaped me. It frustrated me that Hill didn't openly reveal this secret that's 'in plain sight of us all', after all, isn't his book's purpose to give us the 'master key to riches'? Twenty-five years passed before I could metaphorically 'turn down a glass'. An archaic phrase meaning 'in memory of a deceased drinking companion', it's customary to turn down (turn upside down) a glass on the table the next time you go drinking and pause a moment to remember him/her. Thus, 'turn down a glass' means to stop for a moment of remembrance and acknowledge the moment of life-changing revelation. I'll try not to be so cruel by, hopefully, shining a bright light on the secret in plain sight!

Suboptimal mind-training techniques are dictating our life potential. Historical, accidental influences unconsciously limit us, leaving us destined to play the role of an unwitting victim, pushed and pulled by external influences. When we transcend this ego-driven view of ourselves, embracing our gift of universal free will, we can choose our own course, one that resonates with our unique desires. Our mind is not fixed, objectified matter like our body; it's fluid, designed to create from the ceaseless flow of abstract thoughts flowing through every mind like water. Each of us gets to choose the thoughts to which we wish to give attention, thus bringing them to life in the physical world. For most of us, others assumed control of our childhood choices. It's time to take them back—to 'think and grow rich.'

Existentialism and essentialism are two contrasting philosophies claiming to be the objective answer explaining man's reality and life's meaning. Neither offers a complete answer. Our innate ability to create physical matter from the dimension of thought suggests the answer lies somewhere between the two, rather than one or the other. We are outwardly objective and inwardly subjective. The gift of our subconscious means we can train our essential body to competently and habitually perform any repetitive, physical activities we choose, unburdening the conscious mind of repetitive tasks. This frees us to create and refine ways of living that resonate with our unique existential choices. Our mind is the nexus between subjective thought waves and their transformation to objective matter. This nexus has always been in plain sight, represented by the Roman cross, where the vertical element represents the source (wave) dimension and the horizontal element the time/matter dimension, or simply space (vertical) and time (horizontal).

Our dual nature has remained hidden to all but a few. Childhood training focused on developing our essential nature while ignoring our existential development. This has left us at the mercy of limiting-thought habits arising from repetitive suggestions, either by the self or by others. Most of us have been unwittingly trained to use our mind in the same way we train our essential or objective physical abilities—that is, through the repetition of actions to eventually produce involuntary, automatic responses, in the same way as breathing. For example, a child throws a tantrum at the supermarket checkout because they want a sweet from the strategically placed display. Submitting to their frenzied pressure achieves the child's goal, reinforcing their unacceptable behaviour. Repeated success of this manipulative strategy results in a subconscious reaction as habitual as any learned physical skill, like walking or smoking. The process is 'in this situation, respond this way to achieve this result'. However, instead of it being a learned physical muscle memory, where the nervous system links to the appropriate muscle, building on the previous success, it's a mind memory. The nervous system establishes a link to a synaptic pathway in the brain, effectively making its own synthetic 'muscle' from subjective feedback. Why subjective? There are numerous ways to respond to the child's tantrum or bad behaviour, some adaptive and others maladaptive, some by loving parents and others by spiteful siblings. What seems to work so well now can become a future stumbling block or barrier to accomplishment.

Physical habits perfected in childhood support us for life because fixed physical laws exist—for example, gravity. Once learned, riding a bike is a reliable skill that works whether we're six or sixty-six. In contrast, the mind domain is not subject to any perceptible law; it's abstract and dynamic. Unfortunately, our mind has been trained as if stimulus follows definite cause and effect. Our early influencers used our adaptable, creative mind to develop an ego comprising simple, mechanical, repetitive subconscious responses. This turned a complex adaptive system into a simple unconscious reactive system, the thinker left unaware of its true potential. This approach to external stimuli may have been a forgiving strategy during the last decade or century, but today it's stealing our life as a creator from us. Approaching life on autopilot, operating as if we're robots robs us of our unique human ability to adapt, leaving us languishing with an increasingly dated artificial intelligence (AI). While once we were a useful productive resource, time has made us irrelevant as we sleepwalk through life on a programme fed us by others in what was likely an inefficient, random process.

We are captive to this autopilot system because we are unaware of it. Meanwhile, trapped within our reactive ego, we continue the learned pattern of comparing our progress and worth against others. From our point of reference, we experience a grinding cycle of perpetual failure, a living hell with no end of suffering and frustration, while other lives appear to be an effortless cycle of success. Little wonder we wind up depressed, feeling worthless. While our point of reference remains focused on what others are doing or achieving, we're destined to suffer because our self-worth and happiness fluctuates with events out of our control. This renders us a powerless victim of fear, worry, jealousy, anger and envy.

Training our mind to work in an objective, instinctive manner is an efficient approach to survival in a static universe where what you sense is all there ever was and will be. But if that were true, we would've been born just like the lion cub, with an instinctive programme pre-set and ready to thrive in every conceivable situation. Why take the risk of giving birth to a totally dependent species unlikely to survive alone for even a day? Of course, the universe is anything but static. Therefore, treating and training our mind confronted with unrelenting streams of extra-sensory feedback from our external world, in the same way we use objective feedback via the somatic nervous system to train our muscle movements, is a flawed concept. Our muscles respond to corrective repetition to achieve enduring automatic mastery, while the mind requires persistent awareness and adaptive flexibility to reveal the full potential of the ever-changing universe.

Persistent training of our mind as if it is an extension of the body suggests the approach worked as an effective way to advance our species. Until now, our world appeared relatively static; the changes across a single lifetime were insignificant. The interpersonal skills and processes we learned that ensured our survival served us throughout our life span of three score and ten. Workers were trained to turn up and repeat an established, familiar task until retirement. Creative or critical thought input wasn't a factor in their survival or ability to survive and support their families. Perhaps one person in a million would use their creative, subjective capability to make a quantum change leading to improved living standards. For example, Henry Ford's production line innovation played a pivotal role in the industrial revolution, reducing automobile build time from twelve hours to thirty minutes.

The phrase 'generation gap' refers to the difference in worldview between parents and their children, a demographic separation estimated as thirty years. Older generations long for a return to the 'good old days' when their mastered, internalised beliefs and skills aligned with their experience of the world. In a dynamic universe, the value to society of those skills and beliefs erode over a generation. There is little work for a farrier in a city moved by cars, a priest in a culture of atheists or a Gestetner operator in a world with 'cloud' storage. Similarly, how does sending instant messages on Facebook or Instagram even rate as paid employment? Is the live-chat reply on that website from an actual person, or has that role already been replaced by AI, making it one of the shortest job roles in history? Today we encounter an environment of continual technological change, in stark contrast to the incremental changes that occurred last century. It's easy to understand how the elderly have become fearful and alienated, unable to navigate their once-familiar environment automatically on subconscious autopilot. Their once-effortless act of existing is now a constant mental and physical struggle as accelerating change increases their dependency on others in their everyday living. For example, elderly lacking computer skills are anxious about how they'll send their Christmas cards or pay their monthly utility bills by cheque; even playing their favourite music is a challenge!

An accelerating rate of technological development is compressing the established understanding of the generation gap. There is a shift toward an intra-generational gap, as even the relatively young are feeling anxious for their future, worried that by graduation, skills faithfully learned during years of compulsory education will be irrelevant, their career obsolete. This perception is compounded by advances in communications technology that enable mass, instantaneous, global propagation of information by both professional journalists and those who profess to be 'influencers'.

Stories advancing specific objectives can be collected from across vast, unrelated geographic distances, then curated, producing an impression that the events are associated. Collectively, the subconscious message is that this increase in the number of similar events shows a significant, single, sinister cause. Because the information is neither edited nor peer reviewed, it's impossible to tell whether it's fake, fact or sponsored propaganda. Often the pictures are from historic footage or, taking artistic license, snippets from blockbuster movies to convey false gravity. The source's perceived authority is enough to persuade us the information is credible. This technique of simulating gravity by quantity over quality was first used by the recording engineer, Phil

Spector. Called the 'Wall of Sound', Spector engineered in 'far more instruments than was customary ...' (Gold Star Studios and the 'Wall of Sound', Encyclopaedia Britannica) to bombard the senses, giving extra substance to the original music.

Crude, unidimensional teaching methods lock us into learned binary on/off thinking habits, where there is only a right answer or a right way. This suppresses our natural problem solving and adaptability and instils the limiting belief that success is inextricably linked to objective knowledge. Thus it appears that our future happiness depends on our ability to navigate an avalanche of external data, leaving us feeling overwhelmed and powerless, and entrenching the belief that we're victims. Withdrawing to the safety and familiarity of our accumulating memories can bring some respite. We lose ourselves in an expanding backstory— our personal, real-time role-playing game (RPG) of denial—but this is a trap, like a warm bath, it's hard to leave. Believing our best is behind us, we spend more time immersed in memories of the good old days, extracting pleasure from what we were and avoiding the unfamiliar present, while the latter part of our life disappears, unnoticed. That we'll be left behind or have already missed the boat is a symptom of suboptimal childhood thought training.

We have long been aware of the impact on well-being and mental health of progressive change. The silent movie *Modern Times* (1936) directed and starring Charlie Chaplin addressed the difficulty of modern man to cope in a changing world.[1] That we continue to adapt and thrive in an environment unrecognisable from Chaplin's day is a clue we're inextricably connected to this change. Living in harmony with our environment, while maintaining good mental health, depends on recognising that change is the only constant. We are hard-wired to lead and harness this change, having unconstrained access to all the answers needed to solve every problem we encounter. History reflects this; at no point has mankind failed to overcome and prosper.

Dramatic change in the commercial marketplace is the new normal. No one can keep up; attempting to is futile, a zero-sum game. Andrew McAfee from MIT said, 'Our world is increasingly complex, often

---

[1] Charlie Chaplin, *Modern Times*, 1936, IMDB 'The Tramp struggles to live in modern industrial society with the help of a young homeless woman'.

chaotic, always fast-flowing. This makes forecasting something between tremendously difficult and impossible, with a strong shift toward the latter as timescales get longer.' McAfee later proved this with his ill-fated bitcoin price prediction.

Emphasising the nonsense of basing self-worth solely on occupational competence systematically trains us to accept limitations rather than personal abundance. This is the realm of droids—they will be sleepwalking, programmable units of production far superior to what we ever were. Right now, we're at a point where we're about to replace ourselves in the workplace; the future will see our 'doing' tasks become the domain of avatar droids.

CHAPTER FIVE

OUR SUBCONSCIOUS HAS BEEN HI-JACKED

INESCAPABLE CHANGE IS THE GIFT THAT CAN FREE THE MIND OF unwelcome subconscious habit. From the macro level of the previous millennium, to the micro-level today, evolutionary transformation is penetrating every level of life, urging us to wake up and escape the grip of robotic training. Our mind was not designed to act purely from habit, a slave to ego repetition, asleep to dynamic creation. Its ultimate purpose is to imagine new possibilities and transform subjective thought into objective reality by being and observing with faith.

Realisation that we are part of the light from which everything is conceived is the only way to reveal our innate creative power. Still today, we are compared, judged and rated, convincing us that our value is synonymous with performance. While we're captured by this ego-focused system that subconsciously consumes our life, we'll never be spiritually satisfied. Inevitably, we realise on our deathbed—a minority before, that soon after birth we were sold a lemon by someone older, wiser and more powerful, and who seized our life as their own.

Our subconscious mind is a very efficient, programmable tool available to help us adapt and shape our physical environment to our individual needs. For example, consider wood, if we learn to shape it by developing the physical skill to carve intricate, beautiful pieces through repetition and continuous refinement, eventually we become a sought-after carver, an artisan of wood. Development of neuronal pathways in the brain, strengthened by repetition, makes our relationship to the physical world easier. In time, they enable automatic actions, relieving our mind to attend to other matters simultaneously, and once learned, they're never forgotten, just like riding a bike.

I believe this is the intended purpose of the subconscious. Our ability to choose and create personalised, instinctive habits provides us with a commanding survival advantage, allowing us to learn and master complex physical skills; for example, driving a car. The subconscious, through repetition, takes an idea or activity and embeds it as part of the essential being as a habit, an energy efficient, learned instinct. Simple examples include daily activities like cleaning teeth, going to the gym or practicing a daily Yoga flow. Once these tasks become part of our routine, they're impossible to avoid, taking on a life of their own, nagging us until they're done and leaving us feeling guilty if we don't. We can visualise the habit process as a flowchart listing the sequential steps to reach the desired outcome. Repeated again and again, these steps become physical pathways, expressed as the seamless cooperation between chemically connected neurons and muscles.

Through a similar process, repetition of thought concerning our unique interpretation of events leads to a belief that the body and ego are synonymous. We treat interpersonal feedback as if it is equivalent to the objective feedback loop essential to developing habitual physical skills, setting in place unique character habits. What began as a fluid, infinitely plastic and adaptable being, unconstrained by belief, becomes, through repetition of suggestions, moulded by beliefs into a fixed identity, seemingly set like stone. Forming our identity like this worked in a world that remained relatively unchanged for millennia. Developing societies relied and benefited from tribes with refined physical skills, taming harsh environments for the greater good of all. Our ancestors developed survival skills by trial and error, making life or death decisions which ensured their longevity and generational succession. Through iteration, our essential nature developed along a natural and predictable path, taking the form of an intergenerational servomechanism, otherwise known as evolution or survival of the fittest. Surnames reflected the skills that helped the entire tribe to thrive; for example, Smith, Cooper, Potter and Mason to name a few.

Although endowed with the holy grail; the ability to consciously choose our response to every situation, for centuries pragmatic necessity meant our societies trained us to act instinctively. Our reaction to external stimulus programmed in accordance with generalised survival habits or instincts. Our 'essential' side emphasised to the detriment of the 'existential'. From birth, personalised ego formation of the identity or avatar recognised as our Christian name starts in earnest. Existing ego habits are progressively formed and reinforced through repetition of both internal and external instruction, with the goal of achieving certainty of response, with the least amount of energy. This ensures perceived threats are met with a relatively consistent, spontaneous reaction, maximising survival. Before long, our identity is operating on autopilot, outside conscious awareness. Reflecting the beliefs formed from decisions made from our interpretation of the emotionally significant events we experienced as children.

This satisfied the perceived greater good of the tribe, ensuring its survival—appropriate if you're an animal lacking creative potential, longevity being dependent on instinct. This was true of man for millennia. Necessity limited the scope to break out of our career, town or society. Survival depended on learning essential skills, habitually repeated until we keeled over.

Today, while our potential experiences are overwhelming compared to the past, they seldom relate to life and death. In under a century, we have moved from a life with limited options to almost limitless. Movies like The Bucket List leave us with the impression that a successful life is measured by the number of foreign shores visited and the experiences and material possessions we spend every living moment accumulating. Our mind is still held captive through the suggestion of others who subtly prod us to do what they want while belittling and taking for granted the safety and security into which we're born—thanks to those before us.

Despite this remarkable shift, we persist in teaching our children to function as if they're a computer. In their formative years, we program them with a culturally imposed operating system (OS) in expectation that it will remain relevant throughout their life. This learning approach ignores the brain's connection to an infinite, evolving intelligence. Our subconscious is not designed to perform as the operating system, but as an application running on top of the OS, enabling us to adjust and train our bodies to master the physical world.

An analogy is Microsoft Word, an application running on MacOS or Windows. When the OS environment changes, the app must also change via an upgrade to remain compatible. The old pragmatic way of teaching served us well, enabling mankind to adapt and prosper, but now we need a better way. So far, the education system has only achieved stage two of Goldstein and Maslow's five-stage theory of self-actualisation: the basic needs. Continued collective prosperity needs us to claim more, requiring an evolution of teaching methods. It's time to emphasise the existential or subjective nature of our mind and its connection to the universe, Source or God—the OS of which we are all part. Some in the know already harness this ability to their advantage.

Through time, the few who recognised the unique human ability to create from within, who knew that a thought conceived and believed will be achieved,[2] exploited those who didn't. This law, recognised by religion and the aristocracy, offered an opportunity to influence and even control people through the subconscious programming of their suggestible ego. For example; stage hypnotists convince willing adults that they're eating a tasty apple, even though it's an onion. Unsurprisingly, elites use programming techniques unrivalled in their simplicity to influence children's identity development. This gives them a competitive advantage that allows them to control and manipulate the skills and thinking of future generations.

This overt indoctrination process successfully develops teams of people who can be directed to work in areas society believes will benefit most from its view of the contemporary common good. This pragmatic approach to achieving meaningful change focuses massive muscle power and, more recently, massive brain power. Used unscrupulously, it deceives populations into compliance, directing them in tribes, like pack hunting animals, operating as if by instinct rather than free will. An example is Hitler Youth—a WW2 group designed to indoctrinate children into Hitler's ideology such that they would eventually be willing to sacrifice themselves for the sake of the motherland. Even in advanced

---

[2] Napoleon Hill, *Think and Grow Rich*, Sound Wisdom, 1937.

economies today, this suggestible quality of the human brain is abused. By instilling a programme that sets the individual up to be dependent on his or her past response and bound by their self-image, wealth is channelled from mass production into the deep pockets of controlling elites. This self-image is constructed by chance during our early years of total dependency and based on our interpretation of the opinions and memes shared by our peers and elders.

Once upon a time, developing populations of static victims worked. The slow pace of change made it practical. Replacing them with newer, upgraded models via mass education of subsequent generations was more efficient than retraining the old. As Jason Isbell and Bradley Cooper say in their lyrics for 'Maybe It's Time', from the movie *A Star Is Born*, 'It takes a lot to change a man—hell, it takes a lot to try.'

Unfortunately, centrally coordinated training has left most under the impression that they're unable to meaningfully change their behaviour—'It's just the way I was born. I can't change who I am.' Disempowered by this learned thinking habit, we struggle to cope in an increasingly foreign environment that requires constant adaptation and development of not only new but also previously inconceivable skills.

CHAPTER SIX

'So i AM That, I AM.' DEFINED

COMPREHEND THE MEANING OF 'I AM THAT, i am' AND YOU WILL understand our role as creators in total control of our destiny and freed from the fear, worry and anxiety that arise from feeling unworthy and believing that our 'THAT, i am' is insignificant compared to others. If we understand this, then we accept that we've always created our own experience and unwittingly been complicit in playing life's victim. Realising we're all independent creators releases us from the pressure to measure up to contemporary standards of success. We become self-directed, motivated by our own goals and dreams, no matter how big or small, and appreciate that we're born equal under the stars, free to choose our own path. Meeting life any other way means we're controlled by others' values and create what they want, with our life and its creative energy captured in their vision.

How can this simple phrase 'So i AM That, i AM' help you break free from the childhood programming controlling your present reality? 'So i AM That, i AM' is a practical revision of, in my opinion, the misinterpreted 'Book of Exodus' 3:14 phrase, 'I Am That I Am'. A simple comma added after 'That' dramatically changes the phrase's emphasis, revealing a new approach to life described by 'The Semantics of i AM That' (abbreviated to 'So i AM That' with 'So' being an acronym for 'Semantics of'). This simple edit provides a clue to how to consciously and continually use your limitless, existential creative nature to control and define your life experience—to assume the role of driver rather than the passenger asleep in the back seat.

Leaving out the comma gives 'I am that I am' a significantly different meaning, implying that we are conscious because we're aware of our individuality. We recognise who and what we see in the mirror as the self who has our name. While 'i AM That, i AM' implies that we're conscious when we realise we're one with what we observe. The hidden power of mankind is in the ability to consciously create a self or ego bearing our Christian name. We can construct self around the repetition of intentional observations and thoughts arising from observations (say an area of interest or passion), because we're inseparable from 'that' on which our awareness is focused right now. We are the thing! This ability is always available. Objectively, we are what we perceive through every one of our senses and we choose our experience by free will.

Hear that plane flying nearby, hear it fully conscious of its presence and you, in that moment, become part of it and it part of you. Stay in that awareness for as long as you can remain one with the moment. If you lose awareness, you'll drift off into another dream or wish of the ego illusion. Awareness followed up with repeated intentional thought is the formula that will manifest the thing. With this creative method we can take what we love from observation and become it, taking it wherever we go. This is how we created ourselves. The ego carrying our Christian name is just as much a thing as that tree in our garden. But unlike the tree, we can reimagine it into something different.

Get in the game, learn to play with eyes wide open. Immerse yourself in sensual moments, your real now, and embrace our gift of being conscious of objective form. When you fill that jug with water for your cup of coffee or tea, listen to the water, feel it take you over, experience all that it is, its smell, sound, feel, taste, flow. Stop being distracted, living in make-believe mind stories, lost in never land while things happen unnoticed around you. Cast attention on the butterfly that just fluttered by or the bird soaring above and realise that we're one with where our attention goes. Placing our awareness onto our physical environment; to be conscious of the object of our attention or 'that' in 'i AM That, i AM', as in 'that—butterfly', releases us from the incessant, unconscious thoughts that capture us in memories or future dreams, both parts of the unreal. This is how to escape feelings of fear or anxiety, meditation unpacked, no need for expensive courses or gurus. Meditation is not a complicated 'doing thing'; it's just mired in mysterious and exclusive marketing speak.

Under our normal setting, a never-ending stream of thought competes for our attention. It flows continuously—like a river, approaching, here, then gone—with each independent thought labelled in our native language. Because semantics is everything, if our language or vocabulary is limited by a lack of educational opportunities, so is the richness of our life experience. The semantics of i AM means that the greater our vocabulary, the more precise we are as a creator. Just as an artist can produce an infinite array of new colours from primary ones to create a unique masterpiece, we can do the same with mastery of language. The nature of thought means that those managing education and language control the collective and individual potential of societies.

We engage our creative power whenever we are conscious of this moment—the 'i AM That, i AM'—rather than dwelling in some unconscious past, future story or dream state created by the habitual or subconscious mind—the 'I Am that I Am'. Realise this and we assume complete control over our life's trajectory. We're no longer a spectator spellbound by the past or the future, owned by the illusory dimensions of time which consume our life. Being conscious of this moment gives us conscious control to harness the power of the moment in the same way we used this power to master the art of driving a car or riding a bike. In this fully present state of consciousness, we become seamlessly connected to the eternally expanding universe, one with it.

The semantics of i AM releases us from the limited objective ego (I am), which is bound by the beliefs we chose to be part of our 'I am' since emerging into the world. Our absolute dependence on our carers left us no choice but to blindly accept all input from our new environment. This began the construction of the 'i am, ego' illusion in earnest, an ego representing a belief in a limited, objective self, and the source of all future suffering. Ironically, those we love most reinforced this illusory self when they gave us our name as a proxy for 'That' in i AM That. We became it, answering to it, like one of Pavlov's dogs.

Practically, we see how the ego assumes our life experience. Survival requires interaction with others. This inevitably leads to comparison, some we initiated and others initiated by society's contemporary value systems—predominantly economic. By trial-and-error community leaders designed measures they judged to be of value to the stability and progress of the broader system. One constant, though, is that they all seem to be adept at labelling us as good or bad, better or worse, useful or useless, bright or dull and so on when compared to our peers. Yet in the words of Theodore Roosevelt, 'Comparison is the thief of joy.' The intended (unintended?) outcome of the system is to train us at an early age to accept comparative evaluation as the success standard.

As soon as an elephant is born into the circus, it's tethered to a small stake by an insignificant rope. At first, the elephant calf struggles and pulls to loosen its binding, but unable to break free, it eventually gives up. Even as an adult, the same insignificant stake is all that's needed. An illusion masquerading as a rope now captures the elephant. It's limited by unnoticed habits formed in the past, rather than responding to the reality which is only seen after waking to now—The 'i AM That, i AM'. We're trained to be just like the circus elephant, progressively conditioned by, and conforming to, our early life experiences and with our emotional wellbeing tethered to society's systemic and institutionalised standards of comparison. We're raised in a system that presents us with conclusive, objective evidence that scholastic performance accurately reflects our worth and determines whether we'll be a productive member of society or a burden to be carried by those adjudged more capable.

Standards, while arbitrary, motivate us to strive toward society's ideal and to achieve recognised benchmarks along the way—for example, home ownership—which show we're on the right path to achieving ultimate success. These future-focused benchmarks guilt us to achieve more by trying harder. A feeling of accomplishment, self-sufficiency and fulfilment is the implied future reward. Unfortunately, this competitive process, accepted as a natural part of life, dooms the majority to a futile, never-ending race to an unfulfilling end. The promise that life will be better when the future arrives is as much an illusion of the ego as the past.

The adult ego is on a pre-programmed journey, always seeking to become an objectively dominant 'I am that I am'. It has an insatiable desire for more money, power and status. The implied programmed mantra is more, seen as more accomplished, more worthy and even immortalised. This programming sentences us to live our life in the unreal, stuck in a state of imagination, removed from the grace and beauty in which the universe wants us to share, not by forcing or striving, but simply by being. Objective achievement is not the goal; it's the by-product of being one with, and accepting, every unfolding experience and met in faith rather than resistance. Our education only reveals part of the picture, leaving us short-changed by a grand lie.

Because our pragmatic education system is designed around the greater good, it's easy to understand why performance feedback received in our formative years is interpreted as hard evidence of our ability and potential to succeed. The nature of standardised, comparative testing means that most of us will end up believing our ability is average or below. From a practical standpoint of service delivery, the system is adequate, but by definition it cannot deliver excellence. Mass education is a financially efficient means of transferring the minimum required level of communication skills which allow us to survive and coexist in a functioning economy. However, an objective life is far more than a function of the economy. After all, money won't buy you happiness.

Ego has no room for the subjective; to seamlessly rule our life, it must break down every event to an objective cause and effect. It decides that you are or you are not, just as computers are coded in 1's and 0's. Shades of grey not tolerated. This either/or feedback system works well in mastering automatically performed physical tasks, but not so well when it leads to the formation of habitual personality response. Whether the instantaneous response to a stimulus is anger, sadness, despondency or joy depends on the dominant early experience. For example, early on they teach us that performance assessments provide a critical benchmark to future potential, so if we continually fall below the benchmark, we naturally form a belief that, when compared to our peers, we're less than; we're dumb. Rating children against social/ educational benchmarks that are subjectively selected is a disincentive to achievement and detrimental to human progress.

Children who consistently score below average naturally form an enduring, low opinion of not only their ability but also themselves, believing the two are linked. Even well-meaning performance feedback from those within our sphere of influence reinforces our unflattering self-assessment. By the time we're early teens, our self-constructed life model is our operating ego, a reflection of, and a window into, the emotional events we experienced throughout childhood. Yet these were mostly unrelated, random events over which we had little or no control.

The probability of transcending the objectified 'you' is low unless we're aware of the 'you' or personal-construct (ego) creation process. Being oblivious to the constructed personality is the source of our relentless, damning self-opinion. It's rare to escape the hypnotic grasp of the apparently seamless ego without external intervention. Some shocking, perspective-changing life event is usually needed to reveal the 'ego illusion'. Bandler and Grinder, the fathers of neuro linguistic programming (NLP), in their acclaimed book *Reframing* (1982) called this a 'pattern interrupt'.[3] The shocking event or events jolt us from our learned, habitual pattern of thought where a trigger action guarantees a consistent but maladaptive response. With a pattern interrupt we get trigger, pause, awareness (Tip: The moment of i AM That (and I don't want to be), I am), opening a gap of opportunity to break the old, unhelpful thought pattern so we can replace it with a new and better reaction. This new awareness begins the process of taking back control from the ego.

Noticing, then changing your reaction to a new, progressive response is rare because the ego illusion of 'you' is entrenched through unconscious repetition. (Hence the strong opinions for and against the question, 'Can you teach an old dog new tricks?') For those experiencing effortless success congruent with their 'self-view—everything they touch turns to gold and all feedback from the material world combines to stroke their ego—this is certainly true. Why change what isn't broken? Matthew verse 19:24 (KJV) explains this idea as a parable: 'And again I say unto you, It is easier for a camel to go through the eye of a needle, than for a rich man to enter into the kingdom of God'.

Though this doesn't make you immune to a visit from the black dog of depression. For example, an athlete who is idolised by a captive audience of excited fans has a higher probability of experiencing depression once his/her athletic career ends. Boxing legend Sugar Ray Leonard famously

---

[3] Bandler and Grinder, *Reframing: Neuro-Linguistic Programming and the Transformation of Meaning*, Real People Press, 1982.

said, 'Nothing could satisfy me outside the ring ... there is nothing in life that can compare to becoming a world champion, having your hand raised in that moment of glory, with thousands, millions of people cheering you on.' To overcome extreme bouts of depression, Sugar Ray made repeated comebacks, attempting to affirm an identity that now existed only as a fading memory. After retiring, the achievements of famous sports people are dispatched to history, collecting dust in back issues of *The Guinness Book of Records*, while their new economic reality forces them to reinvent their identity, learning new skills while enjoying significantly less influence. Lavallee & Grove noted that 'changes in athletic identity were found to be significant determinants of adjustment for athletes upon career termination. Individuals with a high athletic identity at the time of retirement were more likely to experience a higher degree of emotional adjustment difficulties because of a profound sense of loss in their lives after putting their competing days behind them.'[4]

The developed world's existing education system focuses on learning styles that maximise productivity and value to a capitalist economy while failing to educate us about our infinite mind potential, let alone how to harness the inexhaustible superpowers of conscious creation. This educational shortcoming blinds us to our god-like subjective creation skills, leaving us a servant to our ego mind. Understanding this is the doorway to accessing and utilising our infinite potential.

Until recently, responsibility for spiritual belief/values education lay with the family, because parents are most likely to have their children's best interests at heart. Typically, parents, aware that the teachings of the wisdom traditions contain valuable keys to living a fruitful life, entrusted this training to their faith of choice. Unfortunately, however, their fear-based teaching approach failed naïve congregations. Now that Western religious networks have less influence, awareness of the need to nurture and understand our existential nature has been lost. This assists a surge in political and corporate evangelism that exploits our spiritual poverty via popular social policy indoctrination, which is influenced by contemporary political beliefs. Politics become just another dangerous

---

[4] Lavallee, Grove, and Gordon, *The causes of career termination from sport and their relationship to post-retirement adjustment among elite amateur athletes in Australia.*, Australian Psychologist, 32: pp 131-135, 1997.

ego-fuelled religion that mines and moulds plastic minds to its intended way of thinking.

Exploitation of young, fertile minds by anyone with the access and will is an established abuse of power that must be called out. Children must be educated to understand that personal power and self-love are their birth rights, and a sense of wellbeing is not something assigned by another—particularly not by those who believe that their inherited sense of power gives them the right to exploit the defenceless child-mind in order to enforce their world view and make the child comply with their version of right and wrong.

In a tweet, the Dalai Lama said, 'Modern education is premised strongly on materialistic values. It is vital that when educating our children's brains that we do not neglect to educate their hearts, a key element of which has to be the nurturing of our compassionate nature.'

Historically, poor individual outcomes result when the politicised state or religious denominations dominate egoistic or existential-nature training. Inevitably, the temptation to consolidate their power and wealth by influencing collective behaviour through the syllabus is irresistible. Any group who seeks to radicalise children by discreet indoctrination aims to appropriate their power. Eventually, they form—with help from a politician's most powerful weapon, the passage of time—an army of like-thinking disciples who can realise the governing group's vision, whether benign or malignant. Almost all of us are vulnerable to coordinated suggestions because we're unaware that thinking processes are habitual, predictable and dependent on the society in which we're raised.

This homogeneous, curriculum-driven education system fails at least half its students. It deliberately pits us against our peers, openly ignoring children's healthy long-term development in an obvious expression of Darwinism. In this environment there are three broad outcomes:

1. Success feeds further success;
2. Mediocre performance encourages approval seeking, fear of failure (judgment) and perfectionism;

3. Consistent failure leads to despondency, anger, and eventually disengagement.

A 2002 research paper published by Jennifer Crocker, PhD, a psychologist at the University of Michigan's Institute for Social Research shows up to eighty percent of students base their self-worth on academic performance. The study also found that adolescents with low self-esteem reported 'more stress, anger, academic problems, relationship conflicts and had higher levels of drug and alcohol use and symptoms of eating disorders.'[5]

Today it would be difficult to design a better system to cause endemic anxiety in young adults. Little wonder we spend a lifetime building an impenetrable, emotional wall to hide behind, believing our perceived deficiencies are fixed personality traits that would damage our chance of success if the truth got out. Hell, our educators told us they were, so what chance do we have of discovering the truth! Awake to this process and you'll be on your way to designing your own life, rather than being destined by central design to consume your vital energy in accomplishing another's life mission.

Who you think you are is a habit of repetitive thought conditioning, in the same way that walking is learned by unrelenting repetition. While our subconscious habit of walking on two legs is a skill learned with accurate, unbiased and objective feedback, effortlessly keeping us upright for a lifetime, the same can't be said about our ego habit. Learned values and beliefs, personified through our ego, are a snapshot in time of the dominant cultural view at the time we were educated. However, beliefs and values aren't static; they change with new discoveries and shifting public attitudes. Widely held beliefs that once represented foundational community ideals, and taught within the standardised school curriculum, are now no longer appropriate.

Unfortunately, involuntarily learned childhood beliefs are for all practical purposes hard-wired, a seamless part of identity, as tough to change as it is for a smoker to quit their habit. And yet contemporary leadership condemns, vilifies and discriminates against previous

---

[5] Crocker J, *The Costs of Seeking Self-Esteem*, Journal of Social Issues, Vol. 58, No. 3, pp 597-615, 2002.

cohorts for holding onto beliefs sponsored by their predecessors. This life experience, and the enduring presence of the 'generation gap', is assured in a standardised, education system that conditions, rather than guides, individual ego development.[6]

For so long as we believe that the source of our power comes from our cultural education, our lives will continue to be compromised because man's counsel has always proved to be opportunistic and inconsistent. Only after we recognise that the true source of personal power radiates from our inner subjective nature will we design a value system based on independent critical analysis, rather than political dogma, science, or trending pop culture.

Progressive, inclusive society must teach everyone capable of understanding the process of critical thinking that we're not defined by narrowly focused, comparative performance tests; we're greater than that! When developmentally appropriate, we must nurture our intrinsic creative capacity to forge a unique path in the world. Parents can play their part by taking back responsibility for their children's spiritual training and empower them to take control of their mental development and wellbeing at an early age. This needs to be done with a healthy symbiotic approach that recognises our individual equality, rather than the destructive, aggressive and parasitic 'winner takes all' approach favoured today.

---

[6] Montessori Method of Teaching

CHAPTER SEVEN

SO WHO AM I?

A T SOME POINT WE ASK, 'WHAT MAKES US WHO WE ARE, AND WHY are we a certain way?' Are we stereotypes of pragmatic society memes, like 'girls are made of sugar and spice and everything nice, while boys are made of puppy dog tails'? Or are we pre-set, determined by unique evolutionary genetic adaptations that enable us to thrive on our planet Earth?

For my first fifty years, I thought I knew what and who I was. I'd been well educated in a Western, democratic, socially responsible capitalist society modelled on the English Westminster political system. I unquestioningly accepted that I was an independent, unique human, with physical skills and IQ defined and limited by my DNA, enabling my ultimate potential—over which I had little influence—to be mapped and compared to others in my peer group. Reaching my full potential depended on my environment and access to a good education, factors over which I had no control.

In the same way that we accept the earth is a sphere, spinning in infinite space, we accept the idea that each of us reflects genetic traits fixed at conception, trusting the source of this idea implicitly and forming an unquestioned belief. However, believing that our ego is genetically determined and that we have no conscious control over our dominant traits can act as a crutch when our life isn't working out as expected. Such a belief can provide a convenient excuse to give up when the going gets tough, a sure-fire path to self-hate and loathing. Some express doubts about this dominant worldview after experiencing a radical transformation, but most reject alternative views at the subconscious level for being incongruent with the involuntarily accepted childhood beliefs that formed our ego's foundation. The argument that we're subconscious self-constructs (ego) acting automatically from habit may be accepted logically while still not comprehending the implications. Unsurprising, considering we're raised in the same learned macro model as our generational peers, this explains why repeated affirmations fail even when we accept the logic behind them. Regardless of how believable they seem; they're rejected by the person we believe we are.

While genetic inheritance plays an undeniable role in determining our essential physical attributes, the capacity to succeed is self-determined. Initially, because of our conditioning, the idea 'that our limiting thoughts are self-imposed, and we are free to renew ourselves infinitely in every moment' is as believable as being told the sky is green. You would think the messenger had lost touch with reality; undoubtedly the sky is blue, it's not open for debate! But where does this undeniable core belief originate? Was it instinctive at birth? We looked up to the sky and just knew that's blue? Of course not, we're taught it's a colour called blue. Someone coined the word blue, representing part of the visible light spectrum, and it became the accepted English language usage, facilitating communication and understanding. As a child, those with older siblings may recall them playing sneaky mind games, feeding you false information they convinced you was true. Later you discovered they were telling lies for a bit of fun at your expense.

Even if we accept the idea that we're products of our environment, what about attributes that are seemingly unrelated to upbringing? For example, 'My memory is terrible,' or 'I'm so uncoordinated', or 'I can't run to save myself,' or 'I can't speak to the opposite sex; I freeze up' and so on? In the ninth grade, Mr. Bevan, our music teacher, called me out in front of the entire class and said, 'Because you're obviously tone deaf, there's no chance you'll ever play a musical instrument.' This endeared him to my classmates at my expense. Being a bit of a runt, I was an easy target. The classroom erupted in fits of laughter, leaving me feeling small and embarrassed, and killing any desire to learn an instrument. I interpreted his words as 'because I wasn't born musically minded, trying would be a waste of time'. We're always the ones interpreting the feedback, making the decision that we don't have a lot going for us, and envying those who from the outside appear to have been born good at everything. Whether fact or fiction, my decision made the music teacher's statement true.

When we realise that our core beliefs aren't serving us to navigate our perceived reality, it opens the way for a better explanation of life. But we only let new ideas slip through our normally impenetrable wall of established beliefs when our ego gatekeeper is distracted by moments of intense emotional stimulation. These moments are our opportunity to be free of the old limiting construct, to experience being one with the beauty that is the universe or grace, and released from being triggered by spontaneous feelings of hate, fear, greed or envy.

I had not long turned fifty, when a new idea of who I was slipped through: *Each of us is a combination of both a fixed genetic form (essential by law) and a fluid personality construct (existential by choice) that arose from personal translation of the sensory information/suggestions that originated from my various guardians and influencers.*

Historically, construct replication is enabled either through random unconscious habit, or led by an influential and knowledgeable few who understand the mind's suggestibility. Because the concept of duality between our true unbounded nature and the limited ego is the basis of all scripture, I favour the later explanation. The central theme being that there is a physical and a spiritual element to us all. The illiterate were lectured from scriptures repurposed as stories of fire and brimstone, using fear and the threat of eternal damnation in hell. These threats—and the invention of an omnipotent, embodied god, who played favourites—was marketing genius, empowering the church to organise and control the uninformed masses. Using carrot and stick motivation psychology, the church convinced believers that compliance with God and their leaders' law would be rewarded, while noncompliance led to an eternal afterlife in hell. For the greater good? If our past is anything to go by, its purpose was more likely to have been to enrich the elite. Throughout history, dictators have indoctrinated their people, channelling their collective power for personal gain. The uneducated masses were the equivalent of livestock, herdable, exploitable and expendable.

We're oblivious to the personality construct development process. To illustrate, I'd floundered in second grade, so in a rare decision they made me repeat, drawing unwanted attention and leaving me feeling dumb, but worse, separating me from my friends. The accompanying feelings of embarrassment and shame reinforced and personalised my perceived comparative deficiencies. The naïve child mind is incapable of accurately processing overwhelming, negative emotional experiences objectively. The conclusion that something was wrong with me, while clearly false, was made an enduring fact in my mind. It explained the situation, ensuring it became buried deep within my subconscious, part of my constructed 'Geoff' avatar. Such limitations formed from interpretation of subjective evidence continue to affect us throughout our lives.

Whenever we're challenged by a situation, associated subconscious feelings resurface, reinforcing harmful mind chatter in an escalating feedback loop. This causes stress and anxiety and paralyses our ability to take appropriate action. Although self-destructive, this feedback is not intentionally malicious; it's just supporting the core beliefs or constructed view formed in childhood. Through repetition of thought (literal fertiliser), these significant emotional events sow the seeds that grow into beliefs of limitation, fear of failure and self-abuse. Negative self-talk expressed when in an emotional state—like 'I'm so dumb, I wish I was never born'—is destructive and disempowering, reinforcing the disease of limited thinking. Though we're too young to know this, we set the impact events, past or present, have on our future potential.

It's too easy for children in our hierarchical society to conclude they missed out genetically. A creative way for the ego to rationalise failure is with excuses. This absolves us of responsibility for our apparent shortcomings and affirms the belief that we're powerless victims, at the mercy of uncontrollable events acting on us from out there. In this view of life, success or failure is just about hereditary luck. We have all searched for excuses to explain our comparative failure. In such moments limiting emotional thoughts are rigidly attached to our avatar or Christian name, which can lead to self-consciousness and low confidence. Destructive self-talk disconnects us from all creative power, guaranteeing us more of the same. In time, playing victim becomes a disempowering conditioned reflex, as if it's part of our DNA. Repetition of any thought causes it to manifest in reality, in the same way as a physical habit is formed through repetition of actions. This is how personal beliefs are constructed, one brick at a time. That's why blaming our failures on anything out there or neurotically identifying as a victim is a path to perpetual anxiety, persecution and failure.

In a competitive world, the seed of any limiting self-talk is fed by day-to-day activities. Constant harassment of a child's unprotected mind by their peers and influential adults undermines healthy mental self-development, leading to a range of personality disorders and delinquency. For example, some children hurtfully label kids from children's homes as maggots (*Urban Dictionary*: Maggot (n): a name used to degrade somebody). These so-called 'normal' children confront them with repetitive suggestions that their parents rejected them for being born defective, likely nipping in the bud an innocent life equally endowed with unlimited potential to enrich humanity. Ignorance of constructs, luck and circumstance co-operate to ensure that, even as adults, those born into more fortunate circumstances mistreat them. Their own self-suggested mental abuse eventually blossoms into self-loathing—after all, it is a law of nature that the fruit has in it the seed that will produce a harvest after its own kind.

Even the government is not averse to indiscriminately attacking the vulnerable when they're in a tight spot, marginalising them in its constituent's minds. The vulnerable are easy targets, and they deflect attention from any real cause of mismanagement. Even the most fortunate in our society are quick to play the victim, believing they'd be better off if they weren't required to support the lives of the useless. In begrudging them even a subsistence level of survival, governments entrench the marginalised person's shame and low self-worth.

These are just a few examples of how early input influences our constructed life model (ego or personality) and affects our spiritual passage to becoming a well-balanced and contributing adult. Without the mental capacity to process them, continued exposure to adverse events focuses us on lack, inevitably leading to a personal construct of scarcity. The belief that we compare unfavourably to others is like a seed, flourishing as we repeat the thought over and over, until it dominates all we do.

We're taught at an early age that our experience results from cause and effect. We make our own luck, so there must be a logical reason behind why awful stuff keeps happening to us. In my first decade, I experienced and interpreted a persistent stream of events as 'bad'. Uncontrolled mental chatter (monkey mind) dwelling on these events convincing me that no good would come from my life, that I should always expect the worst. My mind, craving objective explanations, attached meaning to events over which I had no control. Repetitive self-talk, spoken in our voice, giving it ultimate credibility, guarantees that negative self-suggestion becomes a habit, making the thought 'I'm a hopeless loser' a physical reality. In this case, I concluded that the world was a hateful place, and that I was unworthy; thus I assumed the role of victim. The decision, once made, becomes a self-fulfilling order, a sentence to a lifetime of self-induced suffering. This simple example also carries in it the answer to our success.

Because the mind is complicit in forming limitations, it can't differentiate between a self-constructed limited ego and original infinite potential. From birth, mind is a passive servant, obediently implementing decisions made from the meaning derived from our limited life experience. This is how our past endures in ego, influencing our future potential, either empowering or disempowering us. I was confusing my self-constructed ego potential, with all its conditioned limitations, with unlimited birth potential! My ego was filtering my view of life through a self-programmed operating system (O.S.) constructed from involuntarily accepted, external suggestions. It's highly probable that generational bias caused by faulty, habitual thought habits (genetic conditioning) already distorted this input. Once our own interpretation of the events we experience is added to the mix, it's little wonder we struggle through life.

Favouring thoughts, establishes dominant neural pathways against which we filter all future experiences. Pathways with a negative bias present as self-defeating patterns that endure throughout adulthood.[7]

---

[7] J Young, *Reinventing Your Life*, New York: Plume, 1999, Early maladaptive schemas (EMS).

For reality to be congruent with our distorted, negatively biased beliefs, we conclude that all sensory feedback, as viewed through the lens of these beliefs, is objective evidence that the world is an evil place out to get us—a mind-set that ensures our failure. Through ignorance, we make misinformed personal conclusions drawn from a self-created illusion that, unfortunately, through habit, becomes just as true for us as if it were fact. We could just as easily decide the other way and our experience would be so; the universe always creates what we expect, instantly.

While our understanding of Earth develops through scientific discovery, continually revealing new realities, the view of our relationship within it remains relatively unchanged. In the past, mankind's survival demanded a focus on developing the 'essential' animal functions learned by following instructions from external suggestions, leveraging vast manpower. Meanwhile, our individual capacity to create abundantly from internal suggestions was ignored, left to languish, unattended. Realisation that we possess this creative element, which is far more powerful than our 'essential' earthly self and seamlessly connects us to the singular i AM or universe, reveals that the belief that events are 'personal and out to get us' is irrational. It's merely the unrealistic view held by an ego wanting events to bend to individual will, a narcissistic expectation.

There are no good or bad events, they just are. We're not attracting bad experiences because we're undeserving; that's an idea created by our ego's dominant thinking habits. Thoughts focused on repeatedly become a habitual part of our subconscious and part of our personality, as real and essential as our arms and legs. This is true of all habits, whether manifested physically, like smoking, or mentally by constantly repeating memories of our past unpleasant experiences, thus undermining our confidence in the present. Sorry tales of woe can run rampant through our subconscious mind and be habitually recalled when things don't play out as we think they ought to. These are the ones that make you say, 'If only there were a way to shock my brain and #startagain.' Fortunately, there is a much less painful and confronting way to achieve the same result.

It's not long before the image or ego that we build for ourselves one day at a time, gains total control over all we do, including our actions and reactions. We become the physical manifestation of our interpretation of who we think we are. This is guaranteed by habit force, just like a nicotine habit ensures a smoker will light another cigarette, whether they want to or not. Their actions are habitual, completed without conscious recognition, the ego having a proxy to act on behalf of the conscious mind. This is how I created the objective identity known by my Christian name, Geoff: an avatar or image that by thought habit was less capable than those I saw around me or read about in books, even when they told me I was much more. The characters I longed to be like seemed to have it all worked out.

I criticised and ridiculed myself, condemning my misfortune that I wasn't born a naturally blessed type A personality with the genetic advantage of inherent poise and mastery. I could list all the desirable traits I lacked, preventing my success in this dog-eat-dog world I had to endure. Ironically, I had single-handedly created this 'less-than image' called Geoff using my self-developed comprehension system, which gave meaning to the harsh things others had said or done to me, when in reality, I had needlessly limited myself by incorrect use of my mind.

The lesson in this is that we'll only be free of fear, doubt and worry when we accept that the continuous stream of thoughts running unrestrained through our mind are powerless until we shine the light of awareness on them and decide that they're in some way relevant to our life. With focus and time, like a seed, the chosen thought will sprout, growing until it's part of our physical reality. So rather than another deciding for you what thoughts are relevant to your life, best you choose. Find your own fearless path through conscious, critical awareness, so you can discover the unique truth to a life resonating with your dreams. Anything else is a sideshow.

CHAPTER EIGHT

OUR HIDDEN TREASURE

C OMPARING OURSELVES TO OTHERS IS A JOY-DESTROYING CANCER binding us to an illusion that Nirvana sits at the other side of achievement. Progress gauged against others, comparing our worst to another's best, guarantees we'll fall short of where we think we need to be. Framed this way, happiness is conditional on arriving at a point in the future that is dependent on our becoming something 'they' already are, and we wish we were. Using another's life to benchmark our performance makes happiness an unattainable moving target. It sets up a perpetual cycle that reinforces our self-designated role as a victim of circumstances and amplifies our stress and anxiety, leading to depression or worse. This is the karma of maladaptive thought patterns, or sowing and reaping (Mark 4:10-20 KJV). The idea that we need to improve and enhance ourselves before we can be seen as worthy is a deceit perpetuated by those empowering themselves with our appropriated energy. The great tragedy is that while we're shackled to another's dream, concentrating on lack, rather than being grateful for our abundance, an unconscious fog consumes our life force. We're asleep to the truth that, the moment we're conceived, we possess all we need to be and to flourish.

Unsurprisingly, this comparative belief system is central to the Darwinian approach of Western economic systems. Contemporary neoliberal political ideology illustrates this with its social-investment approach to welfare, where competitive ability determines overall wellbeing and our accessible lifestyle. A key element of this bold new global economic reality was the so-called level playing field, theoretically making it possible for anyone, no matter their background, to decide their own economic fate. Unfortunately, this element was missing from the practical framework; the idea of a universal debt reset was unpalatable. Extreme takes on capitalism may have succeeded had a debt jubilee been embraced.

At the opposite end of the ideological spectrum is the belief that everyone must be treated equally, regardless of merit, all of us having an equal right to all earthly resources. This requires centralised oversight and can only work when our essential animal instincts are totally repressed, that is we are all instantly, equally enlightened and following the same path—again this is unrealistic. Today's prevailing economy is a confusing hybrid. On the one hand, we're taught competition is fundamental to an efficient economy, yet arbitrary rules are applied, sometimes to maintain the status quo and other times to appease popular opinion. This makes a lie of the premise that financial success is entirely a result of personal choice. Economic reality reveals the folly of blindly following society's teachings.

Conflicting signals issued by our governance system are sufficient evidence that those directing us are more aware of mind-development processes than they care to admit, using it to achieve their own personal agenda. This knowledge endows them with a competitive advantage and immense global power. For example, for millennia Kabbalah, a body of knowledge within the Jewish faith which explored and taught the truth around 'i am That, i AM', could only be taught to a select few. Elite elders believed the information would be exploited if it fell into the wrong hands. Today, Kabbalah courses are available to anyone who has an interest in learning more about man's foundation in the spirit realm.

Awareness of our inherent capability to decide our own path effortlessly through critical, right thought is the greatest prize of all, reducing the impact of external influence on our future mental wellbeing. This realisation releases us from a dull, reactive robotic-like life and allows us to take back full control of our mind and destiny. No longer are we subconsciously controlled by the premeditated suggestion and agenda of others motivated by selfish goals of money and power.

The serendipity of an adult rebirth is that we get to reclaim our freedom to play and enjoy the fun that comes from designing our life, our way, one day at a time. We're free to choose a new story, unconstrained by the old and making the most of now, rather than being forever bound to a life decided long ago and despite us. I failed to grasp this fun fact until I went through the suffering that accompanies a family in depression. I was blind to the truth that everything I believed was me was in fact a self-constructed illusion affirming itself daily.

At conception, the 'I' or ego and its expectations didn't exist, only pure grace and knowing did. I was solely to blame for creating my personalised version of hell on earth by attaching meaning to external stimulus as if it were an objective fact, and then focusing attention on the resulting erroneous thoughts. Because my ego is personally constructed, I knew how to push all the best buttons to maximise my emotional pain and confirm my beliefs about my world. I operated subconsciously as the person I am (ego), not questioning how I became who I think I am. In the ultimate self-deception, I thought, 'This is me; I was born this way, and this is the most I will ever be.' For example, walking is a subconscious activity; we unquestionably walk upright, always have. To me, the moment I consciously learned by application of single-minded determination to walk on two legs never happened. We take it for granted that we always walked this way. However, our parents can set the record straight. They fondly recall the struggle, the frustration and the unashamed joy they shared while they watched us learning to walk—proof that I wasn't born walking. I had to learn, just as I wasn't always me; I learned that too!

The person we are today, our ego, was constructed in the same way we learned to walk. Unfortunately, the feedback, unlike the objective feedback we received when training our physical abilities, is mostly subjective. As already noted, the meaning translated from burning your hand on a hot plate is clear, there's no subjective ambiguity, being burned is painful and to be avoided. Compare this with a social interaction e.g., a child smiles innocently at a stranger, in return they're met with what looks to the child like a scowl. While the meaning of this perceived response is totally subjective, the child may translate this as a sign they've done something wrong. Their conclusion is biased by their feelings about themselves, drawn from previous experience, and these feelings initiate internal dialogue that questions why they received such a response. In a fruitless search for a new and better response so the undesired feeling isn't experienced again, they ask, 'What did I do?' Yet, the scowl is probably meaningless; the person may have been born with a 'smiling bitch face' or just had a dreadful day. They may be deep in thought, writing their own sorry tale of woe, oblivious of us or our friendly smile. Even if their negative response is directed at us, it's not our concern. The meaning they interpret from their social interactions is their subjective choice. We can't know their process of determining meaning unless we're able to sit down and ask them questions, otherwise we're assuming through our established bias, making an ass of both you and me—ass-u-me.

We're born unconditionally worthy, but our total dependency at birth conditions us to external validation. Children naturally avoid pain by trying to please their carers. Our initial environment emphasises contrasting labels like yes or no, good or bad, right or wrong and smart or dumb. We interpret these contrasts as objective evaluations of our character, rather than what they are: subjective, impersonal markers assisting us to achieve the desired goal of pleasure over pain, courtesy of our natural self-correcting servomechanism. In time, conditioned personalised response extends to all external events. For example, whenever I was in a hurry to get to an important meeting, it seemed like every traffic light would turn red just as I approached! Impatient and annoyed for fear of being late, I'd habitually repeat the subconscious thought spoken in my voice, 'Typical, I'll be late unless I drive over the speed limit, then I'll probably get stopped by the police and fined! Why does this only happen to me? Blah, Blah, Blah.' The response of a victimised mind running wild with neurotic thoughts, believing all life is personal. This is a maladaptive way to think, showing we're under the control of our child-formed ego mind—the ego loves drama, especially if it means it gets to see us suffer. Life is not personal, while our ego assuredly is. Ironically, this moment when our outrage, our resistance to reality, reaches a crescendo is our best opportunity to make a change. It creates a gap that, if you pause, lets you see that you're reacting from a subconscious and stale script. The reality is that most things have no objective meaning, they just are; it's our script creating the anxiety. The self-destructive and disempowering horror story I've heard so many times before, even when accompanied by all the cursing in the world, will not change a single thing apart from my blood pressure. I don't resist a green light, so why would I resist the opposite? We have learned to resist things as they are, in the mistaken belief that our happiness depends on them being some other way. Linking happiness to things in this way guarantees perpetual suffering as a world that never bends to our will. I realise now that when things seem to go against me, it's just the way it is, there's no one sitting there flicking a switch to red every time I approach traffic lights. If they're red, I accept that everything is as it should be in this moment and that it can be no other way.

Awareness of resisting the moment reveals the 'gap', the space of opportunity usually owned by the controlling subconscious ego. Instantly, the moment we release resistance, we take power back from the ego. We see it (the moment), rather than be it (ego). Recognising the gap is our chance to make alternative response choices and reframe the situation. This is being present to the moment, still and content with how things are, not how your ego thinks they should be. So what if we're late? That's the way it is. Accept the consequences, stay in the moment and deal constructively with what happens when it happens. Accept that we're bigger than consequences. Rather than planning to defeat self-created zombies out to get us if we don't do this, be there, and achieve that. We're better served if we reserve our energy for solving genuine issues as they arise. Rely on effective affirmative action rather than resorting to meaningless excuses like, 'I was late because as usual the lights were against me.' This just binds us to our 'typical' experience.

In the 1960s, my hometown in New Zealand was safe even for pre-schoolers to explore unsupervised. We were outside exploring riverbanks, searching for mushrooms on surrounding farmland and even roaming the railway track, oblivious to danger, rather than being stuck at home being bored and annoying. Stay-at-home mothers were the norm, childcare centres the exception, and our mums always close at hand. The school run of today didn't exist; there were few cars outside the morning and evening rush hours.

In 1963, my parents built their first house. I recall as a four-year-old, independently walking to the house site for the first time and from a distance proudly admiring the timber frame rising, developing into our home. Just as I was about to cross the road to explore the deserted section, a boy on a bike confronted me and threateningly demanded to know what I was doing in his street.

'Looking at my new house,' I meekly replied.

He sneered, 'That's not your house; this is my street, not yours!'

I'd never encountered such aggressive behaviour before, and although I was sure this was the right street and the right house, he left me confused. His assertive claim raised doubt in my mind.

Uncertainty about the truth and an invented, assertively expressed story shows how the persuasiveness as much as the reputation of the speaker influences our beliefs. This illustrates the subjective nature of our personal reality and how circumstances and emotions influence it, especially when we're out of our comfort zone. Our minds are easily convinced that a lie is true and the truth, a lie. Once we believe the lie, we will act on it just as surely as if it were the truth. History shows that we'll even support wars justified by lies when those advocating for them are passionate, outspoken and hold greater power. Our unique interpretation of meaning from feedback data or suggestions received through personal relationships or reputation can distort our ego model, so that our view of reality differs a little or a lot from absolute reality. If a lot, we feel like we're forever banging our heads against a brick wall. This feeling will persist until we notice that it's our own thinking habits leaving us bloodied and bruised.

At four we're clueless of our seamless connection to a super mind, the source of abundant creative power. We're taught from birth that we're distinctly individual, then in school we're subtly introduced to the concept of competition. We learn all resources, including success are scarce, so competitive ability dictates our future. 'To the victor belong the spoils' (Macy, 1831). Scant attention is given to spiritual training, and even then, the focus is on personifying our deities as distinct, judgmental identities, further reinforcing the central belief of discrete separation and individuality. Educators fail to teach us of our connectedness to the collective, creative super mind, because they're unaware of it and the idea is not part of the accepted belief system. In my example of childhood confrontation, I focused only on interpreting the unwelcome feedback received from the boy on his bike. At that moment, I felt powerless and out of control because I had no knowledge of the reservoir of power into which I could tap that would provide the faith that I would survive this disturbance and the accompanying feelings of anxiety and fear.

I was emotionally consumed by the moment, rather than seeing it from a position of grace. There was no feeling of cooperation or play or fun being conveyed in this confrontation, just one of hostility and doom. I felt vulnerable and inadequate. I lacked the life experience that would allow me to defuse this tense situation with empowering, calming language that appealed to his curiosity and sense of superiority. For example, I could have said, 'Hang on, mate, this is our new home; I'll be living next door soon. Let's look together.' Instead, surrendering, I ran for the safety of home.

A state of fear blocks access to the super mind, the source of abundant creative power. Instead, our automatic, adrenalin-fuelled, limiting response of fight or flight takes over. In my opinion, this response is one of the few instinctual survival attributes we share with animals. An element of our innate programming, it ensures we have a lifesaving autopilot mechanism that's not dependent on free will. However, once we realise this is an ancient, pre-programmed safety habit, free will can be applied. I could've thought, 'What right did he, or any stranger, have to intimidate me, making me feel afraid? It doesn't matter if I'm in the right place (which I am) or not; I have every right to be here.'

Time and experience have taught me that bullies will go to any length to invent a story that supports their views and beliefs. Their defiant, emphatic belief in their fabricated story leaves us bewildered, doubting what is undoubtedly the truth for fear of being wrong and looking foolish. This is (f)alse (e)vidence (a)ppearing (r)eal, forming the four-letter acronym FEAR.

I was too young to realise that this isolated event contained no meaning about my ability, and it affected me negatively, leaving me wary of others. Even today the memory remains vivid; its recollection provokes the feelings I had then, as if I were experiencing the event right now. If it holds a lesson, it's that some people find it necessary to force their will on others to validate their own sense of self-worth. Still, no matter how threatening they seem, we always survive their interference to experience another moment. Ask yourself, 'What's the worst that can happen? They can't eat me!'

We must grasp that 'now' is always new, boundless and exclusive of the past. Any perceived impact of an elapsed event can be discounted, its power exhausted. Any influence it has now is a creation of our perception. However, as children we're not aware that external feedback is as likely to be subjective as objective, even in controlled situations like the classroom.

Every person's reaction to a stimulus is unique and relative to their own bias, because of genetics and stored conclusions they've drawn from random events in their life. Another's response to us is always subjective, applies to that moment only and is never a reliable gauge of our potential. Negative judgement received from others isn't binding, nor does it damn us for eternity; we make that choice. Similarly, we're not to blame for another's actions or excuses. Like us, they have free will to choose what to think, say and do. It doesn't matter if their choice was influenced by the suggestive power of another, or arose from their own critical thinking, the impact is the same.

The feelings generated by the confronting, threatening experiences of childhood are arguably universal. Still, we obsess over negative comments prefaced with our name and fuelled with emotion as if they apply uniquely to us. For example, 'What were you thinking, Geoff? Don't be a moron; you're so dumb!' We're prone to accepting unpleasant feedback without hesitation or reservation, even when it's from strangers. Their comments trigger harmful self-talk like, 'They're right! I wish I wasn't like that,' prompting our ever-present, target-seeking servomechanism to search for a solution to 'fix us', thus inoculating us against the pain of future criticism. Being a subjective experience, social interaction is never the same, so the search is a waste of energy. A sure-fire formula that applies in every situation and saves us from the suffering brought on by a focus on our faults doesn't exist. Resisting this truth attracts more of the same, compounding our pain and anxiety.

When things don't go our way, or as expected, we invent excuses to rationalise our failure. Blaming someone or something else becomes a habit. We do it to shift the responsibility for our perceived life failures away from ourselves, thus empowering our excuse, but also halting our progress. While we believe the cause of our suffering is external, out of our control, there will be no end to it. In other words, we are victims of our chosen thought habits. Because things aren't how we want, we're in a constant state of outrage and/or helplessness. Let's call it a 'Pity Party', a state of regret that strips us of resourcefulness, making us a victim of circumstance. This is another thought error. Success or failure has nothing to do with circumstances because they're nearly always out of our control. Time spent dwelling on thoughts of regret is an energy sink, trapping us in the past. Believing opportunity is depleted with time embeds a feeling of lack and indifference, rather than abundance and gratitude. Reliving painful stories in the present blind us to the beauty and potential that is abundant as ever, despite the circumstances that brought us here. This is true regardless of any evil deeds committed in our past and is the motive behind the Catholic practice of confession, which absolves us of all past sins. Our ego maintains its hypnotic grip on our destiny, taking every opportunity to replay painful moments as if they're happening now, torturing us with past indiscretions. Yet all past moments are powerless; they only exist in memory. Any feelings of suffering attributed to them are an illusion, still affecting us now only because we give them permission through learned childhood habit.

I subscribed to the idea that it is 'better to be quiet and be thought a fool, than to open my mouth and remove all doubt' (Abraham Lincoln). The thought of opening my mouth in a crowd left me feeling anxious. I'd rather remain anonymous, avoiding examination from all those eyes focusing on me. Eventually, through repetition, this avoidant behaviour was embedded as a subconscious response. Of course, it was my interpretation that dealing with people is stressful, and that led to avoidance seeming like a solution. At the time this was a seemingly logical, conscious choice made from suboptimal interpretation by a child's mind. It's easy to see why we believe shyness is genetic. 'It's the way I was born,' we say. 'I can't change that'. I was too young to have any recollection of the decision to avoid all potentially confronting situations.

Imagine strolling along a deserted city path fixated on solving our latest problem, oblivious to both the changing scenery and the time. In the distance someone else appears. This shakes us from our trance in order to give this new threat our full attention. Do we know them? What's their name? If not, do we ignore them, say hello, attempt a conversation or prepare to fight or flight? Anxiously, our ego searches our memories for the right way to handle the moment when our paths will invariably cross. Simultaneously, we're annoyed at this interruption; we yearn to be alone again, enveloped in our familiar, comfortable state of trance. Because encounters like this are inevitable, you'd think we'd eventually develop an assured response to deal with our urge to flight or fight, so we can conserve our nervous energy for more important tasks. We learned to tie shoelaces subconsciously, so why can't we deal with this event the same way? Why do we experience the same feelings of anxiety every time?

The answer is in the difference between subjective interpersonal encounters and objective physical tasks, like tying shoelaces. We possess a self-correcting learning system (servomechanism) designed to master essential, objective living processes. Once we achieve competency, these processes are delegated to and operate from the subconscious level, releasing our mind from the mundane, so we can further create and modify our physical environment as it chooses. This organic learning system has allowed us to achieve progressive mastery of our planet. Tying shoelaces, once learned, works effortlessly every time; the more we attempt the task, the better we get. Through trial and error our servomechanism adjusts our muscle movements until it successfully zeros in on the finite goal, achieving unconscious mastery—a reward for our persistence. Now it's automatic; our muscles know exactly how to move and never have to consciously think about tying our laces again. However, our mind is not our physical body. It's not designed to respond as a programmable robot creating muscle memory to unconsciously perform repetitive, fixed physical tasks. The mind is constantly encountering new inputs via other people with infinitely variable minds; an approach that worked with one person today won't necessarily work tomorrow, and is unlikely to work with someone else. Imagine if every time you tie your shoes the length of the laces changed, gravity somehow varied or your fingers became all thumbs! This is the subjective world our mind constantly confronts with unavoidable human encounters. No wonder we're uncomfortable and anxious around others.

These events reveal whether we're living our life in the moment or delegating it to ego, hoping it has the answer to save us. When living from ego, the mind attempts to relieve our anxiety by finding an appropriate response from experience; of course, there is none. It's likely the future event you imagined is a story that never eventuates; the stranger disappears from the path into a house 200m in the future! The perceived threat only existed in a fictional story of pending doom, written by an unconscious, untrusting, neurotic mind to which we've handed control. When we're in the moment, time neither drags nor flies; we live in faith with poise to meet trivial moments without a need to subordinate the solution to the subconscious ego and its old ways.

In my opinion the servomechanism was not designed to create a static model or ego managing our interactions with others, as if interpersonal relationships and activities are a learned skill like tying shoelaces. Imagine being transported to another world where, unknown to you, tying shoelaces is impossible. Experience tells us it's possible, but no matter how hard we try, we fail! How frustrating would that be? Our ego is like this, we're exceeding its design specifications. We must stop giving attention to the ego's habit of replaying old memories or horror stories of past indiscretions as if they're relevant now. Our ego servant isn't malicious. It's doing what it does, helping us achieve our goals, but through ignorance of its function, we've set it unachievable objectives. People are unique, so this one-size-fits-all approach will never work. You can't set an autopilot (servomechanism) to hit an infinitely variable target, yet this drives our futile search for skills and techniques to ensure we're in control of every challenging situation encountered.

An archaic, static model in a dynamic environment is a recipe for suffering, yet this is how most of us were taught to operate. We are like zombies with buttons; when pushed they trigger an automatic, predictable reaction, making us easy to control, influence and manipulate. We mistakenly believe that we can achieve mastery over every situation by learning clever routine responses that will have us always on top of the situation, in total control, never found wanting or feeling inadequate relative to the competition. The infinite number of ever-changing random events makes this goal unrealistic. Still, our dutiful servant the servomechanism attempts, through trial and error, to achieve this goal of habituating an effective response to subjective events. It's an unreasonable, unattainable expectation, like trying to fit a square peg in a round hole. Yet when met with continual failure, we blame ourselves for our seeming lack of ability to deal with life effectively. The feeling of failure is the only thing successfully habituated, giving more power to our internal ego voice to gloat over our shortcomings. This only serves to move us further from our source of power.

Interpersonal encounters are a necessary and central part of a full, happy life. However, the thought of them leaves us feeling anxious, self-conscious and disempowered. Reliance on ego is to blame for our inability to overcome the fear associated with these encounters. It's an expert at autocompleting physical life processes in the background, but at the cutting edge, when we've got no choice but to be present, it fails us. Ego is a library of learned, static snippets, incompatible with chaos, while our life, contrary to what we're taught, is happening in a laboratory of conscious, chaotic discovery. In creative, fast-moving situations like interpersonal encounters, because the target is infinitely dynamic, the ego's biofeedback learning process is ineffective. Because we compare our worst traits with another's best, magnifying our mistakes while simultaneously discounting theirs, relying on ego becomes the source of our perceived inferiority. This is particularly so if they are conscious creators, not bound by self-deprecating thought habits, while we're micro focused on improving our faults in the misguided aim of being accepted as an equal. We're absorbed in freeing ourselves from what we perceive as the painful criticism of others but is more likely harsh criticism invented by our ego—by which I mean the concept of 'you' and known as your Christian name.

The need to improve is driven by the feeling that we lack what it takes to achieve success and happiness. We believe we're missing that one ingredient that allows us to easily conquer those frequent challenges that specifically target us. Skilled marketers highlight this feeling, spruiking the idea that they possess the formula guaranteed to save us from ourselves, the secret door to a grace-filled life. When we realise interactions are subjective and all solutions negotiated, we escape this self-development addiction. Because we cannot fully meet each new moment until it happens, there is only one guaranteed formula to meet life in a way that always gives us what we want; self-love is the only path to achieving grace.

If we had an education dominated by the study of logic and science, it's likely we're prisoners to the belief that success depends on us finding the one way, the right way. This perfectionist attitude means we never get to appreciate the abundance that always exists in and around us. We're rendered oblivious to what's unfolding in our real physical environment, while we're searching around within a past illusion (ego), searching for the solution to a future illusion (ego projection) framed as if it's real. The entire event is merely a horror story magically created by our mind. These thinking habits, projected from our learned core beliefs, are hijacking our experience of the pure moment. Essentially, we're wondering about in a fog of the past as if running on autopilot, asleep to the present unfolding right now in our life. Now our habits, collectively termed the ego, have total control of our experience.

Thinking patterns reflecting our core beliefs define us. They are our go-to when meeting any event. Because the thinking to action process is seamless, we're unconscious of this. So much for free will! This habitual thinking or habit-force process[8] where the ego controls every response by subconsciously projecting past results into the future, dooms our life to an illusion lived in the blink of an eye. If we remain in this trance, these long-established, third-party habits eventually fail. Feeling like an alien in the contemporary reality, we'll be pining for the familiarity of the good old days when we understood society and what it wanted from us. There are better third-party operating manuals than our ego!

---

[8] Napoleon Hill, *Think and Grow Rich*, Sound Wisdom, 1937.

CHAPTER NINE

IS THERE ANOTHER WAY?

WHAT IS THE DIFFERENCE BETWEEN SOMEONE WHO WORRIES excessively about future outcomes and another who meets every event with poise, allowing it rather than resisting it? Poise accompanies the belief that we're more than enough to meet any situation as it arises, aware we're conceived with all we need to prevail and flourish. Poise arises from knowing success is not dependent on techniques or methods learned from others, but a non-negotiable part of our makeup reflected in a willingness to take immediate action.

Compared to the typical ego model created decades before from thoughts of fear and worry, effective people present with a model that reflects their authentic self. They transcend the ego's compulsive habit of searching its back story for solutions that will save them from embarrassment, failure or shame. Our energy, instead of being wasted on unproductive worry that fuels anxiety, is focused on the only place where creation happens, the here and now. This accelerates the manifestation of our consciously chosen goals. After all, what's the worst that can happen when even our desire for survival at any cost is an illusion of the ego? Understanding this releases us to fearlessly roll with the moment, accepting ourselves as we are. When we look back over our lives at the many events with which our ego terrorised us, we realise that these were insignificant blips on our overall timeline.

Children's minds are defenceless against the many distressing events that inevitably happen after taking their first breath. We're not assigned a wise buddy to alert us to bad input and warn us that, outside of now, this event has no power or meaning, unless you choose to attach it. Negative experiences get emotionalised straight to memory. Persistently interpreting negative outcomes as evidence that we're flawed creates a filter that distorts the lens through which we view our world. Focused on the thought that 'the world delivers me nothing but disappointment and pain', we fear life and avoid and resist all it sends. The child becomes sensitised to experiences confirming their belief, guaranteeing the appearance of more feelings of pain. We reveal in the world what we first see in our mind, by obsessively seeking supporting evidence to confirm the beliefs we choose to accept. Through thought, we create it. A magic trick of our own making. With a little knowledge of what we are, this can be uncreated.

We believe the reflection in the mirror is proof of what we are for the duration of our life—a unique, identifiable, solid piece of flesh and blood with specific capabilities and limitations determined by birth. A self-made up of excuses or reasons for why we aren't what we should be justifies our relative failure. These excuses rationalise limitations explained by our genetic uniqueness, thus releasing us from personal responsibility. Yet genetics has little to do with it; our limitations of intellect, power, and capability arise from subjective self-creation, reflecting choices made from childish interpretations of childhood experiences. It's a sad indictment of the human condition when such a powerful creation is encouraged to believe we begin life innately unworthy—worthiness being conditional on doing and accomplishing. This is the tragedy of our lives; but with an understanding of ego formation, we can recover.

We are all entitled to be free of our self-constructed ego prison. By making this information both accessible and understandable, suffering and impoverished thinking habits perpetuated across generations (genetic conditioning) can be eliminated. The collective minds and labour of the majority are the fuel that powers our world. This is a closely guarded secret by some, giving them control over human energy for their own enrichment. An understanding of our role as creators is our birth right, and those that seek to keep it hidden are perpetuating an evil; they are a plague to the future of humanity.

CHAPTER TEN

HAVE I GONE COMPLETELY MAD?

AFTER WHAT SEEMED LIKE A LIFETIME OF SUFFERING, I DISCOVERED that I was living in the self-constructed prison of the illusionary ego. Traumatising events reinforced my belief that I was a spectacular failure, experiencing a living hell. I rationalised my woeful situation by succumbing to the ultimate excuse: I was a victim of my DNA. My destiny was out of my control; no amount of learning or positive thinking could change my genetic potential. The proofs of this were all around me. Rotten luck at birth damned me to the wrong quadrant of the four described by Florence Littauer in her book *Personality Plus.*[9] Her guidelines categorised me as a Peaceful Phlegmatic or the Dove— which to my mind was the equivalent of being the runt of the litter. I envied those guaranteed smooth passage through life, thanks to their genetically privileged dominant 'alpha' personalities.

Now that I'd hit rock bottom with no respite in sight, I had no choice but to embrace my life exactly as it was, with no expectations. Surrendering to this reality proved to be serendipitous, leading to a fundamental change in my view of life. The clue that freed me from the ego trap lay in my perceived life trauma. I was living a lie; I had unwittingly victimised myself through my own belief that I was powerless to change things. Now that a fresh perspective had revealed itself to me, I was done with trying to force life to happen in a particular

---

[9] Littauer F, *Personality Plus: How to Understand Others by Understanding Yourself*, Revell, 2012.

way. I no longer felt the pressure to justify my very existence. What a huge relief!

In the early 1980s, the *kill or be killed* ideology was in the ascendant. Social Darwinism interacted with popular economic policy. Developed nations embraced neoliberalism and aggressively implemented it globally. They promised open participation and transparent distribution of wealth through free-market principles that would reward superior performance with individual prosperity, influence, and esteem. Transparent competition would increase overall prosperity and drive the efficient allocation of resources, reducing the waste of both human and financial capital. Fresh out of university and still wet behind the ears, I accepted this globally promoted dogma hook, line, and sinker! My life's worth now condensed into a set of performance indicators or KPI's.

My mind was fertile ground for this ideology. I experienced first-hand what business failure could do to a family. Childhood disappointment drove me to escape a life of poverty, free from the control and judgment of others, but first, I needed to conquer my feelings of inferiority. I diligently followed the techniques and ideas in popular self-improvement programmes. Still nothing changed. The harder I tried to make life give me what I wanted, the less likely it seemed I could achieve it. Frustrated with repetitive failure, I questioned my ability to reach my definition of success because mental anguish was the only abundance manifesting in my world.

This is especially true if our productivity falls outside society's expectations. The contemporary free-market economy, promising reward consistent with effort and enterprise, arguably fails to deliver even to those within the statistically normal part of the population. Fall outside these norms and you're certain to struggle, survival being reliant on inadequate social-welfare programmes deliberately set well short of the level required for a dignified existence—a state-sanctioned punishment for economic failure, regardless of how it arose. In my family's experience, society's concept of survival of the fittest was alive and well; we felt its full effect! The fear of not being able to make ends meet, provide a secure, warm home in my native country or even have enough food was a constant stress.

This condition remained until I realised that grace can't be learned;

it's allowed. Grace was trying to find me. All I had to do was stop resisting events I labelled as bad, as if they were a personal punishment. I needed to accept that life is not personal, and challenges are the rule, not the exception. Nothing will ever be the way I want it to be, as right now it's already the way it must be; no amount of resisting will change it. My one goal as an objective being is simply to be at one with what's happening around me, accepting all that I encounter without prejudice. I had to reach the point where I recognised that 'all is as it is meant to be right now; the universe around me and in me is expanding perfectly for the benefit of us all and see it, don't be it.'

In the song *The Climb*, Mylie Cyrus sings, 'There's always going to be another mountain.' Accepting mountains or challenges as a normal part of life releases us from a state of constant anxiety caused by the childish belief that everything around us is at odds with how we need it to be. Believing happiness depends on specific results means we're always fighting battles and climbing mountains imagined into our life. The universe doesn't care about how we think it should be, despite our protests, it moves in synchronisation with each recent discovery of what was always possible.

How do we end up so far from the reality faced in the present moment? We all have an expanding storehouse of memories, a series of interconnected neural pathways, proportional to our objective timeline that create the illusion of unified form and consciousness moving through an identifiable past into an imagined future. It's as if we're a single grain of sand flowing through an hourglass that consumes our finite, objective resource of eighty plus years, getting closer and closer to the end.

Stop-motion graphics illustrates the impression of continuity. An animated stickman, comprising a deck of separate, slightly unique pictures, rapidly played in sequence appears to be a single moving object, rather than fifty static drawings on fifty separate cards. In the same way, independent memories masquerading as interdependent events progressing through time trick us into believing our life is a continuous, objective movie with an inevitable ending (with or without a list of credits). This concept of time limits today's experience to the accuracy of our interpreted meaning of the past.

Core beliefs arise from our earliest decisions of who we think we are and endure throughout our personal timeline or life, influencing today's decisions. Time decay arouses feelings of urgency and regret. We believe that our next moment contains less opportunity than the last, reinforcing the perception that life is a competition to secure and accumulate scarce resources before we run out of vitality and time. This attitude of scarcity creates a fear of living—what if we make the wrong choice only to waste another one of our limited opportunities to achieve success? It's not surprising we have an epidemic of decision anxiety, regret and self-criticism. With this learned attitude to life, fear of missing out becomes a self-fulfilling prophecy.

Date stamping memories creates an illusion convincing us that elapsed time applies to both objective and subjective reality. Hypnotised by this collective understanding of time and its correlation with our changing bodies, we extrapolate physical aging, assuming holistic cause and effect, to our mental capacity—meaning that our existential mind must be being depleted and exhausted in the same way as our essential body. Yet they are independent; that which is earthly is finite while that which is heavenly is infinite and interlaced. While age is true regarding the body, it is not with respect to the mind. Being conscious of this is to see that you are eternal and death is an illusion.

We accept the statement that 'you can't teach old dog's new tricks' because we're all unconsciously living in the streets of an ego town called 'Deception'. Ego consists of linear streams of experience arising from events unconsciously interpreted on a continuum from empowering to limiting. We believe that these streams, or vivid memories, represent who we are, and we embrace them like priceless possessions. Yet they only represent who our ego has made us, someone trapped in a labyrinth of self-constructed alleys, increasingly isolated from the only truth, the real moment that is now. The longer we've walked Deception's streets, the safer and more familiar they feel, so the harder they are to escape. We're stuck in our comfort zone, an endless loop of limiting possibilities. Our present experience is unconsciously conditional on past performance, which locks us into a future repeating the past— Groundhog Day without the iterative growth. Some of these memories draw us back into reliving events we regret or would rather forget, punishing us, as if they're happening again, right now. Habitually bound to this past, we're oblivious to pure, real-time sensory feedback, leaving chunks of our life unaccounted for and giving the impression that time is speeding up.

The belief that we are bound to our past is an illusion, a thinking error, becoming more significant with time spent in the familiar embrace of unchallenged, learned childhood responses. The past is unreal; it can't bind us any more than we can stop the ebb and flow of the tide. Its influence is easily erased with the click of a finger, startling us from the comfort zone of memories into which we unconsciously and unwittingly sink, from sunrise to sunset. To escape, 'Stay calm, just breathe and mind the gap'. Until we're consciously aware of our ego and decide to break free of its control, life remains merely a habit created from repetition of the decisions we made from events experienced decades before.

A nagging, distant awareness that we're being tormented repeatedly by the same problem is our mind alerting us through life's noise that we're captured. This feeling of Déjà vu is life attempting to jolt us awake, freeing us of the ego's grip. When we unconsciously delegate decisions to the ego, by continually referring to past events and experiences, and then projecting these outcomes forward, we limit our potential. Recalled memories provoke the same feelings now as when they first occurred; if disempowering then, they're disempowering now. This is how uncontested memories punish us relentlessly, especially if we're plagued by low self-esteem.

We habitually focus on those memories, thus confirming our opinion of ourselves, and over time they accumulate and become our ego. This creates the conditions that leave us feeling inferior and powerless in what appears to be an increasingly unfamiliar and unfriendly world. Meeting life through our ego filter like this, guarantees that in time all that was easy and familiar ceases to be relevant or even exist. We are left confused and angry, or while passively awaiting the final taxi, resigned to a life reminiscing the good old days when we were immersed in fun, laughter and family.

Those aware of the concept of time being a practical construct irrelevant to the timeless mind, where the moment called now is all there is, ever was and ever will be, maintain a joyful spirit despite physical aging. They know that man's environment is at the mercy of those controlling today's popular opinion, pimping their latest snake oil, pushing their brand of salvation and exploiting the sleeping masses to gain power, prestige and wealth for their disciples. They've learned to negotiate change effortlessly, realising that man's world is synthetic, subjective and impermanent, increasingly unrecognisable from their childhood. Awareness of our integral nature allows us to see through the mind-conditioning deception perpetuated by authority that we faithfully adopted in childhood. Awakening is to embrace what is eternal — the sounds, sights, smells, textures and tastes that are timeless, where beauty and God exist, and in whose light we are renewed daily. The rest is a sideshow!

The economic and educational systems favoured by global power brokers reflects the statement that 'absolute power corrupts absolutely'.[10] Economies eventually evolve to achieve maximum output from the available labour, regardless of their underlying ideology and initial humanitarian goals. This outcome takes precedence over individuals' wellbeing, revealing to varying degrees that historically populations have been farmed to expand financial trading systems, mostly benefiting the established elite. Farming in this context refers to the mass, rote education of children with contemporary theories, in isolation of creative reflection of their subjective formulation.

Our worldview, formed and embedded in our subconscious through an education received in good faith, arose from a process of progressive evolution specific to us and our cohort, culminating in today's unique experience. Students in every era obediently study, becoming proficient at what's placed in front of them, trusting that it will benefit them and their communities by expanding wealth and collective prosperity. Being children, we're naive spectators in this moulding process that aligns us with the state's vision for the future. In this way, the human mind is trained as if it's simply a servomechanism requiring filling with instructions before it's considered useful.

This sells us short. We are exceptional beings, born almost entirely free of instincts, giving us the ability to create whatever we will from

---

[10] Lord Acton 1834-1902.

thought. Unfortunately, our training ignores this. Instead, we're taught to depend on an objective, subconscious mind model reliant on a habitual approach to thinking taught within all educational frameworks. With progress, man's evolving collective intelligence eventually makes our earnestly learned skills and values on which these habits were based, obsolete. The continuous flow of new understanding displaces the falsehoods of a bygone era, leading to better visions appropriate to today's technology and economic priorities. This evolves until the new understandings become endemic in the lives of new generations, but they feel awkward to former ones, causing growing anxiety and tension.

Today's elders, who gave decades of honest, valuable service, are now ridiculed by the same authorities who administered their indoctrination. Their offence? The innocent acceptance, taught them by an unavoidable authority, that a fact today is an enduring fact forever. Which it's clearly not. Across a single lifetime, the truth as taught in the school curriculum, including something as seemingly absolute as our history, changes as a result of shifts in demographics, religious, political and corporate agendas. Formerly widely embraced progressive organisations, events and records are renounced as inappropriate or harmful. Collectively accepted wisdom beliefs, having endured for centuries, become targets of suspicion and loathing. Even seemingly fact-based, socially beneficial mores promoted just a generation ago are now categorically and vehemently condemned. This is proof, confirmed by the experience of prior generations, that we're raised within a flawed and disingenuous model, designed to exploit our collective productivity before our inevitable expiration.

No or little regard is given to the effect significant social and technological change has on seniors, who through no fault of their own, lack the skills valued in a modern workplace. It's cheaper to replace than retrain. The discovery of the computer signalled the end of typewriters and typing pools. The development of AI directed, self-drive electric cars will see motor mechanics go the same way.

Automation and the adoption of smart systems in businesses reduces human contact, increasing isolation and feelings of loneliness. Seniors are disproportionately affected by these changes, devastating their mental health and well-being. The mass adoption of email over the last twenty-five years illustrates this; it lead to post offices reducing the availability of public mailboxes. Mobility compromised seniors, who laboriously learned as children that communication involves pen, paper, and 'Postman Pat', are marginalised because they're unable to access new digital technologies. Recent executive policies mean traditional physical mailboxes are scarce or non-existent.

Increasingly, digitally based invoices and payments via smartphone apps challenge analogue-schooled seniors' ability to even pay their bills. Living by their integrity, not being able to pay their bills on time is a major stressor, a situation ignored by digitally savvy policy makers. Late payment and paper-bill penalties add insult, because they are essentially an age or ignorance tax punishing their tech illiteracy. Current law requires business to prioritise shareholder wealth, so they're legally bound to move with the times. This lack of social will or conscience in business leaves the elderly feeling frustrated and abandoned, living within a deteriorating lifestyle in an increasingly alien environment.

Seniors express bewilderment; the world in which they were at ease has evaporated, existing now only in their collective imagination. Now that their hard-won experience and skills are no longer relevant, they find refuge in memories created when they were in their prime. They daydream aimlessly in preference to dealing with their rising anxiety over the increasingly frightening, unfamiliar reality of this moment—a reality in which an unavoidable, finite timeline confirms the inevitability of death. Some end up in secure hospital wards permanently lost in their memories, out of touch with the physical world and longing to return to when they belonged. The trouble is they're stuck in Operating System 3.0 in a world that's advanced to Operating System 16.0. They're been cheated by an obsolete education system that taught them to think in a way at odds with the changing world.

Condemning seniors for beliefs they inherited from an obsolete vision is a response of a sleeping mind. Past and present generations—all blissfully unaware that the way things are is fluid, never fixed—fail to accept that there is no right way, only today's way. Because we're pliant spectators in this unfolding understanding, we're accountable to no one for the common memes taught us within the educational framework promoted during our childhood. Despite us, they endure within our belief system as unconscious bias.

Unless they develop an understanding of their minds' true nature, the same fate awaits today's generation. From our first day of school, we're taught from a belief that life is an objective experience. We learn skills and values embraced as being the 'right way' within the 'big picture' vision of today's popular reality, but eventually they will prove just as fickle as yesterday's. The accelerating advance in technology highlights how this dogmatic system cheats us. Until recently, learned skills and factual knowledge stored in our subconscious memory correlated with our ability to feed ourselves and our family. But today our survival and success aren't skill and knowledge dependent. Now businesses like Alphabet (Google's parent company) control vast database server silos with virtually instantaneous access to all mankind's recorded objective knowledge. This means that man's value to the economic system is shifting from physical skills/knowledge to creative problem solving.

Expansion of the silicon-lead economy means that skills widely taught less than a generation ago, which we expected would serve us in the workplace for a lifetime, are becoming irrelevant. Machines capable of completing complex tasks without the need for onsite supervision are making them redundant. In just a few years, due to 5G technology, the Internet of Things (IOT) will lead to increasing numbers of us offering little or no value to an economic system within which, we were taught, our productivity and success determines our self-worth.

Progressive digitisation of analogue processes means our long-term welfare is unsustainable in an educational framework designed around rote learning of objective knowledge. Repetitive tasks are better and more ably performed with artificial intelligence (AI) and robots. The increasing youth unemployment that comes with accelerating AI uptake shows that this obsolete educational system is failing. Teaching children an objective life model in a subjective universe, as if it's the path to a fulfilling life, is an abuse to human potential; it denies that reality is dynamic. A static model becomes progressively removed from reality. Without intervention we eventually conclude that the world we loved is in ruin, headed for failure. Until we change this training approach, our personal constructed reality and the contemporary social reality disconnect between generations will persist.

Our contribution to improving the collective environment would be more effective if our true creative nature were revealed as soon as we're capable of critically evaluating feedback. Instead, we're left with an enduring 'noble lie' where ageing is merely a slow march toward irrelevance and death.

Franchising leverages the idea that franchisors can increase profitability faster with new franchisees rather than by expanding an existing one. A subtle variation of this idea is found in politics where politicians ignore the opinion of older generations when introducing controversial policies. Experienced politicians understand that those unable, or unwilling, to change their spots eventually retire to die, taking their old ways to the grave. New, pliant generations are educated within the new normal, oblivious to any other way. A frog placed in boiling water naturally jumps out, but if first immersed in tepid water, while slowly raising the temperature, it's calm, oblivious to its fate.

This approach to change is both cynical and arrogant, perpetuating the belief that in life there must be winners and losers and the greater good outweighs the human cost. The historic education framework disenfranchises the majority from their birth right. It entrenches a society where the majority consider themselves powerless victims like Samson (Judges 16:28 KJV), under the illusion that their success is acquired rather than latent.

The belief that an objective lens of right and wrong, good and bad, better or worse gives an accurate picture of our place in the world, creates a population of discontented victims, lacking the tools to navigate a subjective world. We're stressed by change, frustrated in our daily lives and left feeling we're suffering a living hell. Some reach breaking point, where opting out of what feels like a ceaseless, inescapable, nightmare seems like the only path to peace. The thought habits we unconsciously embedded within our ego resist all evidence that conflicts with our view of life, leaving us incapable of even beneficial change and vulnerable to buffeting by the winds of change. No wonder we feel tossed around like a dinghy in a storm. We'll never accept ourselves until we discover that our ego is an inappropriate blueprint or model for living; it is not who we are, not even close!

Habitually blaming all misfortune on some external influence is an error of thinking where comparison and envy override gratitude and respect for our collective creative progress. We benefit daily from natural discoveries, but minimise their contribution to overall wellbeing by taking them for granted. For example, less than a generation ago, simple car computerisation like power steering and ABS weren't considered possible or practical; now they make safe, effortless driving accessible to us all. Wallowing in events from our past and, worse, those that happened before our birth is the ego's way of capturing our life in a perpetual web of outrage that honours our victim beliefs formed in childhood.

Accurate or imagined, these beliefs lock us into a one-dimensional life of pain and suffering, because the ego's modus operandi is to verify its core belief that it's the victim of unfair treatment. Our beliefs will always focus our awareness on situations that objectively confirm our outrage. Unfortunately, while our ego is acting unsupervised according to our obsolete beliefs, we become unconscious slaves to them. Like a pre-programmed windup toy, we habitually act out historic horror stories in the present. Ironic, considering we're born to rule over our ego, but while we're not present, the tables are turned and now it rules over us.

Egocentric living is evidence that we're embracing a model driven by animal desires and instincts, in denial that we're born equal and from love. In this model, we see ourselves as oppressed by uncontrollable, external conditions. We believe that liberation is found in others accepting that they wronged us, explaining our situation by passing the buck, attributing blame and making excuses. This mind-set is our undoing, guaranteeing enduring suffering and eventually obsolescence. It focuses our energy on seeking revenge from the phantom oppressors who make decisions designed to control us, like in the movie *The Truman Show*.[11] This blinds us to the truth that heaven on earth is already ours—the truth at our core when all self-constructed beliefs are

---

[11] Andrew Niccol, *The Truman Show*, Paramount Pictures, Scott Rudin Productions, 1998.

stripped away, leaving our original, innocent, all-forgiving child who is keen to move on. Unfortunately, those beliefs are seldom shed.

The creator of this system into which we're born allowed for the eventual redundancy of learned objective beliefs in a subjective universe by limiting life expectancy. This solution, elegant when linked to the creation of new life, ensures a process of improvement and discovery, unhindered by the bias of redundant thought habits. Understanding the right way is not the privilege of a few gifted individuals born with superior intellect. It's a seed within us all, awaiting the right conditions that will allow it to grow in a process of discovery and revelation. Wider recognition that all humans have an innate capacity to create abundantly, when taught the right orientation of their relationship with the universe, will accelerate and enhance this process.

A new strategy designed to protect our collective long-term wellbeing is long overdue. We need one that leverages the subjective nature of life, one that expects and embraces change, life's only constant. Over time, more knowledge of what is hidden from our understanding within the universe is revealed and refined until it is perfected. From the discovery of fire to the creation of the wheel and development of the internal combustion engine, each progression has driven improvement of the human experience. Wireless communication and solar power generation are examples of revelation having spectacular, beneficial and immediate impact on emerging and underdeveloped nations. Raise your eyes from the pages of your self-composed horror story of limitation, where your character is playing the central victim, and you can discover with a simple shift in understanding that your own mind can reveal such magic too.

Objective ego always played the starring role in our life, a role it's not qualified to fill. Unconsciously given full reign in both the physical and mental plane, ego believes its boss and develops into an uncontrollable monster. Its intended role is that of our servant. It's supposed to make our life easier by automating important repetitive tasks via the subconscious. That releases us to consciously and simultaneously participate in the moment to create whatever we choose. It's our servant; we're not its servant! Unfortunately, over thousands of years, civilisations who discovered that man's mind could be controlled via their ego have abused its role. Using the power of repeated suggestion, the development of a child's ego can be controlled by seeding it with a range of preferred beliefs, leaving them a slave to their thought habits.

Dale Carnegie wrote in his book *How to Win Friends and Influence People*, 'Remember that a person's name to that person is the sweetest and most important sound in any language.'[12] Authorities have always been aware that our name is the avatar for our objective construct or ego. It differentiates each of us, defining our physical and emotional identity. Recognition by the elite that the ego is suggestable from birth gave them a competitive advantage. It enabled them to access and control vast amounts of manpower, further enriching themselves. Just like a computer programmer controls its operating system, early access to developing minds allows one to take advantage of the principle of suggestion to nurture or manipulate an individual's developing identity.

In childhood we have little or no control over what's planted in our mind by mostly well-meaning caregivers and other influencers, whose suggestions leave an enduring impact on our potential and future performance. Our own core beliefs have been skewed to align with our society's underlying belief system and its goals around the economy, government and religion. We've been programmed like a trainer does a performing seal. For example, from childhood, education and the media reinforce our belief that self-worth is pegged to wealth and personal productivity. They suggest that attaining goals and achieving tangible rewards reflect success, and that social privilege is the path to happiness. More likely, though, it's the path to a life wasted accumulating debt to buy things we don't need, with money we don't have, to impress people we don't like. Unfortunately, the performance required as an adult to be ever more productive puts us always under pressure to achieve better results. This is likely the source of our unhappiness and anxiety.

Our ego and our identity are one and the same. When you hear your name called out in a crowd, you respond with who you believe is being called. Your name accompanies your ego, and your ego accompanies your name; they are inseparable concepts. The person calling is met

---

[12] Dale Carnegie, *How to Win Friends and Influence People*, Harper Collins AU, 2016.

with who they believe you believe you are, no more and no less. Your name is a semantic representation of the three-dimensional physical presence that is you, an organic living meme. Though the suggestions of others, many anonymous, motivated the installation of the programme, you unconsciously programmed yourself to be the person you are now, uniquely identified by your name and mannerisms. Failure to recognise this is the foundation of human limitation, but, once realised, is the key to releasing your full power as a creator.

Once we possess this knowledge, we can start consciously rebuilding a new, infinitely adaptable identity. Reading daily affirmations to influence and change performance programming, crystallised in an unconscious past, is a small step toward practical recognition of the principle of suggestion.

The identity programming process is the same as the method used in learning to drive. Initially, there's disbelief and anxiety that anyone can coordinate all the steps needed to safely and competently operate a vehicle. This, the conscious involvement stage, is filled with self-doubt and frustration—it sucks to be me. These feelings reflect our core maladaptive belief that, relative to others, we were born lacking ability. Despite this opinion we hold of ourselves, we persevere with determination, just like when we learned to walk, and we eventually conquer our feelings of limitation. Before long, driving becomes part of our automatic subconscious control system. All necessary tasks happen in the correct sequence, without the need for conscious thought. The vehicle is now effectively an extension of our body—have you ever noticed how a normally shy, petite person driving a large SUV is miraculously transformed into Metroplex.[13]

This progression from conscious thought to unconscious driving habit is miraculous. Once learned it runs like clockwork, always on call to take control, quickly adapting to any vehicle. Think about travelling to work this morning; how much of the route do you recall? After closing the garage door, the next thing we're conscious of is probably greetings from co-workers as we settle into our workday. Unless there's an unusual event along the way, bringing us back to the present, our memory of the trip is limited to concern about how many near misses

---

[13] Transformers ™

we may have caused while driving subconsciously on autopilot. Other examples are 'Did I remember to turn the iron off?' Or 'Did I brush my teeth!' Of course you did—subconsciously.

We naturally find and follow the best route to work, and before long it's a mental battle to deviate from it. Our internal voice offers rational excuses why a route change today, of all days, is a bad idea. Even when we win our mental argument, if we don't remain consciously aware for the whole drive, we'll find the car is mysteriously back on the same old, well-worn route, back in our comfort zone. Folding our arms and tying shoelaces are other familiar examples of this reversion to the accepted automatic habit.

This is how ego works. Cast during childhood, it uses the same learning to drive method and has the same result. It's why our response to life stimulus becomes a subconsciously controlled habit. Repeating this response creates a well-worn, seemingly inescapable groove—can a leopard change its spots? Returning to the car analogy: imagine driving while lost in thoughts of last night or deep in conversation on a hands-free phone, fully engaged in thoughts removed from the skill of driving, and numb to the real physical events occurring in the moment. In these moments, our subconscious assumes control. It releases us from the repetitive physical world, allowing us to linger within the pathways of our mind, either for purposeful creation or, more likely, capture by the random thoughts of ego. The subconscious frees us up to multitask, only for ego habit to lure us into its never-ending house of horror.

Suddenly, someone unexpectedly pulls out in front of us, shaking us from our deep dive into unconscious illusion or 'waking sleep'. The reality of the objective moment faces us, requiring our conscious attention. This is a defining moment that contains an opportunity to grow. It reveals the gap between our ego and awareness, a chink in the ego's armour. Our response to this opportunity? A clenched fist accompanied by a stern glare and a stream of verbal obscenities. This all-too-familiar habitual response, we pluck from the list of potential responses championed by our early influencers and now firmly installed as part of our own ego illusion.

'The audacity! How dare they break into my 'waking sleep', shaking me out of my comfortable, habitual thought patterns!'

Forced to deal with an annoying, inconvenient interruption caused by some ignorant, incompetent moron, we lose our thread of thought. Most likely these are thoughts of the past or future, or ones that promise crucial solutions to our most pressing problems.

Many different behaviours regularly trigger us, aggravating our mood, whether committed, intentionally or unintentionally, by strangers, work mates, our partner or children. My children loved to crunch on ice and click their fingers, both penetrating sounds that broke my concentration, triggering a reprimand. Now that I'm aware of ego-initiated thought distractions that unconsciously consume our immediate moments, I encourage them to click and chew as often as they like. Thought interruptions that trigger us are golden moments we can embrace. By offering a path through the ego's armour, they're an opportunity to be born again. The 'gap' provides the chance to regain control from our robotic lives.

In these awareness gaps we discover real life. Embracing the goal of disrupting our thinking patterns enables us to escape from our unconscious, self-constructed mind tunnels. Alternatively, we languish in the stale tunnels of 'waking sleep' among the living dead. A dormant seed sits in every gap moment, waiting to germinate into the you that was intended at conception. Unless we shine the light of awareness on it, it will remain dormant, unable to grow and blossom to reveal our innate, infinite gifts. From now on, in the moment you feel triggered, take conscious, decisive control of your response, beginning the process of claiming back your life. Finally you can create the experience you choose, rather than one unwittingly chosen by carers over whom you had no control in childhood: teachers, politicians, the media and other random influencers. This awareness carries the seed of your eureka moment, the first time you'll know yourself honestly as a sunray transformed into a walking miracle of revelation. The point where we realise we're a reflection of the universe, and the Earth is our sandpit, is the moment we discover duality and the real i AM.

CHAPTER ELEVEN

DUALITY

A N EGO ILLUSION CONSTRUCTED IN AN ENLIGHTENED ENVIRONMENT may never confront duality. In the absence of suffering, there is no imperative to seek a cure. Yet we're all captured by a construct we didn't choose, sentenced to operate within a finite model, even if a comparatively rational one. As such we're destined to remain ignorant of the key purpose of our presence in physical form, that *it is the expression of free will to create from the never-ending stream of thoughts that flow through the ether of which we are part.* Perhaps this is how it's meant to be. It may be an accident that some realise we're not as we seem; we are much more!

Discovering our dual nature (duality) reveals that, beyond our constructed ego illusion, we are everything and everything is us. Each one of us is a separate dimension within a single moment that is instantaneously interconnected. Each moment is unaffected by those before. It's a brand-new opportunity to create a masterpiece from an infinite palette of overflowing colour and potential that reflects who we are at conception, a model of the universe embodied as gelled, carbonised light. Oblivious to the fact that we extend through the ether to touch everything and everywhere all at once, we're limited only by the idea that we're the finite object observed as our reflection in the mirror. When limited in this way, we can only approach an understanding of our true magnificence in those moments when we're able to recognise and feel spontaneous awe and beauty that takes our breath away.

This sense of breathless recognition, the awareness that we have seen or felt something special, reveals that we are one with the moment. For us to recognise and experience these fleeting moments of awe and beauty, an awareness of its presence must already exist within us. These are the moments of grace, proof of our oneness with the source of all.

I first experienced this feeling when I was working on the NZFS vegetation survey in the summer of 1978/79. I have a vivid recollection of standing atop the Glasgow Range, above the Mokihinui River, deep within the NZFS's North West Nelson Forest Park (now Kahurangi National Park) wilderness area. I gazed across the mountain peaks below us, surrounded by the 360-degree blue horizon. The view, reaching out to infinity, took my breath away. In awe of this magnificence, I felt a deep understanding that what I was looking at was the definition of beauty. My senses blended with the summer breeze, seamlessly connecting with all before me.

I enjoyed a similar experience while camping at Aramoana, a coastal settlement in NZ's Hawkes Bay region. Early one morning our then eighteen-month-old son, Aaron, needed to visit the toilet. We stepped out of the caravan into a pitch-black evening unspoiled by artificial light and looked up at a sky seemingly bright as day. The breath-taking sight of the Milky Way caused us to simultaneously gasp in amazement. These experiences teach us that our goal in life is not material accumulation, but simply to reveal moments of spontaneous beauty and awe, and recognise that they reflect our connection to the source creating the moment.

PART 2

I AM GEOFF

SELF CREATING A WORLD OF PAIN

CHAPTER TWELVE

POOR EGO CONSTRUCT

MY EGO CONSTRUCT DEVELOPMENT WAS LIMITED BY CHALLENGES associated with undiagnosed celiac disease, chronic asthma, and my parent's divorce. While my wife Cheryl's was limited by involuntary separation from her family, being raised in children's homes and sexual abuse from age seven through fourteen while in both children's homes and foster care.

In 2004 my specialist diagnosed me with an inherited auto-immune condition called celiac disease (CD), which explained my lifetime of baffling chronic health issues. When not detected and treated early, CD has an adverse effect on all areas of a child's learning and physical development, including failure to thrive, delayed maturity and poor concentration. Much to the nurse's surprise, I was so delighted with the diagnoses I all but kissed her—apparently not a normal reaction. But for me, it meant I could finally take action to alleviate the growing list of unexplained symptoms.

The gastroenterologist was gobsmacked, noting in his written diagnosis that 'These symptoms go back many years, but he went to university and has a BSc in Forestry.' Typical of CD, my small intestine villi were wasted, causing malnutrition because of poor nutrient transfer. This explained both the stomach pain I experienced as a teenager and recent neurological issues. Although I maintain a strict gluten-free diet to this day, additional health problems regularly appear. In 2011, after recurring rib fractures, I was diagnosed with CD related osteoporosis.[14]

Embarrassment and shame caused by regular outbreaks of diarrhoea—one of celiac disease's more antisocial symptoms—filled my childhood. Asthma, while terrible, also served as a convenient excuse to avoid doing stuff I didn't want to do, like learning to swim in the icy cold school pool. I suffered from anxiety (my nickname was 'Nerves'); a humiliatingly slight build, which affected my sporting aspirations; constant bloating and stomach rumbling, accompanied by intense abdominal pain, which affected my ability to concentrate; tiredness and lethargy; and delayed puberty—embarrassing when you're attending a boys' high school. Four years into high school, my peers had matured from boys to men, but I still looked and sounded like a boy. Back then changing rooms for P.E. were communal, and for swimming classes we were often required to change beside the pool, which amplified the awareness of my relative immaturity.

Our ego magically associates independent issues as if they're linked, leaving the impression that there's a meaningful, life-revealing theme across time that gives insight into who we are and our prospects of success. This reinforces the model we've formed of ourselves, regardless of whether we consider it comparatively good or bad. After all, we can't change who we know we are. Collectively, Dad's departure, poor health and social isolation amplified my self-consciousness, repressed any desire to take part in social activities, and deepened my feelings of loneliness and worthlessness.

The mistaken conclusion that events are related over time limits potential. Ironically, our belief that past events somehow attach themselves to us and are able to maintain influence over our destiny in the present empowers them. Bit by bit, this linking process creates the finite construct that fronts up when our name is called. Subconsciously we accept an experience of heaven or hell that is entirely congruent with our thoughts and feelings.

By the end of my secondary schooling, I was a shrinking violet accustomed to hanging out with a few other misfits, who discussed war-gaming and model planes, safe from the risk of rejection on the

---

[14] For more information on celiacs disease go to www.celiac.org

playing fields. When I was seventeen, I had little self-confidence, and few social skills. I preferred isolation, which allowed me time to indulge in the luxury of self-loathing. A loner, only comfortable in the company of my immediate family, I avoided communication outside my limited circle of acquaintances, theoretically protecting myself from potential embarrassment. Unsurprisingly, this mind set, along with choosing a rural-centred career, contributed to me still being a virgin in my mid-twenties.

After completing five years of high school, I applied for a cadetship with the NZ Forest Service (NZFS, est.1919), the custodian of most of NZ's indigenous and exotic forests. The unique heavy machinery shown in its career's material and a friend working there as a trainee draughtsman fuelled my interest in the NZFS. Craig was an enthusiastic big-game hunter and we regularly headed for the hills together, camping and stalking red deer in the surrounding temperate indigenous forests. After a successful hunt, we'd sell the animal to one of the many meat buyers supplying local restaurants with venison. These trips developed my lasting love of NZ's spectacular natural beauty.

As backup, I also applied for and was accepted into Canterbury University's Agricultural Engineering Undergraduate programme. Both my grandfather and uncle had farms in the South Wairarapa—one at Pukio on the Ruamahanga River and the other at Western Lake. My fondest childhood memories took place on these farms. We spent our summer holidays at Pukio, swimming in the river and playing cricket on the full-size pitch Grandad prepared every summer. This is where dad taught us how to fish and shoot a rifle.

My job interview at the Forest Service Conservancy Office in Palmerston North is forever etched in my brain. I'd just turned eighteen and Mum accompanied me for support. The interviewer asked me what forest mensuration is?

'That's easy,' I said. 'Forest menstruation is the measurement of trees.' I turned a bright shade of red, and the others in the room erupted in fits of embarrassed laughter. I wanted to crawl under a rock. I don't know if any other applicants took their mum, but it must've been a good move, because they offered me a cadetship. I think they believed they were helping this struggling single mum out by giving me a job! (Note the unsubstantiated malicious mental storytelling.)

Production forests tend to be planted in remote rural areas, so accepting the position with the NZFS meant leaving home for what would be my first extended trip away from home. Sometime in January 1977, I left Palmerston North, waving goodbye to Mum, my brothers and my familiar life from a Newman's Coach Lines bus adorned with the wings of Pegasus. The bus took me on a slow, winding, eight-hour trip to the Forestry Training Centre (FTC) in Rotorua for a two-week company-induction programme. Living and working with thirty other youths soon neutralised any bouts of homesickness—an experience I'd recommend to any school leaver. A fortnight later, to celebrate completing our induction, a few of the more worldly trainees organised a breakup party. Apparently, it was routine to invite young women from the city nurses' home—now a long-dead institution—to join in the fun. This was my first party and the first time I'd mixed with the opposite sex since primary school.

Because my well-intentioned brothers banned me from drinking alcohol at home—after all the legal drinking age was twenty—it was also my first drinking experience. For this social recluse from the state house in Palmerston North, it proved to be too much, too soon, and I passed out within the first hour! Embarrassingly, later that night I woke up in my dorm room to discover the party was all but over. It's an understatement to say I was down on myself. My mates spun wild stories about the fun they'd had, fuelling my ever-present fear of missing out and adding to my existing self-loathing. What a loser!

The next day we were deployed to our respective training forests based on our province of origin. I was posted, along with five others, to Gwavas Forest in the Hawkes Bay, a two-hour road trip north of Palmerston North. Although Gwavas is a remote location, we were never alone. Back then, we lived and ate at onsite single-men's camps. This community element, though overwhelmingly male, along with the strenuous manual labour involved in forest establishment, forced me to develop socially and physically. This helped me to break free from my reclusive lifestyle.

Collectively labelled as forestry trainees, our training included, but was not limited to, the finer arts of scrub cutting, planting pine and eucalyptus seedlings, spraying weed killer (unprotected), dosing seedlings with fertiliser, fire lighting, firefighting, tree climbing to collect seed cones from genetically superior Pinus radiata, passing our heavy truck driving licenses (I had to sit on a pillow to see out of the old International fire truck), axe thinning, learning First Aid, looking after tools of the trade, listening to Pink Floyd, playing pool in the rec room, fighting, skylarking, riding our trail bikes, and drinking beer when we were fortunate enough to be rained off (have our shift cancelled due to rain).

The onsite accommodation was palatial—yeah right! We lived in draughty ex-army WWII single-men's huts with a central ablution block on the forest edge. On our first day, the officer in charge (OIC) said, as part of his lecture, 'Like all rural folk you must make your own fun.' We took him at his word! Considering there were thirty young guys coexisting in a confined camp, we got on remarkably well, with only a few fights breaking out. I lost one of those, but then my opponent was several inches taller, and he made the most of his height advantage.

No animosity lingered once we'd let off a bit of steam. We were just breaking the boredom, as there wasn't much to do other than watching TV in the rec room, broken by moments when we'd shoot and kill possums (pests in NZ) and rats living in the ceiling. Some evenings, we'd round up turkeys roosting on nearby farms, sliding around in their abundant droppings while doing our best to avoid the farmers. We'd scald and pluck the birds in the ablution block. There were feathers everywhere, but nothing a fire hose couldn't fix! That May, on the first day of duck-shooting season—a NZ institution—we took our expertly dressed turkeys to the Angus Inn, a hotel in the nearby city of Hastings. We told the head chef they were the first ducks of the season, and he bought all we had. They would've been tough as old boots, but then he was probably a better chef than we'd proved to be.

Our weekly pay-check didn't go far, most was deducted to pay for accommodation and meals provided by the contract cooks. They fed us a variety of home-kill meat that from time to time included nutritious extras, including gravel picked up in their backyard that doubled as an animal-slaughter site. Meanwhile, their carbohydrate-rich meals naturally laced with gluten slowly poisoned me. Constantly starving because the small intestine has ceased functioning may seem like a great way to stay lean, but it's a disaster in terms of endurance and mental function. When axe thinning or doing some other physically intense task, my body would quickly fade, and by lunchtime I was exhausted. One day, as retribution for flour bombing their house the previous evening, our supervisors threw our lunch deep into the scrub. By mid-afternoon I was blacking out for lack of food with no energy to swing my axe or even stand. The rest of the day was spent laying in the 'Passion Wagon', our ironically named J1 Bedford minibus. After work my trainee colleagues plied me with chocolate biscuits from the canteen, and I was soon fully recovered.

One stand-out memory from Gwavas Forest happened on my nineteenth birthday, the 25th of August 1977. We'd been rained off before lunch, so, of course, we headed to our local, the Tikokino Hotel. Unfortunately, Fred, a rough as guts ex-army private, decided it'd be nice to help me celebrate by spiking my beer with vodka. The result is legend: that evening the recreation-room bathroom had a major workout, walls and all. I was terribly ill and passed out, a recurring theme. I awoke at one in the morning to a room full of concerned-but-amused onlookers with a forty-four-gallon drum by my side. I survived, but even today I'm not a big drinker. The next day was Friday, which coincidentally coincided with my monthly shopping day off, so I escaped the clean-up. Instead, I headed home on my electric-blue 125 Suzuki GT motorbike to celebrate my birthday with family in Palmerston North. I hoped to return on Sunday with one of Mum's excellent fruit cakes to share, unaware at the time that I was being poisoned by its main ingredient, wheat flour.

Later that year, we transferred to the township of Turangi in the Waikato where our accommodation went up a notch. It had been built to house men originating from all corners of the world while they completed the landmark Tongariro Hydro Electric Power Scheme. After its completion the NZFS assumed management of the camp as it made ideal accommodation for workers establishing the fledgling Lake Taupo Forest. Today it's private backpacker accommodation adjacent to the local hotel. While based in Turangi, we spent several months working and camping in the Kaimanawa Forest Park, maintaining wilderness tracks and trampers' huts, including digging new latrines. Our highlight was manually forming an airstrip alongside the Ngaruroro River to enable access for construction of a premium Lockwood-designed hut. There were plenty of deer to shoot and huge rainbow trout in the river. If you've ever visited Boyd Hut, I was there before you, before a hut existed. It's a far cry from the original NZFS Noxious Animal Division's huts that dotted the NZ high country, reflecting the NZFS vision for growth in remote-area tourism.

My first year away from home is filled with wonderful memories of comradeship involving a lot of harmless fun getting into trouble. Living and working with forestry employees from different backgrounds, ranging from managers to unskilled labourers and PEP employment-scheme workers, also helped me develop confidence. Regrettably, at the end of 1977, because I'd been employed to train as a forester, I had to leave my fellow ranger trainees behind. To qualify as a forester requires completion of a four-year bachelor's degree at Canterbury University, while they were required to complete a three-year programme for the Forest Ranger Certificate at the Forestry Training Centre in Rotorua. After experiencing life as a lumberjack and forging some great relationships, I wanted to transfer over to the ranger training programme, but my request was denied.

Government student-fee regulations prevented me from attending Canterbury University in Christchurch for the full, four-year degree course. Since Massey, my hometown university, offered all the subjects required to complete the first intermediate year, enrolling at Canterbury would reduce my government funding. So I headed back to Palmerston North for the last nine months I'd ever live under the same roof as my family. I enjoyed being back, hanging out with my brothers and, as usual, Mum's home cooking made study easy. However, living at home meant I was culturally isolated from the university, and because of my gap year working, the students I knew from high school were already starting their second year of study. In 1978 I was the only undergraduate completing the four-year forestry degree on the Massey campus, and in 1982, one of only seventeen students in what must have been the smallest cohort to graduate from any degree course in NZ.

I considered joining either the Massey University tramping (trek) or rugby club as a way to be involved in campus life. An acquaintance from my time at Palmerston North Boys' High invited me to tag along with him and his group of girlfriends on an introductory tramp in the nearby Ruahine Ranges. I still hadn't spoken to a girl since middle school when a neighbourhood girl had invited me to the movies. But the imagined roasting I'd receive from my brothers if I accepted her invitation had trumped the thoughts of fun associated with going to the movies with her. So, fearing what others may think or do, I'd declined her invitation. Six years later, here I was, now an adult attending university, with a second chance. Surprisingly, I had an instant rapport with one of the women. She was away from home and also new to Massey.

The first fortnight of a new semester revolves around orientation parties designed so students can get acquainted with their new surroundings. During the tramp, I learned that one had been scheduled that evening, and they were planning to attend. Dancing was way out of my comfort zone, but after much mental debate, I threw all caution to the wind and, taking advice from the lyrics of Bob Hudson's *The Newcastle Song*, I went. Trouble was, they didn't show! Knowing no one, I sat alone on a mat I'm pretty sure was purposely positioned to highlight any losers in the room. Self-conscious and too young to buy a drink, I eventually summoned the courage to ask a random stranger for a dance. It ended in disaster. After copping a few insults, I slunk off home, tail between my legs, disillusioned and embarrassed. The usual repetitive self-talk accompanied me, dominated by the theme, 'What a wimp, a worthless loser!'

After a year of labouring in the forest, I was fitter and stronger than ever, and I felt I could now have an impact at Rugby. So although the date clashed with the next scheduled tramping-club meetup, I turned out for the team trials. I figured there'd be plenty more tramping trips. Turns out, tramping would've been the better option. In our season opening game, I clearly recall the moment the opposition player's shoulder connected with my left knee in a bone-crunching tackle which ruptured my ACL (a major knee ligament), parting it from the knee. So the game could continue, I was dragged from the field and left to limp back to the dressing rooms. After collecting my gear, I rode my 185 Suzuki trail bike home, sitting side saddle while using my good leg to shift gears. Mum wasn't surprised by the injury; she actually laughed because, apparently, I'd been complaining about knee pain a bit. A trip to the hospital ended with my leg being bandaged from hip to toe, ending participation in competitive sport forever. I spent the entire semester on crutches, leaving me nothing to do except study, which made passing all my exams easy and lent proof to the phrase 'it's an ill wind that brings no good'.

Twelve months later, having finally transferred to NZ's only forestry school located in Christchurch, an orthopaedic surgeon advised that my knee required reconstructive surgery. Although I enjoyed the morphine-induced trips while recovering in the hospital, the operation was unsuccessful. Five years later, to reduce its impact on my forestry career, I had another operation which alleviated the constant swelling and improved stability. But what of the woman I met on the tramp? Our paths crossed a couple of times, once at a lecture when I was still on crutches and again while I was celebrating my twentieth birthday at the Albert Motor Lodge in Palmy with Dad and my brother, Lance. The injury changed everything that year, my knee never recovered. In 2015 I received a total knee replacement.

CHAPTER THIRTEEN

JUST GO AWAY

C ELIAC DISEASE, FAMILY CRISIS AND INJURY, AND NOT YET TWENTY years old, surely my ticket had been clicked enough. But the universe wasn't done with me yet! My choice of career was about to be undermined by a new, populist, political wave gaining global momentum. In 1980, while completing my third year of university, Prof. Don Mead mentioned that he was envious of our timing because the forest industry was on the cusp of a boom. He believed we would oversee development of an exciting, vertically integrated, timber-processing industry providing significant employment benefits to the NZ economy.

When I graduated the NZ Forest Service was a world leader in the research and implementation of intensive silviculture practices which maximised tree-crop value. NZ holds a competitive advantage in renewable softwood forestry mainly because of the rapid growth rate of Pinus radiata, the dominant exotic forest species, and to a lesser extent Douglas fir. Over several decades its industry specific, practical training schools had developed a skilled, safety conscious workforce. These included the Forestry Training Centre (FTC), alongside the world-class Forest Research Institute (FRI) in Rotorua; two woodsmen training schools, one at Golden Downs Forest near Tapawera and the other at Kaingaroa Forest, south east of Rotorua, and the Timber Institute Training Centre (TITC), a training sawmill, alongside NZ's largest commercial sawmill, Waipa, also in Rotorua.

Unfortunately, Prof. Mead hadn't factored in the adoption of neoliberal economic policy being championed by both Margaret

Thatcher and Ronald Reagan. Their policies would have a major impact on the development of NZ's forestry and other key national infrastructure assets dominated by government investment. Sir Roger Douglas, finance minister in the 1984 NZ Labour government, sought to divest all state-owned assets with policies imitating those of his more illustrious heroes. Forests, rail, electricity, earthquake commission (EQC), The Accident Compensation Commission (ACC) and government printing were a few of the more significant ones. He also attempted to privatise hospitals, but after a public outcry his ill-conceived decision was swiftly revoked.

After operating successfully for sixty-eight years, ten years after it had employed me fresh out of high school and, coincidentally, in the same year my five-year graduation bond expired, the NZFS came to a sudden and humiliating end. A range of ownership structures congruent with conservative political policies, not normally associated with a Labour government, replaced it. Within three years of these radical, far-reaching political decisions, seventy years of proud and internationally recognised stewardship of both NZ's indigenous and exotic forests had been casually dispatched to the pages of history. Today, other organisations have appropriated many of the initiatives attributed to the NZ Forest Service and its internationally respected staff. These include new government entities, hurriedly established after recognising that even unproductive government land requires management, several foreign corporations representing colossal pension funds and Maori IWI in settlement for many Treaty of Waitangi compensation claims. The current owners of the predominantly NZFS established Kaingaroa Forest describe it as: 'Spanning 190,000 ha of plantable land, it is one of the crown jewels of international forestry and one of the oldest and largest softwood plantations in the world. It is recognised worldwide as an intensively tended forest that produces up to 4 million m^3 of high-quality logs per annum.'

Elizabeth Orr, in her book *Keeping New Zealand Green - Our Forests and their Future*' about the NZ Forest Service and its history in creating a viable NZ Forest Industry, included the following comment about the competency of the NZFS compared with other global Forest Services: 'Another positive view of the future of the forest service at this time was related to me by Jim Spears who had wide contacts internationally in the latter part of his career as director of the Logging Industry Research Association. He knew the American, Canadian and Australian forest service's as well and was reasonably familiar with those of Scandinavia, Austria and Japan; Spears judges the New Zealand Forest Service to be the best forest service in the world or close to it. As for Bruce Wallace, author of the tale of those two 'Titans', Sir Ron Trotter and Hugh Fletcher and hardly an admirer of public enterprises, he considered that the forest service had created the 'single best collection of plantation forests in the world.'[15]

Thirty plus years on, apart from the memories of a few aging former employees, the forest service's positive legacy in the development of a self-sufficient, renewable wood-based industry has been all but forgotten. Political interference erased its very existence and its internationally recognised achievements from history. This illustrates both the subjective nature of history and the expedient manipulation of the truth, which influences the hearts and minds of the most recent generation in ways that support the popular narrative. Where there's an activist or an ideologue, there's always a young, impressionable target audience being manipulated with 'true lies', influencing them into becoming unwitting, single-minded agents of social change, irrespective of opposition, justified or not. This is how history within the paradigm of Darwinian natural selection work. If you hold a position/power don't let the truth detract from any good story, propaganda or recognition that gives you control over and facilitates maintenance and expansion of your power base.

In 2018, with considerable increases in mature wood supply and concerns about significant reductions in new tree planting from the mid-1990's, the current Labour government is now re-establishing a state-owned forest service with an ambitious new planting goal. Unsurprisingly, we have come a full circle! Prof. Mead was right, the forest industry was at the beginning of a boom, but rather than a boom for NZ, it became the golden goose benefitting several international forestry conglomerates and North American pension funds. Unfortunately, because of political meddling, the prediction of a major

---

[15] Elizabeth Orr, *Keeping New Zealand Green - Our Forests and their Future*, Steele Roberts Aotearoa Ltd, 2017.

expansion in processing capacity and employment never eventuated. We transferred much of the wealth created by the forest service as raw logs to China, India and other low-value markets. These countries' economies benefited disproportionately by processing the logs, extracting their potential value.

The corporatisation of publicly owned assets, beginning in 1984, was the first of many intrusions government made into my life, making a nonsense of its promise that 'a free market would deliver a level playing field and ensure a fair go for all'.

The free market, unconstrained by government bureaucracy, was supposedly an economic miracle designed to deliver prosperity in direct relationship to an individual's enterprise and performance. The propaganda affirmed the theory that a good education, hard work, fair play and a bold dream would be rewarded with proportional prosperity. The government removed the subsidies and tariffs that propped up unprofitable areas of the economy, ensuring that everyone started this new economic reality with the same opportunity. Unfortunately, many businesses failed, particularly in the agricultural sector. No support or sympathy was offered those directly affected by the changes. In this new environment, you either quickly learned to swim or be left to sink. Businesses established in the previous protectionist environment were bullied into accepting full accountability for their failure. This ill-conceived, heartless attitude lead to many suicides.

Government believed these changes would reduce costs and improve investment decisions, leading to a more sustainable and productive economy. Whatever the sales spin, the free market deployed so obsessively in the '80's and '90's proved to be only a facade masking the transfer of wealth from publicly owned assets into private hands. In 2006 in *The Great Wood Robbery - Political Bumbling Ruins New Zealand Forestry*, a discussion book about the corporatisation of the NZFS, foresters Lindsay Poole, Hamish Levack, and Julian Bateson noted, 'All the initiators and enthusiastic supporters of the reforms personally benefited greatly from them.'[16]

Taxpayers had already invested in, and now owned, strategic

---

[16] Poole L, Levack H, Bateson J, *The Great Wood Robbery - Political Bumbling Ruins New Zealand Forestry*, Bateson Publishing, 2006.

industries that were heavily capital intensive, time-dependent and susceptible to monopolistic pricing or resource stripping, but now they were for sale. Large, established private companies, like NZ's Rank Corporation, Infratil, Fay Richwhite, and other individuals of means, lined up to purchase NZ's 'family silver' at fire-sale valuations. Billions of dollars of government utility and forestry infrastructure were restructured and eventually privatised, putting NZ on a path that mirrored the US economic system.

The US seemed intent on influencing and profiting from all global economies by monetary and social restructuring pressure via the World Bank, IMF and US Federal Bank, and by opening up foreign markets to its investors; for example, the Harvard Management Company, the subsidiary that manages Harvard Universities $32 billion endowment and who made almost $87 million from the Kaingaroa Forest sale in 2011. Subsequent poor private management led to Air New Zealand ($885m in January 2002), the BNZ ($1b in the 1990s) and ECQ (Earthquake Commission) requiring further taxpayer bailouts after the 2011 Christchurch earthquake disaster to keep them afloat. (ECQ was the victim of successive post-1990 governments appropriating its disaster fund behind the scenes for their own pork-barrel projects). The expected trickle down of state asset sale revenue never eventuated, while many lives and careers were cruelly devastated. Three decades later, because of this flawed ideology, homelessness, once a rarity in New Zealand, tops the table among OECD countries (Yale, 2017). A sad indictment of a country that boasts about full employment.

While in theory the US-led global rollout of the market-led economic policies was expected to improve wealth distribution, in practice it entrenched the endemic greed that characterises its brand of 'old money, crony capitalism'. Hamstrung by this historic environment, the term 'level playing field' proved to be a myth. On reflection, the neoliberal narrative naively embraced by NZ's own zealot, Sir Roger Douglas turned out to be a costly experiment that only offered fake prosperity. Over time, in the manner of Hans Christian Andersen's fairy tale *The Emperor's New Clothes,* the truth finally revealed the illusion. The cost of this political intervention can be counted in its human impact. Whether by career disruption or a loved one's suicide, the path of many people's lives was irreversibly changed, wasting the human capital of at least one generation.

In 2008, because of an unrestrained and insatiable love for power and money, many established private global empires teetered on the brink of collapse. This was the climax of a period now euphemistically referred to as the global financial crisis (GFC) and the great recession, both dramatic expressions of failed neoliberal ideology. Global financial experts report that they resolved the crisis, but, as usual, actions speak louder than words. A financial war still rages unabated today, caused by the extreme, unrestrained pseudo free-market policies that failed the 99%. Perhaps if the 1980s sale of state assets owned by the many was accompanied by an initial unbundling and redistribution of 'old wealth' held by the few, deflationary destruction of unprecedented amounts of capital during the 2008 crisis may have been prevented.

CHAPTER FOURTEEN

ALL BAGS GET UNPACKED

C HERYL AND I MET IN MASTERTON WHEN I WAS TWENTY-FOUR, naïve and oblivious to the appalling crime of childhood sexual assault. My fiancé had just broken off our engagement. I worked at the isolated Ngaumu Forest, an island and a six-hour road and boat trip away from my fiancé's family. When she arrived unexpectedly on a Friday evening in November, chaperoned and emboldened by a carload of girlfriends, I thought she'd made the long journey from Christchurch to move in with me, but it was to end our four-year relationship. Soon after, a mutual friend arranged for me and Cheryl to meet at a barbecue. We were perfectly matched lost souls.

Separated from her parents and eight siblings when she was five, Cheryl had been raised in various Salvation Army Children's Homes spanning the length of NZ. Unsurprisingly, this had a detrimental effect on her confidence, leaving her with anxiety issues, including hypervigilance, a symptom of untreated mental health issues. It presented as an extreme response to even the slightest stress. At least that's what I thought was the cause, having no idea that she'd been subjected to severe, serial sexual trauma. To protect herself from her foster father, Don L, she'd stayed away from her foster family for several years. Now, though, with me riding shotgun, she longed for a reconciliation. Cheryl was seven when she'd joined their family, making her their eldest child overnight, accepted as such by all but their son, originally the eldest. As much as she loathed and feared Don L, she loved and missed her foster mother, as we would our regular mum. I tolerated our visits, accepting this uneasy situation, recognising it was Cheryl's only known family. Her foster mum was always welcoming, but I found Don L, unnerving despite being unaware of the predator risk he posed to our future daughter.

I learned from a book by Sir Bob Jones, a prominent NZ investor, that property is the path to financial security.[17] By the end of 1983, I'd saved enough to purchase my first home in Masterton for $11,000. After our wedding in February 1984, this became Cheryl's home too. Less than a year later, I successfully applied for the role of technical forester at the Waipa Statecraft sawmill in Rotorua. I sold our first home for $19,000, a good return fuelled by a buoyant global economy, and bought another in Rotorua. As already discussed, we were about to face a period of significant, disruptive economic restructuring designed to privatise profits while socialising losses. Before its conclusion I would experience three redundancies: in 1989, 1996 and 2003.

The first wave of free-market legislative changes happened in April 1987, coinciding with a new financial year. Overnight, the Waipa sawmill was rebranded Prolog Industries, one of many new state-owned enterprises. (In 1996 it was sold to private investors, becoming Red Stag Timber, the name it still trades under today). A new CEO was recruited from the private sector with the aim of knocking us all into a shape befitting a multimillion-dollar private enterprise. After a brief spell in Rotorua, all staff directly reporting to him, including me, had to relocate to Auckland where he'd leased plush new offices in easy reach of his home.

At the time Auckland house prices were twice those in Rotorua and October 1987s historic stock-market crash was just around the corner. The only way we were going to remain homeowners was to build a new house using staff-discounted Prolog timber. We found the perfect building section for $40,000 in West Harbour, a developing West Auckland suburb. It was our third land purchase in four years. My salary was $42,000 and we had accumulated savings of $40,000. The BNZ bank was prepared to lend us up to $80,000 at 18%, the going rate in 1987. This was a large home-building project with a small budget on a ridiculous schedule. Experienced colleagues on learning our plans soon let me know they believed the budget was unrealistic, leaving me

---

[17] Sir Bob Jones, *Jones on Property*, Forth Estate Books, 1977.

doubting my plan. But there was no going back now; the funds had been transferred to our account. I would make it work, or our soon-to-be family of four would be broke and homeless!

I enlisted the help of an experienced builder employed at the sawmill for a modular decking project I had developed. While Spence organised the technical details, I worked as his labourer throughout the 1987/88 Christmas holiday break. The first sign that I had a heart problem occurred during our first day on the job. While unloading the pre-nailed frames, my heart started racing erratically. It was fibrillating at well over 250 bpm, and the sudden drop in blood pressure caused me to pass out. Not the best start to our building venture! This was an ongoing issue, especially unnerving when driving on a congested motorway, putting both my and other motorists' lives at risk. Over the next decade I saw several cardiologists. None offered a solution, and one even advised me to harden up as men didn't qualify for remedial intervention! I discovered sometime later that they believed I was imagining it, in other words I was a hypochondriac, a common theme from GP's. I've learned to ignore such comments and trust my own instincts when it comes to my health.

In 1999, after twelve years enduring regular tachycardia-related hospital admissions, they finally scheduled heart surgery. The cardiologist still believed my case didn't justify surgical intervention, but Waikato Hospital had an urgent need for a supraventricular tachycardia (SVT) 'guinea pig'. The cardiologist reluctantly submitted my name as a potential candidate to attend an ablation training clinic being performed by a visiting Canadian. Even then, because they couldn't afford to waste the rock-star surgeon's time on uncertainty, just days out from the event, they found a 'sure thing', guaranteed to have a spontaneous SVT, so they bumped me from the programme. Ironically, the surgeon failed to induce tachycardia in the replacement, turning the clinic into an expensive theoretical lesson. A week later, I flew alone to Hamilton to finally receive my long-overdue heart surgery. We were broke, so Cheryl was unable to accompany me. She sat 500km away, at home in Ashhurst, imagining the worst—a habit she'd naturally formed from repetition of her childhood experience.

My pre-op was held in a vacant staff kitchen at a table beside the fridge because the hospital was over full. A lovely nurse took my vitals and requested my signature giving the surgeon permission to fit a pacemaker in the rare event he damaged my heart. I was conscious throughout and could see the whole operation on an overhead monitor as the surgeon passed an electrified catheter through an incision in my groin to my heart, triggering an immediate textbook SVT. Following the surgeon's orders, I squeezed the attendant nurse's hand while he powered up and activated the catheter from his impressive control panel. This immediately and successfully ablated my heart's unnecessary additional electrical pathway. The surgeon, who'd been present during the ill-fated training clinic, was elated for me, himself, and the group that had gathered to watch. The theatre staff were clearly excited that rather than the Canadian rock star, their resident cardiologist had performed the perfect ablation on his model patient. The surgeon said my SVT was difficult to diagnose because it started via a hidden pathway—a reasonable excuse, but little comfort for the many occasions then and since, that Doctors failed to take me seriously. Something that jeopardised my family's already tenuous job security, mental health and potentially, the health of third parties.

We moved into our semi-completed home in January 1988. Six months later on July 31st, we welcomed our second child, Jason. We were lucky that not only did he survive his unscheduled arrival but also that we had any children at all. After trying unsuccessfully to have our first, tests revealed that for us to have any hope of a family, Cheryl needed an operation and fertility treatment. Thankfully her operation was successful, and we were blessed with our first child, Sarah, born at Rotorua Maternity Hospital in May 1986. Unsurprisingly, it was an eventful pregnancy. Sarah was keen to arrive on April first, but by some miracle we dodged that.

Jason was even less co-operative, he decided to turn up two months early. Poor road-maintenance signage contributed to his early arrival. That night, travelling home to Auckland from Rotorua via the winding Kaimai Ranges, I drove through unmarked roadworks. Our car, accompanied by a frightening loud bang, jolted violently when I drove into a large pothole, irreparably damaging a front wheel rim. When I pulled over to the road's hard shoulder, I found several other cars had suffered the same fate. We made it back home hours later, but by midnight Cheryl was experiencing severe stomach pain with contractions. I called an ambulance, which took forever to arrive. They took a wrong turn and ended up on the other side of our dead-end street, losing precious time while they backtracked. Eventually they arrived and bundled Cheryl from the footpath onto a stretcher and into the ambulance. They ordered me not to follow immediately because there was room for only one speeding vehicle on the motorway. I should take my time, relax and make a cup of tea while our good friend and neighbour Karen packed Cheryl's overnight bag.

Halfway to the hospital, they realised Jason was winning the delivery race! Cheryl recalls things getting hectic. Jason's premature status meant it was a life-or-death situation; he wouldn't survive an ambulance birth. So in the early hours on the last day of July 1988, the driver switched on the sirens and flashing lights as they sped to Auckland National Women's Hospital. Meanwhile, back at home, I was oblivious to the unfolding drama and Jason's eventual birth in the hospital foyer. When I finally arrived, I was shocked to hear he'd already been born. They led me to an emergency ward, where I was distressed to see a tiny naked body stretched out on an open panel, looking very vulnerable and all but hidden under the wires and machines assisting his breathing to try to save this unexpected, new life. Next, they led me to a large linen room where, because there were no beds available on the ward, they'd taken Cheryl to recover from her sudden birth. I found her sitting alone and distressed in a wheelchair. At that moment we had a sudden urge to name him. Surrounded by towels and other hospital linen, with our new baby desperately clinging on to life, we urgently discussed the options and settled on Jason. The staff performed miracles that night, and six weeks later, Jason made it to his own room in the house that Geoff built. He'll soon be thirty-two and has never looked back since his tenuous start.

One year later on Jason's first birthday, I received my redundancy letter from Prolog Industries. By then privatisation of the forestry corporation had come to a standstill; Treaty of Waitangi land-ownership issues were frustrating the government's attempts to complete the process. In lieu of a sale of the entire state-owned enterprise in a single coordinated operation, the government made the decision to sell the timber processing assets as a separate parcel, giving the electorate the impression that privatisation was proceeding to plan. The change in sale process led to different employment contract treatment of forest and processing-sector staff. Arguing that this was an unacceptable inconsistency cost me my job! I arrived at work Friday morning to be told to empty my desk drawers.

Redundancy turned out to be the ideal opportunity to work full time on completing our house. I spent many enjoyable hours with Mick Hucknall and Simply Red blasting from the radio, while spray varnishing the Douglas fir cladding lining the spectacular cathedral ceilings. Within two months I had a job as market manager, Lakepine Superfine MDF at Fletcher Wood Panels. Finally I had a role that was both challenging and exciting, free from the toxicity that now pervaded the new-look public sector. This was as close as I'd come to my dream job. It offered unlimited career development and the carrot of relocation to the central volcanic plateau region in NZ's North Island. The region's main tourist town, Taupo, sits in a picturesque location flanking Lake Taupo, the southern hemisphere's largest lake, which rests in the shadow of the internationally renowned Tongariro National Park, home for the majestic tri-mountain peaks of Mt Ruapehu, Ngauruhoe and Tongariro. During the next eight months, I was lucky to lead the launch of several new MDF products, an uncommon opportunity in the wood-product manufacturing sector, where even a single launch is rare.

Early in the new decade, Cheryl fell pregnant with our third child. The pregnancy came with its challenges, which, along with her history of not reaching full term, meant spending several months as a prenatal inpatient. The continual employment uncertainty we'd experienced over the past few years was catching up with her. Becoming increasingly stressed and depressed, she isolated herself from our worried friends and neighbours. Out of the blue one day, she announced that she wanted to move to Palmerston North, where her foster parents had settled after selling the Rob Roy Motel in Rotorua. As I was enjoying my new job, moving cities again was the last thing on my mind. Although our home was nearing completion, it was far from sale ready, particularly considering we were amid a deep global recession. However, I agreed to apply for one job which if I got, we'd move. I was pretty confident that in the prevailing economic climate I had no chance!

Disappointingly and surprisingly, considering the salary was twice what I was getting, I got the job. Although it was a senior marketing role within the NZ Electricity Corporation, I wasn't keen on learning a new industry, especially another technically challenging one. Even worse, it was government owned, and in the middle of a messy corporatisation. But I'd promised Cheryl, and I felt she wouldn't cope if I changed my mind. Over the next several months, I put in a superhuman effort to lift the house up to an acceptable renting standard. We left the 'house that Geoff built' on June 17th, 1990, Cheryl's thirtieth birthday. Karen still recalls my sad tears as we drove away, our little 1985 Holden Gemini packed to the gunnels with two children and Mindy, our 8-year-old cat, on what was one of the saddest days of my life.

We soon rented the house to an Israeli family, who before long stopped paying rent so their daughter could continue to attend her Jewish private school. Our rental managers, just as useless then as they are now, failed to collect a rental bond, so out of necessity, in 1992 we listed the house in what is the second-worst housing market on record, only behind the 2008 great recession. Despite having views of the Waitemata Harbour, the Auckland Harbour Bridge and the Sky Tower, we had few offers, so out of desperation we accepted $138,000, which just covered our original land and material costs. The 1992 buyer still owns the house, which in 2017 was valued at $1.1 million. In March 2018 the Reserve Bank of NZ (RBNZ) wrote: 'Real estate prices increased by over 200 percent in real terms between 1992 and 2016.' The 'house that Geoff built' has returned well above that.

Free of our Auckland home, we could now escape the perils of being renters. We bought a timeless Cape Cod-style house on a half-acre in Ashhurst Village (Pop 3000). Like our Auckland property, the owner had designed and built it. The asking price of $152,000 was $13,000 more than our Auckland property. I couldn't believe that a house in this insignificant rural township would cost more than our house in a city of one million. I doubt this has ever happened before or since.

Ashhurst is an environment reminiscent of my childhood, an ideal place to raise our three young children. In a throwback to my Pahiatua school days, its school was semi-rural and catered to children up to high school age. This one-stop approach benefited our children's education. All four of them passed through its familiar corridors over the next fourteen years.

The house was surrounded by mature trees, including sycamore, golden elm, liquid amber. Two large silver birch framed the east-facing entrance way, which looked out to unimpeded views of the Ruahine ranges, the distinctive and enduring backbone of Aotearoa, NZ. The lounge and master bedroom had breath-taking views of Te Apiti, Manawatu Gorge, and the Tararua Range. It felt as if you could literally reach out and touch the horizon where the green pastures of this natural geography kiss the clear blue sky. The outlook had the same natural calming effect I associated with the landscape while growing up in the region. It was the perfect place to plant roots, a place our children would hopefully be drawn back to with their own families. It became our sanctuary or *wahi tapu*. In our fourteen years there, we experienced many great times raising our young children but also many extremely heart wrenching ones. Again, it was significant that the worst times arose from influences outside our control.

According to employer psychometric testing in the early 90s, the self-improvement books I'd actively studied since 1982 had transformed me from a shy underachiever into the perfect capitalist citizen. An ideal employee, I was focused on a better future and motivated by a positive, goal-orientated attitude. At the other end of the spectrum, by 1995 Cheryl had been driven to self-destruction. It appeared she no longer wanted to be part of our family and, trapped by dependency, decided she only had one way out. Each day when I came home after work, I was never sure if she'd still be there. This caused confusion and uncertainty, which affected my concentration and motivation. It couldn't have happened at a worse time; the Electricity Corporation (SOE) was preparing for privatisation and required all employees to reapply for their positions. Circumstances at home meant I wasn't confident of holding on to my job, so I accepted redundancy rather than go through the shame of being replaced. Our situation became more complicated when Cheryl fell pregnant with our fourth child, six years since our last.

Twelve months later, coinciding with the birth of our fourth child, Aaron, a good friend called telling me that her daughter had repeated some disturbing comments our daughter Sarah, (nine) had made during a recent sleepover. Her words raised suspicions that she'd been molested. When questioned, Sarah immediately recounted her heart-breaking story. While we were away receiving a significant Amway leadership award in Auckland, her grandfather (Cheryl's foster father) sexually assaulted her. Her grandmother and mum told her under no circumstances was she to tell me what had happened. They said it was an imaginary story, a dream. This revelation explained Cheryl's self-destructive behaviour over the last twelve months; she was conflicted by shame and guilt for not exposing the assault. It also revealed why Sarah, our normally bubbly, happy nine-year-old was now withdrawn and underperforming at school.

Knowing it was wrong, for months she'd tried to communicate what had happened to her to anyone who would listen. I immediately contacted the police who organised for a children's counsellor to interview Sarah. Fearful of speaking out, Cheryl was reluctant to make a statement, after all, since age seven, she'd been groomed by Don L to never speak of his vile attacks. Now thirty-five, the threat of retribution still lingered as a long-standing belief, no doubt recalled as a terrifying demand in her assailant's voice and tone. She'd promised this disgusting secret would go with her to the grave.

Unfortunately, if her abuse, suffered a generation ago wasn't detailed in a signed police statement, Sarah would have to testify in an open court, subject to cross examination. We didn't want that. Cheryl was in a difficult position. In order to save Sarah from an unwelcome and undeserved court appearance, Cheryl had to break her childhood promise by disclosing her own experience of abuse, and that risked retribution and public shame.

To his credit, Don L pleaded guilty, saving us from the drawn-out drama of the open court process. He expressed his love for Cheryl and said how Sarah reminded him of her. Several months later he was convicted of all charges and imprisoned for two years, serving one.

Because of name suppression, most of his friends and acquaintances are unaware of his crimes. His extended absence was explained by some elaborate story involving travel abroad. No one suspected anything or wanted to believe that a pillar of the community was capable of such monstrous acts of evil against children. Don L came into Cheryl's life via a flawed foster system. His evil was finally revealed because of the persistent courage of our little girl, who spoke out despite the lies her trusted adult minders had tried to convince her were real. This unforgivable behaviour confused her reality and forever damaged her trust in others.

Over the next twenty years we sought compensation through the Accident Compensation Corporation (ACC) which provides compulsory insurance cover for personal injury for everyone in New Zealand. However, its skilled manipulation of the legal system denied us our day in court. Long out of prison, Don L lives a comfortable retirement behind a facade of respectability, his lifestyle protected by the legislation that was supposed to compensate everyone who suffers loss from an act that is no fault of their own—that's a system failure! Lozells sentence is irreconcilable when compared to the permanent devastation to our lives. People, unaware of our history, say that if an adult abused their child, they'd hunt them down like an animal, making them pay in kind, while we trusted the legal system to dispense justice—if the treatment we received from those empowered to help us is any guide, perhaps their approach would have provided a sense that real justice was served.

Amid this carnage, I was lobbying to prevent construction of a state-sponsored, subsidised wind farm planned to bisect the horizon dominating the view from our home. Meridian Energy, a state-owned enterprise (SOE) created from the NZ Electricity Corporation, planned to replace the static natural geography with perpetually moving wind turbines. Project funding included an allowance for income received from carbon offsets, traded as credits to foreign third parties. Wikipedia published the following statement regarding these offset credits:

'The Te Apiti Wind Farm is also a carbon offset project. In 2005 the British bank HSBC purchased 125,000 tonnes worth of carbon credits from Meridian generated by the wind farm. Meridian Energy also sold the Dutch government 530,000 tonnes of carbon credits from Te Apiti.

In both cases, the carbon credits for Te Apiti were from New Zealand's assigned amount units allocated under the Kyoto Protocol. The New Zealand Government granted the AAUs to Meridian Energy as an incentive for carbon-neutral power development under the Projects to Reduce Emissions programme (or PRE)'

Assigning carbon credits to this project effectively valued the visual amenity that motivated our house purchase fourteen years earlier. These arguably belonged to all stakeholders whose views were jeopardised by mining the credits. However, the crown inequitably transferred ownership to its SOE, Meridian Energy, who immediately sold them to HSBC London for $6.6 million and the government of the Netherlands for a similar amount (E5.5/tonne, NZ MOE 2005). This reduced our quality of life in order to subsidise an uneconomic, crown-sponsored vanity project, while HSBC signalled virtue to its clients, claiming its operations were carbon neutral. The government of the day arrogantly destroyed the longstanding visual amenity, providing further evidence of objectionable government interference in our anonymous, private life. We were the powerless, innocent, collateral damage of a project that appealed to the guilt-ridden, well-off wallet activists living in large urban electorates.

The planned generation facility comprised fifty-five of the world's largest wind turbines, the Vestas V90. These turbines are as large as a Boeing 747. With a blade diameter of ninety metres, each revolution sweeps an area of over half a hectare, equivalent to the size of the section our house stood. The nearest turbine installation, two and a half kilometres uphill of our home, was included as a strawman. Meridian Energy intended to sacrifice it if the Environment Court directed removal of some turbines to meet the terms of its publicly notified resource consent application. It needn't have worried; the Environment Court rubber stamped the project, ignoring all public opposition and accepting the proposal without amendment. The government labelled long-standing residents opposing the erection of these huge, overtly kinetic, industrial machines as NIMBY (not in my back yard) regressives, disregarding the impact the project would have on them. In fact, submitters were more likely to receive a courtesy visit from the parliamentary arm of the NZ Police than have their concerns taken seriously. An example of state-sponsored selective discrimination, where through lies, deception and exaggeration, opposition is marginalised with no regard to the human cost.

Strategic use of moral grandstanding and impact exaggeration, driving irrational, emotional support, is a systemic expression of Heads of State pretentious need for global significance. This disproportionate approach to esoteric issues, while warm and fuzzy, comes at a high cost to those people crossing paths with their subconsciously programmed worriers fighting their moralistic battles.

For comparison, imagine a private Telco seeking to establish 55 rotating cell towers, the size of 747 Jumbo Jetliners in an urban area. It wouldn't be allowed or be financially viable because of the compensation costs. Today, urban area policy requires retractable stadium lighting towers, protecting visual amenity. Compare urban visual amenity comprising rows of houses, with a complex, rural landscape where we lived; there's no contest! For further evidence that wind farms are more about ego virtue signaling than effective power generation.[18]

I recall the corporate wind-turbine propaganda masquerading as homework our children brought home at the turn of the century. Thus began an era where renewable power is emphasised in the primary school curriculum with simple, repetitive suggestions reinforced by the mainstream media. This is how leaders achieve a generational change in line with their long-term cultural objectives, forming an unshakeable, dogmatic army, pre-programmed to achieve calculated change. Filled with the latest ideas of what will benefit our species future most, they are essential cogs in the long political game of cultural change. As adults, they innocently believe all they were taught was, and still is, objective truth, imagining they are saviours, tasked with implementing change for the greater good. Some are so convinced of this that they completely ignore the opinions, rights, or feelings of others who don't adhere to their righteous beliefs.

This revealing transcript of a 2019 TVNZ Q&A interview by Jack Tame (JT), questioning Secretary-General of the UN, Mr. António Guterres of Portugal illustrates the danger of contemporary, populist indoctrination within the education system:

---

[18] Michael Shellenberger, Forbes 6/5/2019, *The Reason Renewables Can't Power Modern Civilization Is Because They Were Never Meant To.*

JT: 'But if we consider targets previously, and I think of the likes of the Kyoto Protocol, countries have failed dismally in their attempts to reach (Interjection)

Guterres: 'New Zealand is on track in relation to the commitments made on the agreements. So, I hope that this will be the case also for these objectives, at the end of the century. *The problem is that it's not New Zealand that will tip the balance. What we are talking about is the big contributors to emissions and to climate change. And that is where we see this lack of political will that is very worrying.*'

JT: 'It's interesting to consider New Zealand's position because *many people here like to think of us as a small country that is still a global leader on issues such as climate change.* However, our emissions have risen in recent years. We're currently in the middle of an emissions surge. Agriculture in New Zealand, which is our biggest contributor to, um, to, to emissions is still subsidised.'

Despite Mr Guterres repeatedly emphasising NZ is not a threat to the global climate, Tame remains resolute throughout the interview, sticking to his prepared line of questioning. Evidence, that his views regarding climate are subconscious and habitual, inflexible to even rebuttal by the head of the UN! Guterres spoke, but Tame couldn't hear him above the sound of his involuntarily established childhood core beliefs. As Aristotle said, 'Give me a child until he is seven, and I'll give you the women/man.'

Overnight the proposed wind farm undermined the reason we had purchased our home twelve years before. It spoiled the significant visual amenity provided by the rural outlook, while causing an intermittent, audible noise nuisance. Soon after wind-farm commissioning, the landlord/farmer had to abandon the family home unexpectedly because of unbearable low frequency seismic vibration. The family received significant additional compensation for their permanent psychological damage. The full extent of the noise hazard and the cost of settlement is a closely held secret, the lessors muzzled by a confidentiality clause required by Meridian Energy. This conceals evidence relevant to and contrasting with its public statements and environment court submissions.

The seismic effects of this and an adjoining wind farm are so intrusive, that in April 2017, the threat of catastrophic landslides forced the NZTA to close the 150-year-old, arterial Manawatu Gorge road permanently. An essential segment of the regional state highway network, it connects the east and west coast of the lower North Island. The closure disrupted the movement of freight and the motoring public—adding thirty minutes to the usual fourteen-minute travel time, and had an estimated impact of $22 million a year. The long-term detour necessary while they construct an alternative route caused a significant traffic hazard to the normally quiet town of Ashhurst. Vehicle volumes on the Saddle Road detour, passing our former property, increased from 150 to 7600 a day. Just one or two car accidents would occur annually, but now they exceed thirty three, including several fatal and serious injuries. They expect design and development of a green field replacement to cost over $620M, with completion not expected until at least 2024.

When the wind farm was proposed in 2003, side-effects were considered unsubstantiated, irrelevant and acceptable to climate change worrier's—after all, there were only 1000 homes in the sleepy hollow of Ashhurst. The following statement by Mighty River Power, another SOE, illustrates its belief that the end justifies the means, despite the social impact. It reveals their attitude to local communities and its inappropriate use of public money to soften attitudes with deliberate, persuasive psychological propaganda:

'A Social Impact Assessment can be useful where a proposal may have a significant impact on demographics, such as schooling or other social issue, but the results are likely to be far less useful or conclusive where the community is pre-conditioned to the type of development, such as wind farms in Palmerston North.' Mighty River Power 2015 submission to the Palmerston North City Council (PNCC) District Plan.

CHAPTER FIFTEEN

THE FINAL MELTDOWN

T HE COMBINATION OF THE STRESS SURROUNDING POLITICAL
reforms targeting industries in my area of expertise plus my
deteriorating health issues and the disastrous outcome of Cheryl's
reconciliation with her foster family crushed Cheryl. Collectively, these
issues eventually exceeded her mental-coping capacity and triggered
frequent attempts at self-destruction that, in turn, had a damaging effect
on the entire family, resulting in our isolation from society. A close friend
compared our life to living in the twilight zone, neither in the land of the
living or the dead—an accurate analogy. We reached this tipping point
after enduring the resurfacing and unbundling of the psychological
impact from suppressed memories of sexual assault. Through wrong
thought, we were unwitting victims of a stream of seemingly never-
ending, unavoidable disasters, our survival increasingly dependent on
state support.

Life was a struggle for Cheryl parenting four children alone each
day, while I travelled an hour each way to a distant town for work.
Almost ten years after Sarah revealed her abuse, I received a call at work
advising they had admitted Cheryl to hospital after another attempted
suicide. Her specialist became concerned at how quickly she adapted to
the mental health care unit's daily routine, attributing this to her time
in children's homes. He felt the longer she stayed in the ward, the greater
her risk of dependency. Because we were offered no other practical
alternatives, in June 2004 I quit my sixth job in six years to become her
full-time carer, responsible for managing her chronic condition. I also

needed to ensure our four children focused on their education, rather than their parents' situation.

We had endured over two decades of fallout from both the long-term effects of multi-generational sexual abuse and my attempts to engage meaningfully with government agencies. I'd hoped they could provide resources to ease the traumatic psychological and economic impact that had progressively devastated our lives; this hope was misplaced. Constant political interference in our lives amplified the impact of sexual abuse on our wellbeing, triggering impulsive decisions not in our best interest. Coinciding with the rising popularity of the neoliberal ideology, the will within NZ's political class to support beneficiaries declined markedly, culminating with introducing data-driven social-investment policy that treated beneficiaries as state liabilities. Politicians aren't averse to encouraging the public to selectively discriminate against certain vulnerable groups. Championing biased media spin, reinforcing the attitudes they want accepted as the populist view, while arbitrarily denouncing others. In our case, they reinforced popular opinion that beneficiaries and bludgers are synonymous.

Hypocritically, investors facing ruin from their poor investment decisions are portrayed as guiltless victims of unforeseeable circumstances. Media campaigns that groom public opinion minimise outrage when their losses are compensated via urgently legislated, tax-funded bailouts, appropriately called schemes! We didn't experience the same understanding and generosity during our own irrecoverable disaster, unravelling since 1996.

While our family were victims of a convicted sexual predator, bureaucratic technical barriers prevented us from accessing the appropriate ACC legislated compensation designed to assist in the recovery of injured survivors. Now we were all dependents of the state, our income and lifestyle were conditional on the popular political will administered by the NZ Ministry of Social Development (MSD). This lumped us in with the rest of the society's perceived failures, a condition it ruthlessly emphasised. The downward spiral this began affected us for the next fifteen years and beyond. Although Cheryl and Sarah were innocent casualties of sexual violence which left them with chronic psychological injuries, as their carer, they expected me to attend repetitive, regular compliance meetings at our local MSD's work and income office. Its austere decor was intentionally designed to convey that we were worthless, little better than common criminals. The environment left no doubt that it now controlled our financial destiny, leaving us feeling like beggars entirely to blame for our situation and that we should be grateful that we were receiving any help at all. We were hardly 'living life large' on a weekly benefit intentionally set well below the poverty line, removing any dignity or security, an objective of contemporary social investment welfare policy.

In 1974 the NZ government enacted ground-breaking legislation which streamlined the process of victim-liability compensation, intended to protect those facing ruin. Its coverage included citizens, residents and temporary visitors to the country. They established a world-first universal no-fault accidental-injury scheme administered on behalf of the government by a single crown-owned entity, the Accident Compensation Corporation (ACC). This eliminated the need for expensive, time-consuming litigation by removing all other reparative pathways to recover compensation from the perpetrator directly. A compulsory levy on every NZ employer and employee funded the scheme, creating a fund now valued at 31.4 billion; 15% of NZ's GDP (2019). Now larger than the NZ Superannuation Fund, it means that the ACC is NZ's biggest investor, steward of an asset that belongs to all New Zealanders supporting their recovery from unforeseen accidents and injury.

Ongoing political interference eventually diluted the original legislation. Irrespective of political persuasion, the fund's extraordinary capital growth means governments see it as a cash cow, supporting their balance sheet. Multiple parliamentary amendments led to the ACC taking a grudging approach to historical sexual-assault claims, stressing its corporate ethos that it owns the fund, rather than being an administrator on behalf of the legislation and covered claimants.

As early as 1995, it accepted that the assaults sustained by Cheryl and Sarah were covered claims under the act. Knowing that we were covered by this fail-safe legislation, impartially administered by an ACC eager to deliver relevant, appropriate compensation, gave us a feeling of certainty and security for our future. Unfortunately, our actual experience was the polar opposite. As well as dealing with mounting economic, relationship and family stress, I was navigating the unrelenting, corrosive culture of an ACC aggressively evading its responsibilities and withholding entitlements. Dealing with them was time-consuming, demoralising and costly. In a peculiar, far-reaching, damaging decision in 2004, its consulting psychologist concluded that professional inpatient care would not be as effective in Cheryl's recovery as having me look after her. Thus he denied Cheryl the professional support to which she was entitled. In our experience the burden of proof set by the ACC was impossible to meet, far beyond what they could consider reasonable doubt in a court of law.

Cheryl's desperation to self-harm meant her survival depended on medications being locked away, but even that didn't always deter her. She was inventive in her search for medications on which to overdose, proving that strong intention is always followed with creative response. She wouldn't swallow all her tablets and hid those she saved in indoor plant pots until she thought she had a fatal dose. Her choice of poison was also creative, ranging from mixing Ivermectin scabies cream with yoghurt to cooking up the magic mushrooms (Amanita muscaria) sprouting from under our silver birch trees. She found a way in spite of any safety measures I put in place!

One day I asked Cheryl to meet me at Ashhurst school to watch our son Aaron play in a school representative cricket match. There were two small grocery stores on the way, and although she had no money, she stopped at each one to buy a box of twenty Paracetamol tablets on account. She swallowed the lot before getting to the school. Several hours later, realising what she'd done, I called an ambulance, and she was admitted to hospital for observation.

Society praises success and is intolerant of poverty, making my failure an embarrassing, bitter pill to swallow. I'd reached the absolute bottom—at least that's what I hoped. My earlier training in goal setting, positive self-talk and affirmation hadn't helped our situation much as it failed to account for the influence of others. This situation couldn't be solved by repeating a few slick, positive-thinking mantras; we were knee deep in the brown stuff. To me, the cliche 'you make your own luck' was a myth busted! The only chant working in our world was 'soldiering on' in what seemed a living hell, facing total failure in every waking moment, staring at a hopeless future, living but not alive. My reality now mirrored the depressing beliefs I'd expressed in a letter I'd written to Dad thirty years before. This confirmed for me that accepted, emotionalised beliefs always manifest in reality. Whether a vision of heaven or hell, whatever the mind of man conceives and believes will be achieved.

By 2006 our life had descended deeper into despair, worsened by the gloomy Manawatu weather! Constantly battling authorities was exhausting. Unhappy and isolated, I was desperate for a solution to escape the storm. I decided a change in scenery would help drag us up from our deep, dark pit. As a first step in creating a new reality, I began focusing on the thought of moving to another place in NZ. The Hawkes Bay had a better climate, but real-estate was comparatively expensive and anyway who would give us a mortgage; we were state beneficiaries! Our home was valued at $300,000 but after fourteen years of damage control, two-thirds of that belonged to the bank and the justice department for legal aid accrued fighting for weekly compensation from ACC. After repaying debt, if we sold, we wouldn't be able to buy back our existing house, let alone one in another location. I used one of Cheryl's regular counselling appointments to raise the idea of moving to Australia with her caseworker, expecting he would pour cold water on it, as he'd done when I'd recently applied for a senior role at the FRI in Rotorua. That way, I could blame him when I packed the silly idea back in its box. At the time Cheryl was still heavily sedated with the SSRI Citalopram and Quetiapine (Seroquel), an experimental treatment to control her depressed mood. This left her lethargic and distant, seldom engaging with her caseworker at her sessions. She was excited at the prospect of a move to Australia and having the Tasman Sea between her and her assailant. (She told me later of her resentment toward me for staying in Palmerston North for so long after Sarah's assault). She wasn't aware of what it would take to change countries, nor did she care—the logistics were not her problem. Surprisingly, rather than killing off the idea the caseworker added his support, thus breathing more life into the idea.

On reflection, moving countries was a sign of desperation. Although close to NZ, apart from a visit to the Gold Coast as theme park tourists a decade before, I didn't know what I was getting myself into. The move was irresponsible; we would leave our entire support network behind, taking our children into the unknown. However, now the idea was out, like a genie released from a bottle, it took on a life of its own.

No one realised the issues leading to my decision—any rational observer with the case facts would see it was outrageous and dangerous. Then again, the radical change could be the spark shocking Cheryl back to life and jolting me from my pity party. Something had to change, Cheryl wasn't engaged with her outpatient treatments, preferring to cram her pain back into a bulging closet filled with terrifying childhood memories. Something the clinicians didn't realise or didn't want to know.

After searching several Australian locations, I settled on SE Queensland because of its great climate. Our ideal city was coastal, a population around the same as Palmerston North, and not excessively humid. Google returned results including Emerald and Maryborough which our second eldest son Brendon (fifteen), narrowed down further to the city of Hervey Bay. Mainly because the rental housing was modern and affordable, costing under $300/week in 2006. Hervey Bay is recognised as the whale-watch capital of Australia and the gateway to Fraser Island, the world's largest sand island. Its affordability, demographics and facilities looked ideal. Australia's size makes it difficult to comprehend scale and how isolated a place really is, and as there weren't many pictures of the area available online in 2006, I made the final decision on blind faith and gut feel.[19]

Settling on a new location was the simple part, the hard part, making it a reality, was just beginning. Living in a deepening state of poverty, I chose the 21st January 2007 as our NZ departure date. Over the next eight months my feet hardly touched the ground as I worked through a seemingly inexhaustible list of tasks needed to make our shift possible. These included:

Preparing and listing the house for sale; clearing our belongings; organising payment of overseas attendant care from ACC; getting a hospital discharge letter and an introduction to Queensland Mental

---

[19] If you're considering a sea change to Hervey Bay, Qld. go to www. herveybayholiday.com

Health from the DHB for Cheryl; getting enough medication for several weeks, while organising new prescriptions in Australia; booking flights; organising temporary accommodation in Hervey Bay; applying for passports; researching welfare payment entitlements available to NZ citizens living in Australia, organising international access to our money while we established local bank accounts and choosing schools before the start of the 2007 academic year.

The removalist's quotes made it clear that we'd be better off buying what we needed in Queensland rather than shifting our existing climate-challenged belongings across the ditch. Unsurprisingly, over fourteen years, we'd accumulated lots of 'stuff'. I planned to sell it all, including the house, on Trademe, NZ's ebay, although selling houses online was unheard of in 2006. Shifting countries meant I faced multiple large projects within a self-imposed, limited timeframe. Unfortunately, after an accident, they all came to a standstill. A potential buyer arranged to inspect our house on what dawned a freezing cold, wet day. I decided to light a fire to make the house feel warm and cosy, but I'd run out of suitable fuel. While rushing to cut it, I slipped on a wet log and the razor-sharp spinning chain on my Husqvarna XP 372 chainsaw effortlessly sliced deep into my left foot. Luckily, I was wearing safety boots, so rather than losing my whole foot I only severed my big toe tendon. Because Cheryl was paralysed with shock, I dialed 111 for an ambulance while sitting on the front doorstep carefully removing my tattered boot in case my foot fell off. Later that day, a surgeon successfully repaired the tendon, then four nights later, I was discharged, starting several weeks home convalescence laid up on the sofa.

While I lay incapacitated in hospital, no one in authority made alternative arrangements for Cheryl's care, or to administer her medication. Family and neighbours helped where they could, but before and after school, our fifteen-year-old son, Brendon, was left with the responsibility of looking after both Cheryl and Aaron who was still only ten. He did an excellent job, but again, the health system let us down. One afternoon Aaron came home to find the front door locked and Cheryl lying inside on the couch, motionless. Left alone, she'd taken the opportunity to overdose on her suddenly accessible medication. Eventually, Brendon arrived home from high school, and with our neighbour's help, they found a way into the house. Our neighbours drove her twenty kilometres to our doctor's surgery in Palmerston North, where she was held briefly for observation. By now the authorities were very familiar with her condition, so steps should have been taken to ensure not only her safety but also our boys'. Even after this, they were left home with their unsupervised, sedated, ill mother recovering in bed.

What could I have done differently from my hospital bed? Both the ACC and the health system were bludging off the goodwill of our neighbours, both nurses. One, a professor of nursing at Massey University, wrote a scathing letter about the situation to the health authorities, but to no avail. These events left me believing that the authorities don't have a lot of time for suicidal patients. If they survive, they say they just wanted attention; otherwise, they wouldn't be here. If they're successful, they require no further health-system resources; if they're not, because they're 'just attention seekers', they get minimum attention, so their addiction isn't encouraged. Victims only survive because they underestimate the resilience of the human body. Based on the quantities and types of drugs Cheryl took, it was a miracle that her body endured the repeated abuse.

My chainsaw accident didn't stop progress, but it slowed me down for several weeks. I'd already booked and paid for five one-way airfares to Brisbane, 2006's Christmas presents, so there was no time to waste feeling sorry for myself. Between nursing visits to dress my infected wound and the odd rest up on the couch, I kept to the plan, feverishly sanding and painting. I also continued the time-consuming task of listing everything I could on Trademe, including all but a few of our children's things. Their travel allowance was one suitcase, everything else had to be thrown out, given away or sold.

In all this turmoil, I failed to take into account our eldest boy, Jason (eighteen), who was on a sponsored student exchange in Wynnewood, Oklahoma (Infamous for the Tiger King). For many months he was unaware of our decision to move to Australia. He didn't get to say goodbye to the home and room we raised him in from age three. Because he couldn't choose things himself, I was a little more lenient about what we kept for him. Until the day we left for Queensland, I did the same thing day in and day out: list, sell, organise, carry, deliver and move.

Failing to sell our home before we left, meant having to cover our NZ mortgage in addition to paying rent in Hervey Bay. At the eleventh hour, I was forced to list the house with our local real estate firm. We urgently needed to find a buyer; a successful transition required it!

As planned months before, on Sunday 21st January 2007, we finished cleaning and clearing what was left of our belongings. We cut it fine. Our flight left at 5.30 am, and at 1.30 am, Cheryl and I sat on the floor of the empty entrance hall, tearfully saying our goodbyes to the inanimate house that held so many great memories for me and our children. Although Cheryl's recent memories were tarnished, we both had fond recollections of that day back in 1992, when we turned the key in the lock of the fourth, and last, house we would ever own together. Both moments were captured on video. The first, filled with so much promise and joy in our hearts; then fourteen years later, leaving our home exhausted. We ceremonially switched off the light in each room, filled, at least for me, with many happy ghosts, but the air was heavy with sadness as our departure deadline rapidly approached. It's easy to say we're not our possessions, but that's hard to reconcile once they're all gone. After all, the things we hoard are central to the story of our objective ego, with every trinket a memory inseparable from the past we've loved.

In that moment we were victims of both an evil, self-centred man and a governance that failed us. Don L destroyed our idea of family, while our treatment by the ACC between 1995 and 2015 aggravated and prolonged the effects the abuse had on the entire family.

Funding generalised information and rehabilitation programmes isn't reparation; it's a failed social-investment experiment that merely prolongs the abuse of vulnerable individuals caught up in this political game of appearances, statistics, employment and power. All because they are innocent victims of crime.

CHAPTER SIXTEEN

NEW START

W HEN OUR HEADS HIT THE PILLOW, PHYSICALLY AND EMOTIONALLY drained, we were out for the count. Over tired, we slept through our 4 am alarm and had to make a mad dash to the airport. Family and friends and two anxious children, who'd spent their last night in NZ hanging out with their mates, awaited us in the departure lounge, all as resigned as us to the likelihood that we'd miss the plane. But the gods were smiling on us! Dads parting words of wisdom were 'to take time out and recharge'. He was right. I was broken; there'd been no respite from the constant harassment of a heartless bureaucracy.

Although I was the pure definition of a victim, I was a competent one. But the hustling was far from over. We still had to: travel four hours north of Brisbane along the treacherous Bruce Highway to the bay we'd never seen; pay the deposit on our short-term rental accommodation with foreign currency; assist Sarah in her urgent need for employment because New Zealanders don't qualify for Australian Centrelink benefits and we couldn't support her for much more than a month; enrol the boys in suitable schools before the first day of the new semester, a week away; purchase school uniforms and stationary; enrol Cheryl in the local mental health system; organise Medicare; open bank accounts; look for permanent accommodation; approach charity stores for furniture; negotiate a successful house sale back in NZ, so we could begin afresh in our new country of residence, and last, but not least, apply for the disability pension, the only form of government support for which Cheryl potentially qualified.

New Zealand retains traditionally generous welfare arrangements for Australians living in New Zealand, despite the Australian Government in 2001 making dramatic cuts to the welfare entitlements of New Zealanders living in Australia. Since then, these rules have been regularly altered, making them practically identical to those applying to all other foreign nationals applying to immigrate to Australia. Despite government rhetoric, as far as Australian bureaucrats are concerned, the special, neighbourly relationship existing since mutual, simultaneous colonisation by the British presiding over both new lands from its Sydney bay site in New South Wales, has ended. The arbitrary, special category visa—the infamous and confusing SCV—has now replaced New Zealand citizens' treatment as proxy Commonwealth of Australia residents. All New Zealand citizens arriving at its border are advised by immigration kiosk screen that they have or haven't been successfully issued a discretionary SCV—a flimsy visa that except for one exception, the disability pension, no longer gives access to social security assistance. Meanwhile, Australia continues to rely on NZ's skilled, mobile labour force, keeping its industry humming while capping domestic-wage inflation in a cynical betrayal of both labour markets and a disservice to innocent minors who become accidental disadvantaged immigrants.

The sale of our entire history on Trademe only raised $5000 to cover us for our first few weeks in Australia. Having the money to cover further time depended on selling our home quickly and Cheryl's disability pension application being accepted by Centrelink. Otherwise, we'd soon be back on the plane to NZ. I encouraged Sarah (twenty) to search for work urgently, as we were unable to support both her and our remaining dependents. Although Cheryl was receiving the NZ Invalids Benefit, to qualify for the Australian Centrelink equivalent, she still had to pass its strict medical assessment. After a stressful four-week wait, we were relieved when Centrelink finally notified us her application was accepted. Although qualification for the disability pension is assessed under Australian rules, the NZ Government pays the entitlement as a monthly, taxable pension. The Australian Federal Government tops this up, matching Centrelink's pension rate, giving us an additional fortnightly, tax-free payment that varied with exchange-rate fluctuations.

The Australian Tax Office also paid us a fortnightly family tax rebate on qualifying school children, giving us a welcome economic boost which improved the lifestyle with which we could provide them compared to NZ.

In our experience, the Australian welfare system is significantly more humane than the NZ equivalent. We felt that they were on our side and were there to help make a difficult situation easier, the polar opposite of our NZ experience. It was refreshing to see Cheryl being treated with dignity and empathy through what is always a traumatic experience for her. The contrast was pronounced, every meeting in NZ was a running battle to prove we still qualified for its leanest-imaginable welfare payment. I always left feeling that it would withdraw our support at any moment on a staff member's whim.

In 2016, after successfully completing ten years of schooling in Queensland, changes to the SCV meant Aaron had to return to NZ to attend university. It seemed like a sensible time for Cheryl and I to move back to NZ permanently as well—at least that was our intention. By now we were expert minimalists, so we again disposed of all our unnecessary possessions. On arrival, we encountered a severe housing shortage, a lack of healthy housing options, and the same callous attitude we experienced before we left our homeland. In August 2017, we returned to Queensland as permanent refugees, fifth-generation Kiwis, scorned by our country of origin. Australia still elects to issue us its discretionary entry visa, but we can never take it for granted because, as the past shows, our entry status is never certain.

In January 2007, we arrived in Australia with the attitude that this was a second chance. We intended embracing our adopted country and, where possible, draw a line through our painful recent past. However, in a situation like ours, challenges don't miraculously disappear. Issues of survival surrounding finances, housing, mental health, medication, mania and the developing problem of alcohol abuse, were ever present. I quickly exhausted our $5000 budget buying necessities like school uniforms, the rental bond and bicycles to name a few. At this point I'd been unemployed for three years. I was both Cheryl's carer and the family homemaker, limiting my employment options, and although I applied for many jobs, I didn't get a single interview. Our income comprised part NZ ACC Carers Payment, part Disability Pension and part Family Payment. By March we were in a critical cash-flow squeeze; if our house didn't sell soon, we'd have to abort the move and dash back to NZ under cover of darkness! Fortunately, in the nick of time, after refusing many brutally unrealistic offers, we received our asking price. No thanks to the real estate agent, who I begrudgingly paid the statutory commission.

My next challenge was protecting the house sale proceeds, earmarked for our home deposit. On professional advice, I invested a large percentage in Australian listed blue-chip companies like JB HI-FI. Since 2002, 'buy and hold' had proven to be a reliable investment strategy, providing impressive stock market returns. Ben Bernanke, Chairman of the US Federal Bank, confidently spruiked that the global economy was in great condition, no financial storms in sight. But by July 2007, dissenting commentators were expressing doubts about the state of global markets. Several respected experts were calling out investment banks for developing extreme, over leveraged products like collateralized debt obligations or CDO's that were driving up asset valuations, causing a global real estate bubble. These opinions resonated with our own experience. We'd survived the tough times by refinancing our mortgage only because our house had appreciated significantly over the previous three years. The alarm bells started ringing. Afraid of losing our money, I dug deeper into the financial market rabbit hole—credit swaps, mortgage-backed security deals and so on. Evidently irrational exuberance had infected even well-established financial organisations, a situation exaggerated by the US Federal banks endemic preference for loose monetary policy, which fuelled bankers and speculators' greed.

Research revealed a developing opportunity to profit from the most significant transfer of wealth in history. If the post 1980 economy genuinely modelled a free market, there was about to be a bear market in stocks. Selling stocks in a predictable bear, or failing, market, and then banking a profit is a sensible, defensive trading position that sees a justified wealth transfer from weak hands to strong. It shifts wealth from the established 'old money' to a new generation of innovative, digitally savvy technocrats wanting a more-inclusive and fairer world. However, not even the boldest commentators were prepared for the desperate measures introduced by those facing total ruin fuelled by their own unbridled ambition. Short sellers were the first to feel the establishment's wrath.

Under normal circumstances short selling is a sound business practice, but Goldman Sachs, JP Morgan, Merrill Lynch (BoA 2008), Lehman Brothers (Bankrupt 2008), Deutsche Bank, Bear Stearns (Bankrupt 2008) and the Bank of America—the world's largest and most respected investment banks—had created a financial environment that was anything but normal.[20] The establishment quickly fed short sellers a dose of reality. Officials likened them to common criminals, denouncing them as immoral parasites, gorging on others unforeseeable misfortune! Ironically, in an unprecedented action, both the US government and federal bank urgently passed regulations making short selling illegal. This ensured that short sellers banked significant losses while those causing the crisis were rewarded, sending the message, 'The Fed has your back, despite the inherent moral hazard.' This continued the recurring neoliberal theme that collateral damage is acceptable as long as it's only felt on 'main street'.

Because of the actions of a paedophile, our family had already experienced financial and emotional decimation that had forced me to make tough decisions that radically affected all our futures. In addition, we'd experienced arrogant treatment from successive NZ governments and their agencies, allegedly because good policy meant that the bigger picture was more important than protecting our rights to humane treatment. Hindsight shows that on every occasion their actions were nothing more than a grab for the family silver, personal gain being the prime motivator for every decision. All publicly owned entities are fair game, open to plunder. In desperation, I'd used a sound investment strategy, but I was too naïve to realise that, yet another quasi-government entity, this time a foreign one, was willing and able to fight to the death to maintain wealth in traditional hands, despite the vulnerable being collateral damage. Its plan to arbitrarily bailout financial institutions revealed its total disregard for the long-term effect these initiatives would have on global social and political stability.

In March 2009, Federal Reserve Chairman Ben Bernanke said, 'The

---

[20] Michael Lewis, *The Big Short*, Penguin Press, 2011.

US Central bank would use all of its tools to stabilise financial markets and lift the economy out of recession. ... At the Federal Reserve, we will continue to forcefully deploy all the tools at our disposal as long as necessary to support the restoration of financial stability and the resumption of healthy economic growth'.[21] With these statements, Bernanke promised to stand in support of a few global elites threatened with the loss of all they had accumulated for themselves and their dynasties—by manipulating entire populations for centuries. Effectively, central banks acted unilaterally to appropriate the future money supply. They were prepared to create additional money (debt) for as long as it took to bail out both national and international corporates, regardless of whether they had been reckless in the discharge of their fiduciary duty to shareholders. In a free market system, these companies and shareholders would have ultimately absorbed the full risk. History shows they were excused culpability or financial liability; this was unreasonably shifted on to sovereign states.

In a true open market economy, we would have seen a natural transfer of wealth to the fittest, accompanied by imprisonment of those found to be negligent in carrying out their statutory obligations. Government appointed economists suddenly controlled major world economies, free to deploy their theoretical policies on an unsuspecting public. Overnight, central banks became converts to modern monetary theory, but participation in this club was limited to the one percent. In full view and total indemnity, it dipped its fingers in the money jar. Unprecedented levels of money printing, in tandem with sponsored global migration, propped up their frat boys, while recklessly risking the impoverishment of existing and future generations and disrupting established, endemic populations in a grand experiment, while ignoring the likely moral hazard it would unleash. A situation still existing today (2018).

From 2007-2009, the aftermath of the Global Financial Crisis (GFC), small/medium investment companies fell like dominoes, potentially leaving thousands of retail investors penniless. Following the Federal Bank's lead, governments around the world hastily enacted legislation

---

[21] USA Federal Bank Chairman Ben Bernanke: 'Fed will use all tools at its disposal',Reuters, March 2009.

mitigating investor losses. The NZ government delivered investor protection through an urgently implemented investment insurance scheme, passed in parliament knowing full well that failures were inevitable. Deliberately redeploying taxation revenue funded these schemes in a bold, brazen that protected insiders and others from the losses accumulating from their ill-considered investments. Loss compensation that specifically targets the affluent class amounts to welfare for the wealthy (minus the stigma). Another example of the skewed playing field ironically called a free market.

CHAPTER SEVENTEEN

TAP, TAP, TAP

THE TSUNAMI OF BAILOUTS POST THE GFC TIPPED ME OFF THAT THE economic system is not what it seems. I realised economies are arbitrarily derived, synthetic models dependent on consumption. Their success requires increasing productivity reliant on an indoctrinated population believing nirvana is achieved by pursuing financial and material goals. The dice are loaded from the beginning. There are no fixed rules of engagement; any path that achieves growth is acceptable. This economic model is congruent with the theory of evolution: mans' enduring success is best served by the concept of kill or be killed, survival of the fittest. Those controlling the labour hold the power. It's an error to believe that you can aspire to become successful by having faith in a free market. Economic failure and subsequent manipulation of the financial system during the GFC reveals that while we are conceived equal under the stars, we don't start with equal opportunity. Unless you're lucky enough to catch a trend, competing successfully at the elite level of business requires a high degree of massaging and manipulation of the playing field.

Interventions supporting elite globalists is now the new normal, deepening the inevitable correction triggered by some future more painful and enduring event. Meanwhile, the global economy falters in the face of cavalier money printing, which distorts market price discovery and artificially props up insolvent, zombie companies. This locks up capital that would otherwise be attracted to contemporary projects that use latent human potential, increasing overall wellbeing.

Instead, cynical, concurrent policies led to an unparalleled increase in asset inflation, accompanied by an exponential growth in homelessness that is now systemic. The central banks blame this on the aging boomer's generation to deflect the ire of the sleeping away from themselves, the true villains of this unfolding, historic tragedy. Together with their accomplices, desperate politicians equally focused on protecting their own interests, they continue their reckless globalist, monetary experimentation, while Western economies endure widespread erosion of their cultural and financial living standards.

A true free market would have delivered a post GFC deflationary environment where cash and savings are king, reducing the number of vulnerable families facing the growing prospect of homelessness. Instead, in what is known as the great reflation or more correctly 'the grand larceny', rather than banking losses, capital asset investors, regardless of their generation, were guaranteed windfall gains.

Unprecedented levels of migration to western democracies continue to stress infrastructure, reducing the incumbent population's living standards and life expectancy. For example, the ballooning number of vehicles on NZ roads now exceeds the road networks design capacity. The NZ Transport Authority states in its 2016 report, that 'Light vehicle registrations increased markedly in 2013 and continued to grow year on year. New registrations have set record after record'. Globally, politicians have let their constituents down, manipulating the playing field to their own advantage. The creation of at least forty-trillion dollars of new currency in just the last decade support the lifestyle of global elites who operate once-dominant, now-moribund businesses.

Contrastingly, the vast majority, equally perfect at conception and naturally possessing all the attributes required to prosper and expand humanity without further enhancement, are powerless, denied the most basic of living conditions. Through no fault of their own, they fail to reach their potential due to educational indoctrination from an early age. Climactic, cyclical economic failure over the last thirty years warns us to question the economic doctrine that increased productivity is the path to a better earthly experience. Crisis like the GFC, are like a fingernail scratching on a chalkboard. They induce a stress reaction that attempts to break into our subconsciously driven life, imploring us to question what's really going on and ask, 'Are policy makers genuinely working for the collective good or selfishly satisfying their own narrow objectives?'

Neoliberal capitalism is an ideology that emphasises individual prosperity at the expense of collective wealth. Its seductive promise of unlimited power, prestige and security keeps the indoctrinated and unquestioning bound to the dream. Yet the promise is an illusion designed to milk every kilojoule of our energy. Repeatedly failing to meet the high expectations set leaves us questioning our ability. Knowing no better, the only logical conclusion is that we're lacking the right stuff. If we blindly believe the system is fair, we're captive to a path that always ends in disappointment. We're raised on sophisticated messages spelling out what we must aspire to be, seduced by endless rags to riches stories glorifying the lifestyles of the rich and famous. Privilege seems to be accomplished merely through hard work and the application of learned techniques available to all who are willing to pay the hefty price tag.

We enrol in every recommended self-improvement course, but still remain frustratingly stuck. Even when armed with the right knowledge, we still fail! Such convincing evidence that we're beyond help leaves us worse off than before. With nothing else to blame, there's no other conclusion; it must just be me. Naturally we compare ourselves to those others following the same process and achieving uncommon success. Faced with their remarkable success stories of overcoming, we get up and try again and again, admonishing ourselves after every additional failure, which emphasises the perception that we're somehow born flawed. If we hear one more story of the fourteen-year-old who designed an app and now controls a multi-billion-dollar company at twenty-five, or the twenty-year-old who amassed a real estate portfolio of ten properties in ten months, we'll throw up. Like a self-fulfilling prophecy, each defeat carries with it the seed of the next. Given attention, feelings of self-deprecation and inferiority grow until they become an inescapable vortex, dragging us down into inevitable inaction, failure and depression.

The key to unlocking our greatest blessing is hidden within these experiences. The act of surrendering to what is, accepting ourselves the way we are, warts and all, ending the need to change in the mistaken belief it's the path home, reveals a tiny ray of hope. We've been living in the ego's shadow, captive to a socially seeded operating system flawed by replicated limitation. This has sentenced us to a life of aimless sleepwalking, captured in a virtual world of self-constructed fantasy while real life races by. On surrendering to what is, for the first time, the path forward is clear, and past failures and future promises can be seen for what they really are: illusions of an ego-controlled mind that habitually focuses our attention anywhere but the here and now. Once awakened, our critical mind reveals the eternal self as the true you and the ego as the great pretender. It's a transformation to being rather than becoming.

Before leaving NZ, I'd booked a three-bedroom holiday home over the internet, so we didn't have to rush into permanent accommodation or buy furniture for a while. Compared to New Zealand peak-season holiday accommodation, at just $360/week, this was a steal. At the time Hervey Bay was recognised as Australia's fastest growing city, and I'd thought there may be a chance to build and flip houses, but it soon became apparent that it was at the peak of an unsustainable property boom, so I gave this idea no more attention.

Soon after arriving, our new neighbour's toddler befriended us. Some mornings we'd wake to find him standing at the end of our bed with a beaming smile. Naturally we soon met his parents, who became our first 'true blue' Australian friends. At first, they represented hope in our new country, but they soon became my nemesis, a disruptive influence on many fronts, almost proving to be our undoing.

They'd recently moved down from tropical Far North Queensland, worked full time and had two young children, and I assumed that, like us, they were devoted to their family. However, I soon realised that at their place, every night was party night. On the surface they were fun-loving, harmless company, and before long they accepted Cheryl as one of their regular drinking buddies. Both were charismatic extroverts, which fuelled Cheryl's own 'under the influence' extroversion, and she fell in love with them and their lifestyle. With their encouragement, she resumed her excessive drinking, and they soon introduced her to their cannabis habit, a substance to which she'd previously been fiercely opposed. For as long as I've known her, she's had an irrational fear of rules, even refusing to cross deserted intersections without a green walk signal. So smoking tobacco, let alone an illegal substance, was totally out of character.

Excessive alcohol consumption in addition to her established antidepressant treatment of Seroquel and citalopram caused her mood to become manic. She reverted to a rebellious, impulsive teenager, and it became increasingly difficult to keep her safe. I was soon vilified as the enemy, a killjoy parental figure out to spoil their fun. Yet, when things turned bad, as they often did, who did they call to fix the situation? I notified the local mental-health authorities of her worrying behavioural changes, but because low dose Seroquel with SSRIs was still a novel treatment for patients having serious suicidal tendencies, the side effect of mania hadn't been reported. Today, it's a recognised side effect.

A friend of Cheryl's since their days at Whatman Children's Home in Masterton mentioned our situation to one of her acquaintances who happened to be a police officer. She concluded that, ironically, as her husband/carer, I fitted the profile of an enabler and was facilitating her maladaptive conduct. This left me feeling somehow responsible for her errant behaviour. I'd become the broad-shouldered, enduring enabler, the reliable go-to guy who'd pick up the pieces when the music stopped, whether that call was made by her friends or government agencies.

Caring for a wayward partner in a foreign country without a support network to call on meant my decision to move to Queensland was rapidly turning pear-shaped. Then, adding to our increasingly complex situation, ACC decided to unceremoniously throw us under a bus. At its discretion, the ACC Act allows payment of attendant care (AC) to overseas claimants. Retaining this payment was critical to our successful transition from NZ to Australia, so months before departing NZ, I sought confirmation of continued eligibility. All it would say was other claimants were routinely paid AC overseas, so we could expect the same treatment. Yet within days of our arrival in Hervey Bay, I received a decision letter reneging on its verbal advice, explaining that as allowed by its discretionary rights, one month after our departure it would stop paying the AC allowance. This shocking turn around began an ugly, revealing dispute that continued for almost a decade.

Our lawyers, JM Miller and Co, sought an immediate reinstatement of payments while executive management investigated the decision. Being discretionary, we had no rights of appeal. Our only hope was that the ACC would show compassion and reconsider. But true to its systemic habit of abusing sensitive claimants, it demanded Cheryl undergo another psychiatric assessment, by yet another ACC appointed clinician, adding to the long list of assessments she'd already endured. In spite of her extreme fear of flying, it insisted the assessment be completed in NZ. Eventually I convinced them this was unreasonable, and finally seeing reason, they agreed to an assessment in Brisbane by a suitably experienced professional. Predictably, besides the continuation of AC, the report strongly recommended additional support. Senior ACC sensitive claims unit officers, aggrieved by this, responded with an illogical assessment summary which concluded with an arbitrary and nasty decision that immediately stopped payment of AC.

Removing $2,000 from our monthly income left us dependent on state welfare.

In tandem with this dispute, we appealed another ACC decision through the appropriate tribunal process. On three separate occasions over a three-year period, our appeal was successful. However, each time the ACC chose to ignore the tribunal's ruling. The crown had always turned a blind eye to its immoral, possibly even criminal behaviour. There was no penalty for evading tribunal decisions, but there was a financial incentive to both the ACC and the government. After the ACC ignored the tribunal's findings, our only option was to lodge another appeal of the same wrong decision, wasting everyone's time and money. But three times justice was perverted by indefinitely delaying our day in court! The original legislation attempted to provide an objective, no-fault solution for victims, smoothing their way to recovery. However, over the years, policy changes led to it being administered in a subjective manner. Our dealings with them were met with inconsistent application of entitlement laws, constant delays, lies and confusion. Its case-by-case approach, helped by a failure to keep accurate case records, seemed to be part of an elaborate, deliberate strategy to enable ad-hoc manipulation of entitlements, leading to inappropriate individually negotiated decisions. The absence of publicly gazetted standard operating procedures made meaningful, independent audit of these impossible. As the months, years and decades passed, becoming increasingly shattered, we lost all hope of receiving the appropriate compensation from ACC.

We simply couldn't match the limitless, publicly levied financial resources that allowed it to access a professional army of litigators mobilised by a corrupt, government-sanctioned system. In contempt of the no-fault ACC legislation, it had weaponised the tribunal review and district court process, using it as a cynical roadblock to defer and delay settlements. With the government's blessing, the corporation arrogantly gamed the system, exhausting us mentally and financially in a downward-spiralling loop of death. Rather like tipping a quadriplegic out of their wheelchair, then taking bets on the time it would take before they gave up trying to climb back on—a bit of harmless fun.

When the government is complicit, ensuring there are no consequences, it makes perfect sense to shamelessly set arbitrary, fluid policies and practices that enable the goal posts to be shifted at will. Though sound business practice, it normalised fraudulent behaviour within a privileged free-market monopoly, sanctioned by both the prime minister and minister for ACC, regardless of the party in power. In our experience, reparation via traditional legal channels would've been a lot less onerous and deceitful. Because they convicted Cheryl and Sarah's assailant on all sexual assault charges, liability for compensation would've been clear cut and decisive, allowing my wife to receive proper, professional care while I maintained a regular source of income.

ACC's deplorable behaviour meant we had to tighten our belts further, and our children bore the brunt of this decision. After learning to live off a meagre income for the past twenty years, I was an expert budgeter. I planned to minimise saving withdrawals, so we'd again be able to own a house, but the ACC's decision left us with a $300 per month shortfall. Its decision transferred its legally mandated burden of support for Cheryl from the NZ ACC to the Australian welfare system. Centrelink provided us with a carer's pension, which covered some of the stopped ACC payment. We used our now-depleted house savings to cover the shortfall. Now we were a family of four surviving on $39,000 per year gross income. In 2007 our home lease cost $260 per week, by 2016 it had increased to $345, and our income had dropped. Now, in

2019, the lease has increased to $360.00, and our income has remained static. Eventually, aggressive, coordinated central-bank asset inflation policies will force us into homelessness. Will NZ see its way clear to assist Cheryl then? Based on its past track record, I doubt it, but it's certain no one will give my situation a second glance. After all, because I dared to question its processes, I had it coming.

Meanwhile, Sarah strived to maintain casual work in the hospitality industry, but haunted by the residual impact of her abuse, she could never meet her employer's expectations. In 2011 she was raped in her apartment and, soon after, her multinational employer unfairly dismissed her. (Her cases were upheld by the court on both counts). With no income, job prospects, or access to financial support, returning to NZ where she qualified for welfare was her only option. Her move introduced additional complexity and guilt from the shame I felt at failing her. Calling NZ in the early hours of the morning to ask the NZ Police and Waikato Health Department to help your daughter, who is perched on the edge of a bridge while you're powerless to assist, is unimaginably heart-breaking.

These experiences ultimately unlocked the door, freeing me from my self-imposed prison, a hellish place I'd imagined into my reality. For nearly three decades, we experienced brutal treatment from those legally required and materially able to provide reasonable restoration for the damage caused by a sexual predator. This was justification enough for us to become disconsolate victims, demoralised by the overwhelming resources of a callous bureaucracy. But if we did that, we'd be the losers, surrendering to excuses that masked the truth that we choose our response to every moment. A detailed description of the experiences that contributed to this revelation would fill several books, but would only serve to shine a light onto the extensive, destructive, lifelong unravelling of events arising from repressed memories of childhood sexual abuse. In hindsight, I now understand the reason for this journey.

The events I interpreted as suffering were actually a poke in the eye, each one a flashing neon sign, alerting me the source of my suffering. Eventually, when in a state of numb resignation, I surrendered to defeat, the true nature of life was revealed. Unfortunately, the same can't be said for Cheryl and Sarah. Cheryl is forever trapped in that child tormented by the monster who lurks under her bed, like the troll in a children's story with no happy ending. She had no protective dad to save her. The monster violently forced her to sacrifice her emerging life to satisfying the deviant nature of his premeditated fantasies. It's true that nothing breaks like a heart.

Even while I visited through the years, even after the birth of his natural grandchildren, fantasies lived on in the offender's mind. He gave those depraved thoughts attention until he acted on them when he re-offended against our innocent nine-year old, daughter of his first victim. Twenty-one years before, at just seven years old, offered up by the Salvation Army, Cheryl had stood in front of him with hope in her eyes. Her heart had soared with joy to finally be chosen by a foster family. The successful, well-known and respected couple had fostered, and then, for her foster father's gratification, broken the heart of a defenceless, gentle, girl. I hope my journey alongside them and the thoughts leading to the revelation described in this book offers them clarity one day. Like breadcrumbs, they could lead them along a path to the only door that can reconcile them with love, a realisation of the true source of their suffering.

PART 3

I AM THAT, I AM

CHAPTER EIGHTEEN

THE WORLDS A PRISON

AFTER I COMPLETED FOUR YEARS OF STUDY, THE UNIVERSITY OF Canturbury's Chancellor handed me an official-looking, signed paper scroll stating that I was duly admitted to the Degree of Bachelor of Forestry Science. Although nice to have, holding that piece of paper did nothing to make me feel any more confident or competent to carry out my role as a professional forester. I still believed I was out of my depth, incapable of fulfilling any useful function.

At the time, Dad was selling goal-setting programmes developed by the late Paul J Meyer, founder of the American corporation, Success Motivation Institute (SMI). After convincing me its programmes would develop my self-confidence, I signed up and began enthusiastically incorporating its techniques of brainstorming, goal setting, and affirmational self-talk into my daily routine. The turning up with a 'steam shovel rather than a teaspoon' attitude to life sounded empowering, but who was I kidding? Deep down I knew that no matter how diligently I applied the techniques, they wouldn't work for me.

I had faith in SMI's programme, but none in myself. The ideas were sound, and considering my starting point, the improvements were measurable, yet still I doubted. I missing the obvious—that firmly held beliefs are an accurate predictor of future outcomes. It irritated me that the programme's enlightening, transformational ideas weren't taught in school—a waste of our most productive learning time. If I'd been exposed to the content earlier, I may have found it easier to accept the idea that we all possess open-ended creative potential. I feel it would've encouraged greater resilience to adversity and increased self-belief. Now, the thought that I was actually capable of success motivated me to read more self-development books. Hooked by the idea that the solution was learning better techniques, I went deep down the self-improvement rabbit hole, searching for the 'right way' that would guarantee success.

Three decades later, four years after immigrating to Queensland, one genre—self-development books, tapes and videos—still filled my bookcase. Yet even with this wealth of information at my fingertips, it seemed I was no closer to success; in fact I'd gone backwards. Why did the same bad stuff return with monotonous regularity? Solving this puzzle was beyond me. My life script was straight out of the movie *Groundhog Day*; but who would be so cruel as to write the screenplay for such a pathetic story!

'Plan for the worst but expect the best' is an excellent philosophy. But no matter how I willed our fortunes to turn, things went from bad to worse. Eventually, when 'worse' seems to be the only outcome, any effort to improve our lives appears futile. At this point, unless we lift our sights, we're destined to manifest into our lives what we fear most.

In autumn 2010, I booked a trip home to NZ with our credit card to visit my aging parents, who we hadn't seen since 2007. By summer, after being conned by a slick salesman hawking a forex trading course, we were living under extreme financial stress. He revealed during his phone pitch that he'd been an Amway distributor and had reached diamond status. Having operated a growing Amway business myself, I knew this was a rare achievement deserving of respect and an indication he was trustworthy, so I confided the full extent of our grim financial situation. He was absolutely convinced his product would save us. Still, I was no push over, since I'd need to commit the rest of our savings. Eventually, after some convincing, I agreed to buy the programme. I woke the following day with a severe case of buyer's remorse and urgently sought a refund. Coincidentally, it turned out that the company's senior trainer not only lived in Hervey Bay, but was also chairman of our son's high school PTA. Living in Hervey Bay! What were the chances? He allayed my fears over a coffee, insisting the programme was genuine and that with his tuition I'd succeed.

The training turned out to be comprehensive, but unbeknown to them, a consortium of elite banks was up to their usual dodgy deals. Through manipulating foreign-exchange markets, they rendered any rules-based, data-driven forex system useless.[22] Not a single banking executive was held accountable for their offences or restorative compensation offered to the millions of swindled traders. The real scammers in this story are the banking regulators, a label they still deserve today. Adding insult to injury, I lost a major trade in the YEN/USD, when the YEN plummeted at the moment the 2011 Tohoku earthquake and tsunami struck Japan. The drop was so significant and sudden that I turned on the TV, quickly forgetting my loss as I watched in horror at the live scenes unfolding.

With our savings gone, there was nothing left to cover our credit-card's monthly minimum payment. I proactively offered to pay the bank interest only, promising that I'd clear the debt once ACC settled our successfully defended review. Apparently, because banks are legally required to collect the minimum monthly payment with no exceptions, it was unable to accept this proposal. Instead, they advised that I should default, spoiling our impeccable twenty year track record and incurring an unrecoverable $20,000 debt. We would've paid the bank back in full if ACC had honoured any of the three reviews that found in our favour. However, maintaining its long-standing policy of evading its legal obligations, it continued to withhold compensation.

Across ten years, I experienced enforced employment change, poor health, family members with diagnosed complex PTSD, BPD and dissociative disorders with deteriorating finances. We struggled against the endless resources that government agencies, including Meridian Energy, WINZ and ACC, deployed against us. I attempted to maintain a normal family environment for our children while single-handedly managing these relentless bureaucracies, which had predictable, compounding, emotionally degenerative effects on the entire family, as identified in the Holmes-Rahe Stress Inventory. It took a toll on my

---

[22] *Record bank fines for foreign exchange market manipulation. Four of the banks—JP Morgan, Citigroup, Barclays and RBS—have agreed to plead guilty to US criminal charges,* BBC.com, May 2015.

will to survive. Expecting compassion, I encountered aggression and conflict! Cheryl had treatment options, including support from health authorities, but I was on my own. Fortunately, love for my children kept a lid on my own depressive thoughts. Not that the state cared, to them I was a faceless, convenient, primary-care scapegoat.

From birth, we're taught that success is a formula. Do this to achieve that; if you don't, then do more until it does. Contemporary memes equate happiness to financial success, material possessions and even how well travelled we are—all indicators that the formula is working. These collective memes, or viral beliefs, keep our thoughts focused on the unreal future, instead of the present. The mind, captured by the learned thought habit that happiness is an outcome of manipulating actions, forces results to align with our expectations and desires. With this view of life, success is conditional on arrival at a planned future destination, which few ever achieve. This definition of success dominates all developed economies. Growth is the mantra, and the standard of living depends on perpetually accelerating productivity. The drive for success and the fear of failure in a competitive job market leads to long workdays, stress and performance anxiety. Researchers list this race to the top in a material world as the cause of low life satisfaction, falling life expectancy and accelerating male suicide rates.

The accumulated effect of resisting a lifetime of events I viewed as bad had taken its toll. Finally raising the white flag, I surrendered to the thought that no technique or process exists that would work for me. Clearly success is bred not learned. Self-improvement authors like Napoleon Hill are born with a golden ticket, the success gene making them type A personalities. While I was born destined to experience oppression, suffering and disappointment—a conclusion supported by a fifty-year track record of failure, which promised a hopeless future of continuing poverty. Homelessness now seemed inevitable. What was the point of prolonging the pain? Fortunately, our youngest son, Aaron, was still at school, and like his older siblings, I'd vowed I'd hang in there to give him a fair chance at a secure future. We'd brought him into the world, so I owed him that.

In this moment of surrender, I had a revelation, a breakthrough, in which I finally understood that the cause of my repetitive pattern of failure and suffering was self-inflicted. Could this be it? I soon confirmed the idea's validity with an internet search that revealed my thinking error. The actual source of my suffering was a maladaptive core belief.

While genuine, ironically, the despair caused by what was happening to my family was also supporting a thirty-six-year-old belief that the world is an intergalactic prison for ne'er-do-wells. This belief, a seed I'd chosen to sow and given regular attention, grew until it bloomed, producing a harvest consistent with the original thought. It cast me as a victim of my own supernatural story that 'the world is a prison'. Had thirty years studying the books written by Paul J Meyer, Napoleon Hill, Jose Silva and the late Wayne W. Dyer prepared me for this revelation? My eureka moment revealed that our childhood belief choices create our adult life experience. Until I recognised and changed destructive central core-beliefs or schema no amount of goal setting, affirmation or subliminal programming would eliminate my suffering. I was captive to a self-injected belief virus that was consuming my life through self-sabotage. The belief hijacking 'Me' had become as much a part of me as any organ. I had formed the belief, then proved it with precision, using my very own cybernetic servomechanism[23] or 'as goes our attention, so comes our experience', an immutable law of nature.

It devastated me when my parents separated; it was a blow to my world model or ego. My life was not supposed to be this way. Dwelling on this state of mind nurtured a thought that set me up in a lose-lose situation. In an emotionally charged period, I attached objective meaning to their divorce, casting me as the lead actor in my own tragedy. The pattern for my life was irrevocably cast when I decided that the world is an intergalactic prison designed for our punishment. I wrote to my late dad (1933-2019) about this belief in 1975. He replied:

'I'm so sorry it's taken me so long to write to you, especially as you sounded so depressed. You say you still can't find a reason or an answer to the question, why are we alive? I know this feeling well, and the question constantly faces me! For me, the answer is to overcome struggle against all the odds, never to give up ...'

Excellent advice, but I was in no state to receive it. I already viewed

---

[23] Norbert Wiener, *The Human Use Of Human Beings: Cybernetics And Society* Ingram, Revised ed, 1988.

my life through this new 'hopeless' filter. I had interpreted, assessed and decided from limited life experience to believe a story designed to punish me for the wrongs committed in some imagined, previous dimension of life. At my own instruction, I filtered all future events in a way that supported this belief, arbitrarily limiting future possibilities. My mind did precisely what it's designed to do: slavishly act to achieve my concept of life. Like a missile locked to a target, its attention was sharply focused on the evidence supporting my chosen belief system, while actively ignoring information at odds with my expected experience. I was accidentally programming my mind to create my own hell on earth—but, serendipitously, a hell leading me to a reward that few achieve.

I gained the awareness that my feelings of overwhelming anxiety and misery were caused by role-playing my life from faulty core beliefs, emotionalised at a time when I lacked adaptive coping strategies. The reason for my perpetual suffering was now clear; interpretation of my parents' situation had turned me into the unconscious victim of my ego. I was fixated on identifying the negative in every event, confirming my ego's view of life that we are victims of a heartless world. The self-constructed model of 'myself' naturally translated all experiences to be congruent with this model (confirmation bias) making my life a self-fulfilling prophecy. This discovery forever changed my understanding of the meaning of life.

CHAPTER NINETEEN

SUCCESS IS WHO WE ARE
NOT WHAT WE PURSUE

TRADITIONALLY, WE'RE TAUGHT SUCCESS IS A DESTINATION, NOT A state of being. Our attention is permanently focused on future attainment, which is dependent on wilfully doing, forcing and changing, hoping to gain approval, recognition, power or material reward. I was slavishly focused on this tradition when the discovery of generational sexual assault blindsided our family. While struggling to come to terms with our world collapsing around us, my ego searched for excuses to explain our sudden change in circumstances. I needed something or someone to blame, to rationalise our fall from grace. I'd always found meaning by doing and fixing; how would I find purpose in this new reality? By creating an ego-contrived environment which would reward me for surmounting the unsurmountable. Overcoming became my new life purpose, a role supporting Cheryl and Sarah, while insulating our boys from the effects of this unexpected family trauma. I wanted to protect them from everything that an undeniably evil world dared throw our way. Doing this breathed life into Dad's response to the question I'd asked him in that letter that cemented my destiny back in 1975: *For me, the answer is to overcome, struggle against all the odds, never to give up.* How could I meet societies expectations while struggling with this train wreck? This perspective provided me with the perfect excuse, one that rationalised my sense of failure when compared against traditional measures. Obviously, I was an innocent victim of 'them'.

Core beliefs established during our childhood and youth continue unconsciously and uncritically. They filter present perceptions, ensuring that reality exactly matches our model or ego's expectations. Our childhood summation that the world is either a kind or heartless place becomes our truth. We see only what we already believe, maintaining congruency with our established life model. Winnie the Pooh might call it the Tigger/Eeyore ego model.

In reality events are neither good nor bad; it's our learned judgmental mode of thinking that makes them so. While physical harm or mental pain caused through no fault of our own is debilitating and unfair, unconsciously dwelling on it can lead to us becoming a neurotic victim, serving only to keep us frozen in time; dead but not buried. Just as the sun's gravity acts on the earth's tangential motion, guaranteeing its consistent, eternal orbit, our interpretation of events throughout life are aligned and interpreted in harmony with our earliest life decisions. This builds our ego personality. We construct a virtual object, block by block with precise form and mass, like building a house. Unconsciously chosen thoughts assume a life of their own in a seamless marriage to the physical body called 'me'. This snowballs with time, gaining unstoppable momentum, and it's not about to relinquish the reins without a fight.

Essentially absent during this childhood process, no wonder we believe we're born blessed or cursed by our ancestor's bloodline. Yet the truth is we're designer items. The horror story we call our life is destined to repeat until it's consciously redesigned. So, yes, with an understanding of ego formation, an old dog can learn new tricks. Change is easy, but not effortless. Earth orbits the sun effortlessly, eternally captured within a well-worn habit without needing additional energy to keep it there. Ego is just a collection of thoughts emotionalised as beliefs against which we evaluate all events. Locked in place through repetition, our beliefs connect to us as the planets connect to the sun. Now, imagine the energy required to disrupt earth from its orbit, breaking its attraction to the sun! It's enormous. Our response to events is like this planetary attraction, locked in a groove inextricably linked to the ego by habit. Repetitive emotional pain is the red light warning that we're trapped in a rut. Victims of our self-constructed ego, we're destined to repeat the same painful experiences, over and over. The ego is no longer serving us; we're serving it.

Realising this is our eureka moment. When we recognise that the bad from our past is, and always was, an illusion, made real by wrong thought, it becomes powerless to control our response today. Realising there is only now erases the word 'regret' from our vocabulary. We no longer fear thoughts of lack and scarcity, both illusions created by a hypnotised mind. Our memories are subjective, relative, existing only in imagination; even the concept of death explained by an objective life model is little more than an elaborate fairy tale.

Through ignorance, we believe our objective body is synonymous with ego. We accept this character, designed in childhood and captured in a subconscious story, without question until the day we leave our physical form behind. As the last thoughts cross our dying mind, we may possibly awaken to the folly of chasing 'must do's and regretting 'could haves'. Without an intervention, we'll never discover that our reality exists apart from the ego, which is a tiny subset of experience chosen from an infinite array of choices. While the body follows the cycle of birth and death, changed only by rare discrete evolution, the ego is dynamic. Discovering that the ego is a clever impersonator, imperceptible from the object that meets us in the mirror every morning, is as effective as electroconvulsive therapy for freeing us of our destructive patterns of thought—and it's obviously less intrusive.

The first step to designing our life requires the conscious application of energy to regain control over our ego and consequently over our outcomes. Ego's life, death and resurrection must come under our continuous control. Awakening from the ego's hypnotic spell reveals our unlimited power to consciously recreate our identity, in the same was as we use Lego blocks or plasticine.

At some point in our lives, we may experience this miracle; some may even understand from the beginning. Perhaps revelations are cumulative across lifetimes, and once a lesson is learned, our physical rebirth begins from a more enlightened point. I think we must endure our share of suffering, so, like water eventually wearing down a large boulder damming a stream, we enable the flow of energy rather than resisting it. Eventually we discover that suffering is a choice. We're like oysters irritated by a grain of sand which eventually becomes a beautiful pearl, or a piece of coal which under intense pressure creates a sparkling diamond. Like these examples from nature, when we're facing what seems like intolerable suffering, if we contain the overwhelming urge to end our life, victory is ours. The complete destruction of the unconscious self comes from realising that ego is a false and insignificant self, and the divine prize is realising this while we still have life. Unfortunately, the door concealing this reward seems to only appear when, exhausted from the struggle, we give up, surrendering to our perceived fate. Paradoxically, the moment we stop resisting, life becomes effortless.

CHAPTER TWENTY

RELEASED FROM THE ILLUSION

THE REALISATION THAT I WAS PUSHING MY OWN BUTTONS, A VICTIM of my own stinking thinking, released me from the ego's vice-like grip. I had a choice to make: awaken from this bad dream into the light of new possibilities or continue wallowing in self-pity. Continuing meant a subtle shift from playing the role of unconscious victim to conscious martyr—not an option! When the flash of awareness happens, revealing that the ego is a mistake of interpretation, it seems so obvious. Yet it's difficult to express how our relative perspective instantaneously changes. Before, I identified with the reflection in the mirror, in the same way unique labels identify familiar objects. Now, I identified with everything! Not just my body and what it represented, but what I could see in the mirror and all that surrounded the mirror, everything. I became the formless observer. My body became simply an objective experience or host to a nameless observer. Significantly, when Cheryl's mental illness was at its worst, when she looked in the mirror, she saw a stranger staring back at her. She was observing, but not experiencing any connection.

During a BBC interview in 1959, Carl Jung described his awakening to consciousness: 'That was in my eleventh year. Walking to school I stepped out of the mist. It was just as if I had stepped out of a mist. Walking in a mist, I stepped out of it, and I knew I am what I am, but then I thought, what have I been before?' To me, awakening at such a young age seems uncommon, but then I can only draw on my own experience; it may be far more common than I realise. The interviewer's specific question to Jung was, 'When did you first become aware that you were conscious?' It's easy to confuse the interviewer's meaning with the dictionary definition of 'aware of and responding to one's surroundings' or the definition of self-awareness as 'being conscious equates to our first remembered life event convincing us we're separate to others'. We are self-aware when we see our reflection in a mirror, but not necessarily conscious. My interpretation of what Jung means by consciousness is *the moment we realise we are creating our own experience.*

If we each create our own experience, there is only one explanation of our reality: All that surrounds us starts within, before it can be formed without. This means that 'I' (ego) is a self-created and fluid illusion. By law of the universal creator, through free will 'I' is what I have created by my thoughts. It follows then that I can have whatever I imagine by sowing and nurturing any idea until I reap the result that matches the thought. Because we're reaping the harvest of our own thoughts, all is as it should be in this moment. It can be no different because our thoughts have made it so. Our life is what we choose to make it, consciously or unconsciously!

Undoubtedly man didn't create everything, but what man has created began as a thought, conceived within, before being born without. The world we see today is proof that thought precedes all things. But first there was the universe. What created it? Because thought precedes all things, the universe could only have been manifested by the source of all thought. The universe is an infinite field of thought from which each of us is conceived *through* man and woman—not *of* man and woman—into abundance. Worthy of the original creator, a being of the universe manifested by the source of all, we can confidently declare that we're always all we need to be. What we are at conception cannot be improved. We possess all we need now to prosper as intended—no need to strive to be better. 'Whatever the mind of man can conceive and believe, he can achieve': these immortal words of the late Napoleon Hill apply to us all equally. It's a law, so it cannot be limited to just a gifted few.

The moment when we're realise we're not defined by the mobile vessel, our body enabling our earthly physical experience with which we've always identified, is incomparable. Realising we're a timeless thought in a limited physical form, nothing yet instantaneously everything, immortal because we never are, so we can never die.

The ego, the objective 'i' identified with our past and our future, is an illusion, hardly worthy of our awareness, let alone a lifetime captivated in a state of trance. The emotional memories, persistently haunting us with our blessing, are subjective, destructive and irrelevant. Only memories full of joy and thoughts of a hopeful future are worthy of attention and brief contemplation. Memories and dreams are a refuge, a resource to draw on to replenish our strength while we wilfully design a life focused on the 'Now'.

Next time you're out driving and inevitably another driver makes a mistake, just as you do from time to time, instead of raging, smile, wave, and thank them for bringing you back into the moment. It's your conscious and creative choice to stop dwelling on the rotting thoughts of the past or fears for the future. Being an adult in a conscious state, you're in control of every response; no one can push your buttons, harming you without your permission.

We only exist when our awareness is on this very moment, in the same way that if a tree falls in a forest and no one is around to hear it, does it make a sound? We imagine that it does, but that's not the same as physically sensing and experiencing it. Compare the feeling of watching our favourite musician on a video stream to being at a live concert. We imagine one experience while we feel the other physically through our senses. The belief in our existence in any point other than right now is a trick of our constructed ego, connecting 'now' moments to give the illusion of longevity measured as physical time. These connected moments become our self-aware or objective ego, inseparable from our name. We have been taught to live our lives acting from this objective ego, habitually relying on past subconscious experience, until we die. Our lives, like the tree in the forest, rarely make a sound. True consciousness is the realisation that we are part of the whole of creation, while being the conductor of our own experience on earth, courtesy of the miracle of our physical body.

Recognising that we are the zone where waves and matter meet, the point of creation from subjective thought to objective particles, adds another dimension to our life. It becomes an entertaining game of build and break, exploring and expanding alternative fictional stories around our fixed beliefs. Projecting sequential possibilities and connecting bizarre thoughts within these stories helps us recognise that significance is a choice of free will. Story telling is an excellent tool to alert others that they're captured within self-constructed stories. We give these stories significance when we accept them as true, the definition of belief.

Tread carefully and be prepared for the sparks to fly if you question the core beliefs of someone who is unaware that their worldview is a variable, dependent on their choice of beliefs. Until they understand this, they'll find your questioning confronting and annoying. Continuation of our ego, our sense of self, depends on these beliefs continuing unchallenged. Convinced otherwise, what are we left with?

Change the belief, change the story, and expand the potential outcomes. The subjective story approach significantly improved Cheryl's perspective of her past. She even adapts it to use on me when I'm needing a reboot, thus releasing me from the headlights of wrong thought! It's hard to argue when you're reminded that the past or the future is a story of imagination dependent on a collection of unknowable variables.

Our memories and meaningless ego personality die with our body, while our i AM is conceived in form again. In his novel *Westworld*, author Michael Crichton theorises this process by creating a world in which android avatars are part of elaborate theme parks. The avatars are born, suffer, then die, only to be reset, to do it all again. The robot characters appear to be conscious within their current life, but in the story's context they are habitually locked within a finite life scenario, destined to repeat the same experience, suffering their destined fate for eternity. Eventually, after experiencing moments of déjà-vu, one or two principal characters notice their lives' repetitive nature. This is their true awakening-to-consciousness moment, a first step in the fight for freedom from unconscious oppression. Is conception a time machine? A path to alternate physical experiences that we live with the aim of becoming awakened to our individual power to create?

With help from Western society memes, there's no escaping the belief that success is measured by the attainment of wealth and accumulation of possessions. Only when we awaken to the natural abundance of what we're born into, does this belief evaporate, ceasing to be a motivator. I realised that the unquestioned pursuit of anything consumes our life. Messages constantly bombard us from all quarters, suggesting we must do certain things in a certain way to have any chance of becoming a worthy part of humanity. This is a lie which keeps us enslaved by doing unsatisfying work to enrich others. We're led in a trance, only realising in the finality of death that all that was required from us is to 'Be.'

There is no need to become, because we already are. Right now, we're asleep, hypnotised like a crayfish in a pot of water, oblivious of the danger while the 'heat' is progressively raised. 'Heat' in this analogy refers to the pursuit of unending economic growth in a system that exploits our need for social validation through the accumulation of material possessions—tangible evidence that we're worthy of our place at the top table. It's a crude motivational ploy designed to extract as much of our energy as possible on the futile pursuit of an eventual arrival. Those who plunder our essential vitality in this way appropriate our lives to enrich themselves and their dynasties. It's time to awake and embrace a better way of thinking, one where we're consciously pulling our own strings.

CHAPTER TWENTY-ONE

WILL THIS WORK FOR YOU?

I DOUBT THOSE ALREADY NAVIGATING LIFE SUCCESSFULLY ARE motivated to question the source of any temporarily encountered suffering.

A hound dog sits on its owner's porch. Occasionally it whines, but only momentarily. A visitor notices and asks its owner why the dog whines.

He replies, 'Because he's lying on a protruding nail.'

The visitor then asks, 'Why doesn't he just move?'

The owner responds, 'Because it's just not that bad'.

It's only when we've wandered far from the path, feeling lost, that we're motivated to seek answers. If we persist with our search, we eventually realise that joy and happiness are our natural state, while suffering is a sign that we need to adjust our perspective or point of reference. We know we're pulling our own strings when we see ourselves not from our point of view, or even another's point of view, but from an everything point of view, a perspective that knows that life is just a question of semantics.—the semantics of i AM or #SOIAMTHAT. Reflect on this; understand it and be released, like the wind, free for eternity.

Imagine you're an eagle and sense its power and freedom, or imagine the sparkling light dancing off the flat ocean on a still, cloudless day. Now, consciously choose the target of your awareness in every moment; focus your attention intentionally rather than randomly. Notice a dragonfly; focus your attention on it; follow its aerial dance, and become it as it darts this way then that. For as long as you dare to hold the thought, that's effective meditation. See it seeing you and you seeing it, even being it. After all, each of us is just light organised into a conscious, cellular organism, creating from the unceasing thoughts that are us. The dragonfly differs from us only in that it can't choose the thought; its destiny is a predetermined blueprint, already set like stone.

The creative miracle, always accessible but seldom used, is reserved for human beings. In every moment, whether consciously or unconsciously, we choose thoughts by casting our awareness, and through constant attention to the idea, we magically reveal it from the abstract into the objective for all to see. This is the inevitable journey of all that is objective, from conception to birth to maturity to death.

CHAPTER TWENTY-TWO

I WILL BE HAPPY WHEN ...
EQUALS NEVER

BOTH NORMAN VINCENT PEALE, AUTHOR OF *THE POWER OF POSITIVE Thinking*, and Paul J Meyer, author and developer of *The Dynamics of Personal Motivation* (DPM), wrote that if you shoot for the moon, even if you miss, you'll land among the stars.

Here is an example of the Paul J Meyer attitude in action (Success Magazine, June 2009).[24] It illustrates his philosophy that anything is possible when you know. 'During his mid-forties, Paul was trying to recruit some peers into one of his businesses. They repeatedly gave excuses about being too old or it being too late to venture into such endeavours. Paul set out to prove them wrong by showing that anything is possible as long as you set a goal, have a winner's attitude, and apply discipline and a willingness to work.

At forty-seven Paul decided he would make his point by learning to play tennis and becoming a champion. Before he even picked up a racquet, he bought a wood-burning set and made an affirmation and put it on his desk. It read: I am a Class-A tennis player. Then he went to work. He bought and repeatedly studied every video from every great tennis player.

'I took lessons from Rod Laver, the world's number one tennis

---

[24] Todd Eliason, *Paul J. Meyer: What it Takes to be a Winner*, Success Enterprises LLC, Success Magazine, June 2009.

player at that time, as well as from Roy Emerson, who had won more tournaments than anyone else at that time, and from Russell Seymour, the top player in my age group.'

He then bought a local tennis club, installed the number one tennis player (Robert Trogolo) as the resident pro and sponsored him on the world tour. He took more than 300 lessons, read twenty books and went to four tennis camps. He even bought a computerised ball machine, using its 7,000 shot variations to simulate the style of his targeted opponents.

'It would shoot the same balls at me that you would hit at me,' Paul said.

Within five years he won the Dallas Open and was one of the top-ranked players in the country in his age group. When asked how someone his age could accomplish such a task, he brought the discussion back to the power of goal setting. 'I put down my goal in writing, listed the obstacles and roadblocks, and then it was about finding a way around them,' Paul said. 'I was over fifty years of age at the time, but that's what I was willing to do to learn. It's what I had to do to be a champion and to be the best".'

This is Meyer's philosophy. It reflects his refined creative skill, fuelled by a high degree of self-belief. Meyer is the godfather of affirmation, something that's at the core of his many self-development courses, but with his steely attitude, who needs affirmations! His self-image, dominated by unwavering faith and confidence in his personal power, rejected thoughts of failure. And he knew he was born of the universe. These attitude advantages acted like rocket fuel igniting under him. When he repeated the affirmation, there was no chatter at the back of it saying, 'Who do you think you are to believe you can do this. Look at your poor genetics. What a loser.'

He'd already decided he was worthy; affirmations only had to focus his awareness, ensuring constant attention to his intention. Using tennis, Meyer proved how to 'progressively realise a predetermined and worthwhile goal'—something taught in his numerous programmes. His mind-set is more than belief; it's one of knowing without doubt that what a man or woman conceives and believes, they will achieve. Napoleon Hill was another with this mind-set. In my experience, this is the exception rather than the rule.

In 1981 I bought into Meyer's philosophy of personal achievement at an intellectual level, but in practice it would never work for me. It wasn't congruent with my decision as a vulnerable teenager to frame planet Earth as an intergalactic prison, intent on punishment. With this attitude, I was always going to prove the self-help literature wrong by sabotaging my success. Many of us decide in childhood that we are unworthy of significant achievement; very few develop the required state of single-minded conviction. During our growing years, our education and the media, particularly film and TV, subtly directs our aspirations. This sets us up for a life perpetually struggling to achieve success measured by material wealth, a symptom of being taught to think within a narrow range of options offered early in our development. Centralised, proactive influencing is not a secret, but before now, unsophisticated and decentralised data collection only allowed broad brush, time-consuming analysis of small groups, which limited the damage. Subliminal advertising technology was developed in the 1950s, offering a covert way of influencing society's goals, desires and opinions. The technology was reportedly banned for fear of abuse by both the state and corporations.

Today, enabled by the all-pervasive smartphone, the tentacles of politics and commerce are far reaching. Contemporary generations gift access to every part of their lives via apps for banking, investment, health, love and spirituality. This leaves them vulnerable to manipulation by 'big data' mining analysts. Unrestricted access to 'big data' enables planners to develop sophisticated control programmes or psyops, capable of unconsciously capturing the minds of entire populations, ensuring majority compliance, while guiding economic productivity along a narrow, prearranged path. For an enormous fee, powerful elites have practically instantaneous access to vast amounts of our unsecured, intimate data. Implementation and targeting of social programmes, influencing our behaviour is fast and precise, herding us to a destination that achieves their predetermined blueprint.

It's already difficult to wake up to the gift of free will, but now that power brokers have access to systems that allow them to reverse engineer our every stimulus and response, the task has become a lot harder. Expect to be led by these analysts/miners, from here to there, in order to help them to accomplish their grand plan. We assist them by unconsciously following the goals and dreams implanted in us from the day we're born, believing they're ours. Many of these goals are unrealistic, unattainable illusions that keep our minds focused on the future, while they consume our lives in the present. Unconsciously, as if in an induced trance, we diligently strive to improve ourselves along a narrow path of endeavour, believing it's the path to success and the cure for our restlessness. No wonder we're always stressed, anxious, feeling inadequate, never able to just be still. This futile endeavour is squeezing the joy out of every second in a controlled, robotic existence, and there's no let-up in sight.

Perhaps this is how life is meant to be experienced. Congealed particles of light in physical form on Earth take us on a journey of progressive discovery, from a state of trance to one of conscious free will. Learning lessons, moving us toward the faith mind set of P.J. Meyer and others like him. Maybe the revelation that we choose consciously or otherwise, creating our own heaven or our hell on earth, can't be forced. Maybe it must unfold, like the butterfly from the caterpillar, after suffering across more than one lifetime. Like the oyster and pearl, is suffering the path to refinement and an understanding of our role within the expanding universe in which we're entangled? I don't have the answer, but by expressing the thoughts from my experience, I hope to help open the eyes of those who are ready to draw the curtain on the imposter living their life—the illusion that they believe, without a doubt, is them.

Any self-improvement philosophies I applied were as effective as plastering over the cracks in a load-bearing wall. Long held feelings of anxiety, fear, loneliness and a sense of suffering caused by a belief in a universe of lack and torment guaranteed that improved performance would be temporary. Searching in the pages of a book or course for the missing ingredient to fix our flaws, hoping to finally achieve success, reveals a complete lack of faith and understanding of who we are. From a young age we're deliberately taught that success is attained by doing things in a certain way to avoid failure, poverty and a sense of worthlessness. This is a lie. Until we rediscover our true north, realising that our happiness is and always was under our control, lasting success will elude us. Success is a matter of faith; it's a state of mind. Believing it's a thing to be achieved guarantees we'll never find it.

When we develop the awareness that birth and worthiness are inseparable, help from books is optional, not the path to a cure. Meyer's affirmations focused his belief on what he wanted to manifest in the physical plane, assuring victory, as described in the Book of Matthew 17:20 — So Jesus said to them, 'Because of your unbelief; for assuredly, I say to you, if you have faith as a mustard seed, you will say to this mountain, "Move from here to there," and it will move; and nothing will be impossible for you.'

Until we recognise that we're under the subliminal control of our ego mind, we'll remain the character lead in our own autobiographical horror story. Waking to this immediately releases us from its tyranny. We see that we're already the successful, effortless creator we've been seeking in all the wrong places. We all emerge from the same thought that created the universe, so believing we're born inferior is a self-imposed lie. At conception we possess the same qualities as the most powerful: all we ever need to be, having all the attributes required to lead a prosperous life. We are born possessing the ability to solve any and every roadblock or hurdle we will ever encounter. Abundance is our birth right, connected to an unbounded universe in a state of perpetual renewal. We arise from light, the enduring source of everything, created perfectly right here, right now and complete in a moment that is everything that ever was and ever will be. With this new mind set, the mantra for more ceases to motivate. Our reasons for being and our traditional society nurtured priorities that promote consumption above all else transform instantly. We no longer seek approval by competing to the death for more of the power, wealth and fame that strokes the individual's ego. Now we delight in having just enough: enough food to sustain, warm shelter and a new sense of freedom from the nagging, judging voice—a remnant of childhood indoctrination. This gives us access to a whole new, exciting world. Not a prison, but a sandbox.

'My head is bloody but unbowed.
Beyond this place of wrath and tears.

Looms but the Horror of the shade;
And yet the menace of the years finds
and shall find me unafraid.

It matters not how straight the gate,
how charged with punishments the scroll;
I am the master of my fate;
I am the captain of my soul.'

'Invictus' by William Ernest Henley.

CHAPTER TWENTY-THREE

SELF HELP IS AN INSIDE JOB

IN 2018 GRAND VIEW RESEARCH ESTIMATED THAT THE VALUE OF US self-improvement industry exceeded 38-billion US dollars. This illustrates the insatiable demand for products that promise a cure to failure, reveal the secrets of success, and light the path to a happier, more prosperous life. Expert copywriters persuade us that it's easy: set goals, repeat affirmations, visualise the result you're seeking as accomplished, keep a journal, maintain a positive attitude, read Oprah's book of the week and most importantly 'learn' to meditate—oh, and there's a right way for that too; for a price! Like millions of others, I spent my hard-earned cash on a growing list of self-help gurus like Robbins, Mandino, Hill, Maltz, Vincent Peale, and Carnegie, but by the only standard that matters, mine, I was no closer to my goal of self-acceptance.

These gurus tell us that our life reflects our decisions and choices, and this doubles as a convenient out-clause. If their strategies don't work, it's because that's what we're choosing subconsciously—a belief that frees them from the responsibility of ensuring that individuals achieve results. This causes a destructive loop that reinforces the belief that there's something wrong with us, that we're an irredeemable victim of birth. What alternative conclusion is there? After all, we have the same access to information and opportunity as society's achievers. If only we were born with their genes or in their family, we could emulate their success and live a privileged life.

The media tease us with the nineteen-year-old who already owns three investment properties, and the twenty-five-year-old who runs a multi-million-dollar online corporation. Shooting stars? Who knows? We're unlikely to hear the 'where are they now' backstory. It's irrelevant to their aim of creating a subconscious picture of hope for the little guy, something that motivates us to stay the course, searching for the pot of gold at the rainbow's end. New Zealand's thirty-eighth prime minister (2008-2016), Sir John Key, like me, raised in state-owned rental housing, weaponised this shaming approach which marginalised those crying poverty. During his term he extinguished concerns cited by the media over rising levels of poverty among the disadvantaged by highlighting his extraordinary international success as an investment banker in the 1990s when he worked for Merrill Lynch Ltd. He returned to NZ as a self-made millionaire in 2001, and by 2008 he'd been elected prime minister, serving two terms before resigning late in his third at the peak of his popularity. There's no doubt about the story's underlying message: Key, from an underprivileged background, succeeded at the highest level. So what's your excuse for failing?

The neoliberal takeaway locked and loaded into this propaganda is that poverty is self-inflicted, caused by a lazy attitude, poor breeding or both—cause equals effect. They want us to believe that we are entirely responsible for our financial situation, and that extraordinary success always reflects hard work and superior performance, which warrants exceptional compensation. We make our own luck, no exceptions. This is survival of the fittest as an economic ideology in its purest form.

Promoting societal ideals, through carefully staged-managed, anecdotal stories, have the opposite effect on those experiencing repetitive failure. It encourages negative self-dialogue like, 'Given their age, how did they achieve that?' And, 'Why can't I do it? I'm so dumb!' Self-development, once inspiring the hope of achieving wealth and privilege by fixing us, becomes a cruel reminder of how hopeless our lives are. It reinforces our belief that we're a victim who chooses to focus on thoughts of suffering, and this raises our level of anxiety. Unfortunately, political ambitions control our interpretation of these stories, supported by a captive media with access to technological trickery. With a global population exceeding six-billion people, there's always going to be someone achieving the spectacular, making our life appear insignificant. It's the nature of the randomness of large populations.[25]

For those driven by an agenda and having access to globally interconnected social media like Twitter, it's easy to inflict extensive psychological manipulation on the global population. Deceptive alternative or independent media sources already influence opinion by repetition of a consistent narrative as a proxy for the truth, causing predictable herd-wide reactions. For example, daily news reports can be designed to give us the impression that the world as a whole is experiencing an increased incidence of disaster, increasing violence and unrest, record-breaking floods, fires and pestilence or some other crisis. Technology that enables simultaneous reporting from even remote corners of the world can easily be abused to facilitate a perpetual, exhausting illusion of a pending catastrophe. Already today, mainstream media outlets have been caught using scenes extracted from disaster movies and decades-old library footage in place of actual footage. Techniques like this may be used to prepare the way for our minds to accept seemingly appropriate expert solutions that promise to deliver us from the latest catastrophe threatening to destroy civilisation. Perhaps to keep us focused on a belief that we're victims in need of saving.

Recent research[26] concludes a sense of anxiety is clearly seen in millennials, who are experiencing unprecedented social change through accelerating advances in technology. With technologies like AI, robotics and voice recognition becoming widely adopted, careers are becoming obsolete overnight. Job insecurity makes them vulnerable to organised political groups and zealots, who promise solutions spread via persuasive viral memes promoted on social media platforms like Twitter. Protecting ourselves against manipulation requires an understanding

---

[25] Biondo, Alessio Emanuele & Rapisarda, Andrea. *Talent vs Luck: the role of randomness in success and failure*, World Scientific, Vol. 21, 2018 and Scott Barry Kaufman. *The Role of Luck in Life Success Is Far Greater Than We Realized—Are the most successful people in society just the luckiest people?* Scientific American, March 1, 2018.

[26] American Psychological Association *Stress by Generation*, Harris Interactive Survey, 2012 and Moody's Analytics for the BlueCross BlueShield, *The Economic Consequences of Millennial Health*, 2018.

of our duality and how we're captive to our ego illusion. Being captive to our ego illusion makes us vulnerable to deception by promises of a better future that victimise us and use us as a resource in political power games. Nothing new, but the tools being used today are more pervasive and sophisticated, which allows the covert persuasion of groups by promising solutions to their particular brand of suffering.

CHAPTER TWENTY-FOUR

PIGS DON'T KNOW PIGS STINK

THERE IS A SAYING THAT 'TRYING TO TEACH A PIG TO SING SIMPLY frustrates the teacher and annoys the pig'. Or, in the case of the self-help industry, enriches the teacher while leaving the student deeper in despair. The pig will never sing, and I will never change. It turns out I didn't need too, and nor do you! Clever techniques aren't the answer; a better understanding of model development and the self-construct is. I needed a new view of what I was. First, my core self-construct needed realigning and then the rest would follow. Once we know that our primary setting is to be creators, not reservoirs, we see through the manipulation of others. While simple to achieve, it seems impossible because pigs don't know pigs stink.

From the beginning we're immersed in a society that defines wealth in terms of money and emphasises the pursuit of money. As adults validation against this benchmark is unavoidable, reinforcing the idea that comparison to others is the measure of success. This path is tailor made for the ego—unsurprising when the financial system is also a synthetic construct, designed over many generations of sovereign rule. We're captured within non-essential jobs, striving for financial wealth to buy material goods and services that enrich a few. Even the goal of security for ourselves and our family reveals a lack of understanding of our relationship to our physical existence.

Pursuing material goals isn't bad; if you consciously decide to follow this rabbit hole with all your ability and power, then do it. However, unconscious pursuit of financial or material goals will imprison you in a world where happiness is measured by attainment. This focuses us on a non-existent there, leaving us powerless in the present. Chasing goals chosen for us through suggestion from another, or for fear of what others may think (peer pressure), is stealing our life from right under our nose. While we're focusing on fulfilling society's goals and dreams in some vague future, ten years pass in what seems like the blink of an eye. If we give it freely, others will gladly accept our unique, precious life force as their own. The need to judge our success by materially comparing ourselves to others vanishes when we're awake to our eternal 'self'. The goal isn't to consume our life by blindly following the crowd, mindlessly motivated by the suggestions others have planted in our mind, but to forge our own path intentionally.

The key to life is realising that happiness isn't conditional on achievement. At conception we're given everything we need to 'Be'. A plant doesn't need coaching from other plants for it to mature and bloom as intended by its seed; neither do we. Like the plant, we will grow to maturity following the plan, but better than that, we're given free will to do much more. This birth right gives us the creative power of the universe to create the life we choose. As Napoleon Hill said in *Think and Grow Rich*, 'Whatsoever the mind of man can conceive and believe he can achieve.' We are victims or victors of our own making. We have all the attributes needed to flourish without additional enhancement, but if we run with the dogs, we'll catch fleas. Where we were born, a function of luck and randomness, governs our ability to harness our free will to create our life. None of us has control over our childhood learning environment; these choices were made for us.

More economically developed countries (MEDC) have thrived for centuries by influencing children's core values and beliefs via the early education syllabus. From a young age, values taught cultivate the belief that success is correlated to scholastic ability, thus linking our happiness to comparative performance. Our self-worth depends on achieving approval and validation from others, making us unconsciously susceptible to the carrot and stick theory of motivation. Hoping for recognition while avoiding punishment we try harder, focusing our minds on regret for past failures and anxiety for future results. Failure to measure up leaves us feeling that we're somehow lacking or inferior.

Focusing expectations on lack in an abundant universe encourages greed, exploitation, jealousy and fear of loss. Because we learn that success in a financial world depends on others' failure, we become victimised, unable to see past our selfish desires.

Since the global recession of the early 1990s, the extreme, exploitative form of capitalism practiced in western economies has reinforced the belief that personal success is synonymous with financial success, and so we idolise consumption. Decisions made during the 2008 great recession leave no doubt that the wealthy control the narrative, manipulating conditions and protecting their financial position, whatever the cost—even if it means indebting us all, including the unborn. Framing ourselves as victims of this economic game and its arbitrary rules obscures the knowledge that, from the beginning, the oak tree is in the acorn, the key to the source of all magic. Faith that we're born with all we need to thrive and unfold without effort or embellishment gives us the confidence to live with an abundant mindset that knows we can access all we need, when it's needed. When we shift our focus from desiring to hoard power to confidently distributing it, our wellbeing is no longer threatened by the success of others. Love becomes our focus. We can work together symbiotically, developing our abilities to ease the suffering of others, providing for them from abundance. We are the objective conception of an expanding universe, gifted the opportunity to learn unconditional love. Our purpose is to awake to our singularity, extending this unconditional love to all and setting universal prosperity in motion.

CHAPTER TWENTY-FIVE

THE LOVE FORCE SINGULARITY

IMAGINE THE PALEOLITHIC PERIOD, POPULARLY REFERRED TO AS THE caveman era. Did Neanderthals see themselves as powerless victims, persecuted and mocked by unseen gods? If so, they could be forgiven, because everything before them existed despite them. The natural landscape was unmodified at the hand of man. The environment offered no hint of their creative power; like their surroundings, they just were. Having no concept of their origin, explaining their existence with belief in an unseen omniscient, all-powerful creator, makes perfect sense.

Their life seemed to be at the mercy of an unseeable, unknowable magic force. In the Book of Genesis (Genesis 1:1 KJV), magical thinking describes the creation of the universe: 'In the beginning God created the heaven and the earth...' The concept that there is a personified, greater power was a fortunate model. It lead to a system of cooperative progress, making development of an increasingly enlightened civilisation possible.

Today, unwavering faith that we're a vessel manifesting the creator's grand design through belief in infinite possibility is all but gone. Unfortunately, contemporary man through its reliance on science and religion to explain everything, has influenced an increasing denial of creation. Now the pendulum has swung back from an objective God view to its opposite, where ego man is the omniscient creator. By taking exclusive credit for our own objective, creative brilliance, we've lost sight of the forest for the trees; our spiritual cup is empty. Instead, mankind's enduring success is attributed to individual brilliance, refined by evolutionary selection.

Considering mankind's objective revelations since the first days walking on earth, dwindling faith in the existence of a singular omniscient power is, at most, arrogant and, at least, ignorant. Those subscribing to and actively propagating the idea that we are an isolated deterministic model, dependent on pedigree, perpetuate the idea that for life to develop and thrive there must be winners and, inevitably, losers. They argue that man's progression from the cave to circumnavigating the globe in hours was only possible because of the competitive process of natural selection. That supposes that mind and body are one, independent of all else. Yet evidence surrounding us suggests that our body resembles an intricate wheelchair giving form and movement to a subjective universe. Evolution of our objective form is the tip of the iceberg, the enabling preface to the never-ending story.

Conscious, iterative discovery across what appears to be a linear progression through time got us where we are today, not just unconscious natural selection. One discovery spawned another, then another, mostly by mistake of an enquiring mind. A recent streaming video advertisement for the software simulation game Civilisation depicts a sports car making an impressive 180-degree handbrake turn, stopping in front of a Neanderthals thatch hut. A couple sitting at a table outside the hut eating breakfast, naturally startled by this apparition, look up in shock and awe. Considering the era, perhaps they may not have been capable of comprehending the cars existence. Alternatively, they may have fallen to their knees, praying to the gods for their lives to be spared. The stark contrast illustrated by the advertisement between the two eras accidentally provides the perfect example of iterative possibility. Just as ENIAC—the first programmable, digital computer—eventually spawned the smartphone; not in one step, but in several smaller iterations, each requiring the input of many enquiring minds.

All that is revealed to us now was possible in the beginning. However, ancient civilisation lacked the thought, not understanding themselves as creators. All objects they sensed were created before the evolution of their consciousness. It's easy to understand how they perceived that all suffering originated from some powerful, external force punishing them personally for their indiscretions. Identifying as victims of their environment, they submitted to many gods, worshipped the sun and any number of deities. They had no small steps of progress, or history of their own thought-creations to project from, which made it unlikely that they would make the leap of faith to realising that 'I'm a creator in his likeness'. Probably, origin man's mind was consumed by surviving for just one more day rather than contemplating his ability as a creator. Now, though, there are no excuses!

Modern man doesn't have nearly the same pressure to survive from moment to moment. Today there is an extensive documented and visual history of man's progressive discovery. Widespread urban migration during the 20th century means today most of us have been raised in heavily modified landscapes dominated by manmade objects, overshadowing the natural environment. Everywhere we go we are surrounded by extensive, intensive environmental modifications illustrating our capacity to create from nothing to dynamic urbanisation. This is proof of the love force singularity or God and that we are his reflection. Yet, because of past influences, mentioning these three letters challenges our contemporary beliefs in objective science or other popular explanations of our accidental existence, putting us on the defensive, closing our mind to what's in plain sight.

The creative process from thought, through concept and objective creation is undeniable. Throughout time, each advance has happened progressively, step by iterative step, as the mind of man searched deeper down the rabbit hole, captive to the thought. In fact, becoming the thought, quickly associating new ideas, each refining the initial objective creation, like dominoes falling forward at an ever-accelerating pace. Consider creation as being represented by a mind map--branches are creatively added here, another there, bearing fruit from ideas offered up in cooperation with like-minded colleagues. For example, the discovery of the radio tube led to the transistor, IC, and the 3D IC. Now the race is on to develop the first viable quantum computer.

Even in the face of this wealth of creative discovery, not even contemporary man could seriously consider the idea that we have the capacity to create the earth and all its resources. Yet his arrogance is revealed by a willingness to believe that he alone possesses the ability to create an objective reality from a subjective thought. This is reflected in the increasingly accepted belief that the natural world, not formed by his hand, magically evolved in a random process, culminating with a human being, who routinely creates.

We see evidence of a singular power every day through past, collective creative endeavours. Still, dominant opinions abound, denying such an indisputable presence that is so apparent in this century, that we're left with one conclusion: that contemporary man is more ignorant than our ancient ancestors, who accepted an organised creative source. Proof exists everywhere in everyday objects. Look out your window. Actually, just look 'at' the window! First, it was a thought within man's mind, maybe not acted on initially. Like all thoughts, it floated around in the ether, the subjective environment, until someone fell in love with that particular thought. Perhaps they saw a need and decided it would offer mankind a real survival benefit if they manifested it into the objective world. However, notwithstanding that one man may have taken credit for the invention of the glass window, it was always a subjective possibility, waiting to be objectified.

The clues that we're all physical creations from the predetermined intention of the source of all are as abundant as the air we breathe. So why is it difficult to accept that we are part of a universal, unlimited power congealed from the light of our sun? Are we afraid that believing would take away our freedom, holding us accountable for our sinful thoughts, condemning us to a pure, bland, oh-so-boring life, or is it fear of ridicule by those we hold near and dear? Perhaps the idea or meme that it's uncool to believe we're the fruit of a single creative power, reflects our overwhelming need to conform to our tribe's beliefs. Would we rather deny the obvious than risking criticism and being excluded?

Throughout life fear of abandonment is a powerful emotion. It's derived from a child's dependence on their adult minders, which we accept as evidence that we're incapable of surviving by our own wits. A childhood thought error, it reinforces the illusion of our own fragility. Because our experience relies entirely on our interpretation of events, this emphasises thoughts of scarcity and confirms that life is what our chosen beliefs make it.

Undisciplined memory recall of the thought that we're 'not enough' forms a belief that's perpetuated, allowing it to unconsciously influence our present. Fearing abandonment leaves us vulnerable to persuasion. In the light of such fear, we're prepared to compromise our values and boundaries in return for the security of being part of something and its implied illusion of certainty. Choosing this path of least resistance leads to inevitable lifelong suffering, just as cigarette smokers surrendering to peer pressure develop a habit which leads to the cancer stick owning them. Addicted to nicotine, they keep lighting up, denying the obvious truth that every breath is killing them and those breathing their exhaust.

We become susceptible to emotional manipulation by the loudest, coolest group on a roller-coaster ride, and we remain this way, unable to find true peace, until we discover that we have ready access to the solution for every challenge confronting us—and we have done from the start. Ultimately, we all seek a spiritual path in a search for meaning. When that moment arrives, we need an open mind so we can draw our own conclusion, free of third-party bias. We need to be awake to the malignant, ideological chants and incantations seeded in our suggestible mind via popular cultural memes and propaganda. Memes intent on leading us further into darkness and confusion, further away from the love that lifts us from emptiness into light.

Only by taking back control of our thoughts can we reveal our innate, timeless belonging flowing up from within—a centring faith grounded in knowing that we're already everything, before, now and always. By replacing God with less loaded words like love, source or singularity, we can disrupt the ego's past God associations which blind us to the obvious. Framing God this way may help overcome our craving for external validation that leaves us in the grip of group think.

The systematic process used by man to achieve physical creation is clear evidence of a singular creator. If every man-made object we see was first a thought, what is the origin of all that's natural (mostly everything)? Where did the animals, trees, even Earth come from? Our creator, the singular intelligence. This is an irrefutable conclusion; thinking otherwise is the ultimate ego-trip. Unfortunately, this ego attitude of denial is common. It's the source of continued poverty and war afflicting mankind as power brokers seek to maintain the illusion that some are more worthy, because of their superior heritage and breeding. Truth is, by this proof, we cannot deny our inherent personal power. It is law that everything without starts from within.

The belief that we need to add to what we are is a disempowering thought error. It may have originated from a seed planted in our suggestible mind by another, or it may have arisen from our own childish interpretation of a traumatic event. Whatever its origin, though, once we're aware of this, we cease being a victim, finally awake to our birth right as co-creators. We're free to create whatever we choose, whether choosing to experience poverty, isolation or chasing fame and wealth. At least now we're deciding consciously, rather than unconsciously as a bitter, vengeful victim.

We're created from the thought of the Almighty, of the same elements as the Earth, the planets and all that exists in the universe. Conceived by the seed of the most powerful, our birth right is to create. Denying this as our true destiny is caused by faulty interpretation of our early environment. It's likely this happened with little or no input from your adult mind and now needs revaluating. A children we absorb unchecked lessons from adults who once endured the same process of education by association and who now accidentally project their own ego belief in lack onto us. This leads us to the conclusion that we're born inferior to others, the fall guy or girl, a perpetual victim. In reality, it's just another lame excuse explaining our failure, allowing us to relinquish responsibility for our situation while blaming people and circumstances for our seemingly disadvantaged existence. If we're living a life in despair, it's because we've decided to, believing we're unworthy of anything good. We perpetuate the lie that we're born broken, lacking what we need to thrive, unable to experience joy as a normal emotion in our life until the chain of belief across generations is broken.

Perpetuating the illusion of lack benefits other key influencers. Both the state and activist groups, whether motivated by religion or politics, know that belief in scarcity and negative emotions generally are useful mechanisms of behavioural control. Financial systems designed around perpetual productivity growth depend on broad acceptance of this belief to succeed. This is no accident; they have refined the indoctrination methods over millennia. When modern media sophistication is stripped away, revealing the subliminal intent, it turns out to be just another variation of carrot and the stick motivation, coercing compliance.

Ten years on from the global financial crisis, during a 60 Minutes interview in 2019, the US Federal Bank Chair, Jerome Powell stated that the United States has a lower labour force participation rate than almost every other advanced country. Asked why, he listed a range of causes including evolving technology, poor comparative educational attainment, globalisation and the opioid crisis.[27] Surprisingly, he failed to mention the overwhelming reason for the high 'nonparticipation' rates--the GFC, caused by the reckless actions of the 'too big to fail investment banks' fuelled by prolonged dovish Federal Bank monetary policy. Powell implies (I'm paraphrasing) *they're unemployed because they choose opioids (derelict) over working, they didn't educate themselves (lazy) and expect high wages (offshoring/globalisation).* The plutocratic line that by design everyone gets a fair go because they base the economy on open-market principles, so workers are entirely to blame for their failure.

Meanwhile, the federal bank still creates currency at an unprecedented rate, distributing it to the same too big to fail investment banks who retain the right and privilege to participate in the federal reserve's open-market operations. Although These currency transactions are supposedly backed by equivalent security swaps, the negative stock market reaction to the banks attempt to tighten the money supply in late 2018, showed the likelihood of the Fed ever recovering the debt is slim to zero.

In the same interview Mr Powell remarked: 'Well, the financial crisis did a great deal of damage to many people's lives. And, of course, not all of them will be made whole. People lost their houses. They lost their livelihoods, lost their jobs, and there's no way that they're all going to be made whole. So, I think what we can do is learn our lessons from that crisis. That was the worst financial crisis in 75 years. We tried very hard to learn the lessons of what went wrong and to build a much stronger, more resilient, better capitalized financial system so that it will be more resilient to the kinds of shocks that happen in the economy.'

---

[27] Scott Pelley, *What is the Federal Reserve Chairman's view on the health of the U.S. economy?*, on "60 Minutes", CBS News, June 2019.

The stubbornly high long-term unemployment rate is an effect of pre 2009 neo-liberal economic policy. The 60 minutes interview purposely subverts the historic facts causing the GFC, blaming its victims as if their bad outcomes resulted from their personal shortcomings, while reinforcing the subliminal carrot-and-stick message that success is exclusive of luck or insider information. In a world designed on the premise that 'he who has much survives best', or survival of the fittest, this is a bald-faced lie, perpetuating injustice. Bad economic outcomes happen to good people simply because the economy is not a natural system; it's synthetic, based on man-made theory. The concept of personal accountability is only valid in a congruent world, where we are awake to an ego construct significantly influenced by third party interests and where we recognise that we simultaneously exist as essential and existential beings, the animal and the spiritual. Through conscious choice, our reaction to adversity is always under our control. The choice to grovel or thrive then becomes ours, because we're born of the universe as the universe.

CHAPTER TWENTY-SIX

OUR EGO HAS US IN A HEADLOCK

THE CONCEPT THAT LIFE IS A CONTINUOUS, LINEAR OR DIMENSIONLESS timeline moving from the past into the future is an enduring cultural model that forms the illusion of an i-AM ego known as 'I'. It's a convincing model, seamlessly blending yesterday's 'I' with today's via a natural process of continuous, time-stamped memory association. This leaves an impression that our future depends on past performance, as if we possess energy able to reach through time and influence future moments, limiting their potency to our ego's understanding of our potential—as set in childhood. If we have low self-esteem, we project low expectations onto the screen of our future possibility, making us a victim of our past.

In the same way that the illusion of passing time leaves us believing the past affects the potency of today, time-decay memes promote an irrational fear of ageing that reinforce the idea that our power diminishes with each day. Experiences accumulating in our memory represent our past, creating a timeline that leaves us feeling like life is being depleted, as if it's a scarce resource. A timer relentlessly ticks down toward our last moment, creating time pressure, which contributes to mounting anxiety and/or regret, while we rush to accomplish what we think we should. This view of time limits future experience to past results, when in fact each moment is an opportunity to create from a blank page, unburdened by our perceived potential, physical deficiencies or past results. Our unique 'free-will' ego miracle was never intended to cause us to see ourselves as time limited, as if our opportunities are dissolving like sands through the hourglass. It's a lie sustained by the science of genetics and evolution, which, while applying to our body or essential self, doesn't limit the creative potential of the human mind. It's like saying that a wave and a particle are equivalent, when in fact a wave is unlimited in its potential outcomes, while a particle is somewhat determined in its role by thought—a particle is formed from a wave, which comes from the intention of the thinker's creative thought. The mind is a continuous wave-to-particle generator, limited only by the thinkers' consciousness.

The ego is an organic servomechanism that enables us, through trial and error, to attain proficiency over the physical world in the only moment that can cause any change in matter—that is, right now—by giving repeated attention to an intention. Ego obediently strives to manifest what it thinks we want, and each new attempt takes us closer to our desired outcome. Taking conscious control of our ego-development process restores the ego to its rightful place as our personal assistant, where it automates the skills we decide to master, bringing them to the front of our experience. The ego tamed, now riding shotgun as the ultimate 'continuous-improvement' mechanism, ensures we become progressively more competent and effective at achieving what's important to us. No longer are we a victim to our past.

Shaun White, US snowboarder, businessman and gold medallist in the halfpipe at the 2018 PyeongChang Winter Olympic Games, demonstrates this process of attaining enduring excellence through trial and error. Several months prior to the games, a horrific, normally career-ending accident in Queenstown NZ hospitalised him. He refused to let this rob him of his chance to compete in Korea and miraculously recovered. He overcame adversity by not only realising but also harnessing his power of habit force—by having complete faith in his ego's ability to accurately duplicate learned patterns of excellence. Alex Honnold, rock climber extraordinaire, is another example of this attitude to life in action. His free climb of El Capitan in Yosemite National Park is a remarkable expression of the oneness of a trained body and mind (*Free Solo*, 2018). This is life in its purest form, as God intended. Have fun, explore your limits, push the envelope and reveal, through right thought, what you're gifted at conception. After all, what are the consequences? Death of the body and the ego; yet both are simply momentary expressions of the one-mind, eternal spirit.

In contrast, wrong thought perpetuates suffering. Willingly regurgitating painful memories is like rerunning a horror movie that leaves you feeling emotionally disturbed every time you watch it. To illustrate; hate and revenge are two destructive, ego-centred emotions guaranteed to bring suffering. They consume our outraged, offended ego mind in an attempt to justify why someone must pay for leaving us in this unbalanced state. While we're fantasising, lost in destructive thought, we're emotionally absent from physical reality, unconscious to its gift of unlimited possibility. Revisited emotions, masquerading as reality, run rampant, dragging us down a rabbit hole of suffering with our permission. We become captive to our ego for hours, days, perhaps lifetimes, trapped in this unreal moment which holds no power to expand our reality. Out of habit, we're repeatedly tricked into playing along, captured by the promise that our 'will' can change what's already done. We think that if we change it to fit how things need to be, then we can be happy with the world.

Painful experiences of the past are harmless, but the memories associated with them empower their influence over us. Habitually recalling the experience and our interpretation of it, reignites painful emotions, sabotaging hope in this moment. We attribute our persistent suffering to the original event, yet we're to blame for repeatedly recalling them into the present. Our ego preserves our suffering by giving repeated attention to limiting memories, reinforcing the view that we're a powerless victim held back by a past that prevents us from achieving expectations. Through ignorance, mismanagement of our thought habits accidentally turns our ego against us. It takes on the life of an abuser, more damaging than any real offender. Our unbridled wrong thoughts are the cause, sometimes even acting out to destroy us.

CHAPTER TWENTY-SEVEN

EXCUSES - VICTIM BY ANY OTHER NAME

EXCUSITIS IS THE DOMINANT SYMPTOM OF WRONG THOUGHT. WE ALL have logical excuses that justify our comparative failures and rationalise our particular situation. Apportioning blame to everything but ourselves absolves us of responsibility for making bad choices, but it's the path to a habit of quitting. The habit of calming our mind with excuses reflects an ego construct with the dominant belief that our past failures are due to congenital deficiencies; that is, our potential is determined by hereditary, the biggest delusion of all. Truth is, in predicting future success, genetics is near the bottom of the list, while thought habits learned in childhood sit at the top. It's a law of the universe that we're never faced with an insurmountable problem; we just interpret or frame them that way. Meeting a problem with a belief that we inherently lack the ability to solve it makes it so. But if we accept that we're seamlessly connected to the source of all creative energy, then at some level of consciousness, we already possess the solution. Hence the Persian adage, 'this too shall pass'. Problems, like solutions, are all just a part of the totality; therein lies the solution. The yin and the yang.

Dredging up painful memories, recreating unpleasant experiences and their related emotional suffering is a self-destructive habit, ingraining our neurosis. In reality, memory is an unreliable, subjective interpretation of past events. Our judicial system is expert at revealing how relativity and personal focus change interpretation—what seemed undeniably true from our point of view is suspect under critical examination. Nothing we do now will transform any part of the previous moment, but dwelling on its memory steals the potential within this new moment from our awareness, disconnecting us from the source of creative power that only exists in now. Repetitive recall of past suffering eventually traps us down a rabbit hole. Confined within its familiar passages, we're captured as expressed in the words of the 70s classic Eagles album, *Hotel California*, 'You can check out any time you like. But you can never leave!' Dwelling on a recalled past, filled with implied suffering and regret, eventually imprisons us in a hell of our own creation, blind to the infinite beauty in which we are, and have always been, immersed.

Such a state arises from poor knowledge and application of man's creative capacity. We're captured in a story, created by our constructed personality or ego, identified to the outside world as our Christian name—an avatar for our stale, unquestioned, maladaptive core beliefs formed in the distant past, packaged up and running around ready to be released to run amuck when our name is called! While we unconsciously embrace this state as the 'real I', we remain victims committed to it, just as we're committed to our skin, our hands or our heart.

That's why it's so hard to change. How do we change what we are? While we're committed, others see our subconscious decisions from an impartial point of view. Frustratingly, not bound by our model, they plainly see the maladaptive choices keeping us stuck and ever the victim. From their perspective, outside looking in, our mistakes are obvious and easily overcome. However, all their lecturing and solutions are doomed, because how do we get over ourselves, over the model with which we seamlessly identify, other than by self-destruction? Which unfortunately, is often the chosen route to relief, because pigs don't know pigs stink!

Until we separate the ego label from the abstract, flowing self, nothing can, or will change. Change requires us to metaphorically turn ourselves inside out in order to gain a new perspective, one that lets us see the unconscious ego for what it is, a self-constructed, limited model we unwittingly designed. The moment we recognise this, we instantaneously become master of our fate in an effortless rebirth, more significant than the original. We finally stop playing the victim, awake to the truth that we're the conscious author of our own life, even in situations where the persecution we feel is real. Thinking that we're a victim denies our innate power and connection to the infinite universe, guaranteeing a life of self-imposed discontent.

In an awakened state, we may decide to change our life status from victim to martyr, so we can continue to accuse and blame others for our current situation, but at least now this is a conscious decision. The difference is that a neurotic victim is an innocent bystander, oblivious that they are perpetuating their own suffering via their maladaptive life choices. In contrast, a martyr chooses to accept their persecution in the name of some passionate cause, neither expecting, nor deserving sympathy, because by definition, they choose the role of victim.

Full consciousness is accompanied by the realisation that all actions have consequences, but those consequences have no meaning, other than they may set us along an alternative path of discovery, offering new challenges to overcome with new and enlightened responses. Everything we do is a lesson, expanding understanding of our relationship with our surroundings, evolving as it is intended to be in this moment. How can it be anything else?

After all: 'The Moving Finger writes, and, having writ, Moves on: nor all thy Piety nor Wit Shall lure it back to cancel half a Line, Nor all thy Tears wash out a Word of it.' Omar Khayyám

Thinking otherwise is delusional, illustrated by the mass hysteria exposed after Donald Trump's election as President in 2016. Even now, deep into his first term, many still cannot accept the way things are. This leaves them vulnerable to victimisation by the unscrupulous, who pursue their own selfish agenda, looking to profit from the distracted mind of the masses. If this is you, watch Byron Katie unpack, 'I'm Afraid of Trump' on her YouTube channel and consider completing her programme—The Work by Byron Katie®.

Many live with the belief that our view of the situation is absolute and this must be reflected in the present reality before we can be happy, rather than lovingly embracing the reality facing us, warts and all. This arrogant, narcissistic view of life is a sure indicator that we're the unwitting victim of an unmonitored, controlling ego. Fortunately, these moments present a golden opportunity to capture and conquer the slippery ego once and for all. Suffering is a construct of comparison, of a feeling of injustice, of loss, of things being different to how we imagine they must be for us to be happy. Paradoxically, this keeps us in a perpetually unhappy state, controlled by the opinion of others seeking control of our energy.

The view of 'I' as the centre of our world needs to be replaced with a better one. Others have grasped this and taken their opportunity to awake, realising that the world doesn't care for our personal outrage at the injustices we perceive life is delivering us. It moves on at its own pace, regardless of our interpretation of events we've cast in stone and on which we continuously bang our heads, proving our martyrdom. They accept everything is perfect just the way it is now, embracing their gift to choose happiness despite circumstance. They move forward, knowing that they are conceived with the power in every cell of their body to overcome and conquer all obstacles, no matter how impossible that may seem right now.

CHAPTER TWENTY-EIGHT

ACCEPTING WHAT IS

IS ANY EVENT GOOD OR BAD, WHO KNOWS? (TAOIST PARABLE). ANNI-Frid Lyngstad of ABBA is an example of good, out of the seemingly bad. During WW2, Anni-Frid's mother Synni hooked up with her father, Alfred Haase, a young sergeant in the German Army. Their brief liaison led to Synni being branded a traitor, being ostracised and forced to immigrate to Sweden. No one could have predicted the joy their illegitimate child would bring to so many. ABBA became one of the most successful music groups in history, a band made possible by Hitler, one of history's most evil leaders! So how can we be certain what will turn out well and what will turn out bad? The right philosophy is to accept that 'it's an ill wind that blows nobody any good' and let life unfold as it will, without resisting.

Napoleon Hill said it this way, 'Every adversity, every failure, every heartache carries with it the seed of an equal or greater benefit.' Even death, the pinnacle of 'bad', is an illusion of interpretation—after all, the cells with which we're born are soon shed, replaced by new ones in an automatic, programmed cycle, until one day the collective group of cells known as 'I' die together for the final time. For all life to exist and be sustained, constant death and renewal is necessary. It enables a churn of life that continuously expands from one moment to the next, revealing new possibilities, because everything is happening right now and all that is possible is already here, but no one has yet conceived it into our objective world.

How do we accept what is without resisting when it's not what we ordered? Easy! By 'knowing' that we can come to no harm, there is no beginning or end, just eternal meaningless expanding space. We're nothing; we control nothing except the choice of colours with which we choose to paint the moment, dark or light based on our personal interpretation. It's this that creates our unique experience. However, regardless of our choice, reality is always beautiful. Those moments when we feel awe and grace (when a child is born, or the sun sets over a mountain top), we're one with reality, seeing it for what it is, not distorted by our arbitrary filter. We see that life unfolds as it should, in its own time. We're in control of one thing only: our reaction to stimulus. Realising life isn't personal turns it into a game we can't lose. We're creators, just like a child in a sandpit. Think it, make it, refine it, break it at will and repeat.

What is the worst that could happen right now, our death? Resisting or fear of death misrepresents reality. What we fear is the loss of the timeline associated with the memories of our relationships. We stitch this timeline together sequentially to form the seamless continuity that defines our objective life. A construct of imagination, it imitates an institutionalised model developed by the society into which we're born. Dementia illustrates this 'stitched' timeline well. A sufferer's ego, along with its memories, are progressively lost, changing their sense of self. Their behaviour mirrors sometime in the past where a portion of their timeline remains intact. In this state, they have no fear of death, because their constructed self-identity, built from memories flowing through time, is gone, the objective perspective lost. Death is the ultimate renewal of the old, frail matter, a shell of the original given us by the ultimate creator to master during our lifetime. Comprehend this and there's no turning back. You will have a renewed sense of consciousness, sensing the awe in every moment, viewing the world as an innocent child. Knowing this, we transform our purpose from attainment to a journey of discovery. We become a seeker, searching for others who are awakening to the infinite abundance gifted us all at conception, so we can learn together about this new, expanding state. When awakened, even the seemingly derelict and broken among us can return from the living dead, instantly transformed to powerful creators, serving for the good of all.

What is awakening to ourselves or realising that we stink? The clue is every interaction with others is possible because of long-established, evolving language conventions developed by communicating and comparing sensory stimuli that form a consensus understanding of the experience. For example, people would question our sanity if we called the sky green, when it's undoubtedly blue. While we could steadfastly stick to the belief that it's green, *verte* or *kārerarera*, language conventions are necessary for effective communication, and that enhances our tribe's survival. The label blue is the accepted name based on the global convention that there are three primary colours, correlating to the presence of three types of photoreceptor cells in the human retina. Through repetition of our native language, eye light or rod cells connected a pathway in our brain, translating the colour it saw, based on the simultaneous verbal feedback of carers. The colours accepted name was initially arbitrarily assigned as illustrated in this puzzle:

Q: If air is called green, green is called blue, blue is called sky, sky is called yellow, yellow is called water and water is called pink, then what is the colour of clear sky?

A) Blue   *B) Sky*

C) Yellow   *D) Water*

Answer: B) Sky

If, as a tribe, we teach our children that the colour of sky is 'sky' then to them all blue will be forever sky. The more sophisticated the language (feedback), the more accurate the translation of what we see, feel, taste, smell or hear will be. From this we're able to construct and progressively refine an inter-dependent, relatively accurate, three-dimensional, semantic model of our physical environment. All this happens from electrical feedback via our sensory nervous system becoming subconsciously accepted as visible particles with form and mass.

From our earliest memories, we remember things from the model as our reality. When I was three, I remember playing with a skink lizard in the garden of our home in Northcote, Auckland, NZ. By translating electrical feedback from my senses, I approximated what this thing called a skink looked like. It's likely the nature of a skink appears different through the eyes of an eagle. Neither is right nor wrong, just different. Our senses have allowed us to thrive through at least two millennia by giving us an acceptable representation of the world.

To illustrate, close your eyes and remember the second-last home in which you lived, then recall walking through each room. Open the door to your bedroom, turn on the lights, feel the flooring beneath your feet, hear the sounds that you typically heard. The feelings from this imaginary walkthrough are as strong as if we're actually there. Our senses create efficient memories, which give us the ability to accurately, subconsciously predict in advance our explicit reaction time (like reaching for the light switch in a familiar, darkened room). We can create imaginary scenes as if they are real, allowing us to be anywhere we want right now, even bouncing around in the fine dust of the moon's surface. Again, recalling that familiar room, change a few things around, reimagine it, mentally remodel it without lifting a finger, or raising a sweat.

Have you noticed that reading books is so much more rewarding than watching movies? A book allows us to create personalised worlds from the author's word descriptions. This illustrates the difference between living in an ego-generated world and an infinite world. We're often disappointed by movies depicting our favourite books because the movie script and scenery limits our own imaginary interpretation to the director's portrayal. With ego, as in a movie, our view of life is chosen for us; we get to watch what's practically complete. In the infinite, like in a novel, we get to be the co-creator, choosing colour, depth and meaning from the words. Any piece of art has as many interpretations as there are people. A book is a more intimate, personal adventure. Our interpretations bring the author's words to life, resonating with our unique world model. From here, it's not a huge leap of faith to realise that what we first imagine, with focus, can be manifested into physical reality. All things start within, before they can become, and I mean ALL THINGS physical!

We could develop a uniquely personal language to describe both the subjective and objective things encountered and experienced, but it would be a relatively limited perspective and definitely not as rich. Having shared communication techniques enables us to consider and reflect on our personal experience with others. Our agreed semantic tokens enrich and broaden our understanding of what we encounter. This accelerates our model formation, model accuracy, social growth, survival and development as civilisations, giving us an altogether, more rewarding and rich experience.

Unfortunately, we take our native language for granted, because like everything else, it's been spoon fed to us in our childhood as a fully formed structure. In those early years, we're installing a foundational communication system. We learn it by rote as if our lives depended on it; there's no time to discuss its purpose or formulation from first principles. However, after enduring several years of this learning style, education becomes a tedious and repetitive task of memorising facts. The focus remains on the accumulation of knowledge, rather than on the creative thinking process endowed to us by the human brain. It reduces language usage to identifying objective contrasts in our physical world. For example; there's a tree, this is a forest, I'm kind, they're not. We're taught just enough to allow us to understand instructions and take direction, with the purpose that we'll eventually play a useful part in a society where collective economic growth is valued above all else. Learning language this way emphasises the physical plane, that part being sensed outside of us, so naturally when we use language, we focus habitually on what already exists, rather than on what we can create. In other words, if we can't label it, it doesn't exist. This is undoubtedly a desirable use of public time and effort but leaves us with a language programme that is more useful to economic expansion than personal growth and achieving our latent potential.

Depending less on our minders as we develop competence, we could expect that the education system would adapt, expanding with our thinking capacity, but it doesn't. Using language to identify and label for one purpose limits interpersonal communication. Language skills determine the richness of our creative human experience, the magic that takes imagination and turns it into physical matter for the enjoyment of all. Fundamental to achieving our potential, words are a shared code or interface. They are tokens of our collective sensory experience, turned into a vast tapestry of understanding and continually expanding with our awareness. First our imagination brings awareness, then language brings it into reality, through active intention.

CHAPTER TWENTY-NINE

CREATING THE 'i AM'

ORGANISED EDUCATION SYSTEMS HAVE ALWAYS EMPHASISED THAT existence is an entirely objective experience. Our rank within the system depends on our ability to learn and regurgitate specific and important facts. We're rewarded for being right but feel humiliated when we're wrong. There's little time for individual attention; we either sink or swim, left in no doubt that our performance is being constantly compared to our peer group. The way this pragmatic, economy centred, education system works means we lose many capable people along the way. It's not designed to build and nurture children with strong self-images. It disadvantages those born into suboptimal conditions or with some form of disability, and they are unlikely to close the gap between them and their peers, leaving them feeling like victims of an intolerant system, a feeling that manifests in a range of social disorders.

An education system entirely designed around standardised testing robs the world of creative genius. The judgmental, competitive process leaves many feeling like worthless failures, when the truth is, we're all born with infinite potential! Low self-esteem is a by-product of this system and a life sentence to suffering. Some cultures still exist, where the pressure to not only meet, but exceed competitive standards leads to extreme levels of anxiety, fearing failure will bring shame to their family. The pressure so great, that some see suicide as their only way of escape. These people are victims of a lie, robbing them of ever discovering their true creative identity; that they are the Universe embodied.

Throughout life, language programmes us to take instructions, effectively inoculating us all with a user interface (UI) that's marginally more advanced than the passive, prescriptive, AI operating system in contemporary robots. Robots use a limited, iterative intelligence, bounded by existing objective knowledge extremes. Our education leaves us operating in much the same way. Preferred systems of education are focused on developing our outer objective or essential nature, while ignoring our more powerful subjective, creative inner or existential nature. This explains why researchers suggest we only use 10-20% of our brain's full potential. Existing systems fail to reveal the next level; that we're always actively creating our own experience. This is the path to achieving our full creative potential; it's a process of realisation, not searching and forcing. It's trusting that we'll discover the tools we need to take us where we choose to go when they're needed, trusting we're already complete.

Only when we comprehend our role as creators, creating the 'i AM' we desire using semantics, will we escape exploitation. Language used as a simple identifier, labelling the physical world objectively, is uncreative. It's a useful communication tool in a 'particle' based existence, but our paradigm of life changes when we realise that language used subjectively, frees our mind to create consciously. Language is a living thing, continually being reinvented and adapted as thoughts (the subjective), become things (the objective). This is the only acceptable order, or flow of creation, determining the richness of our life. Understanding this causes a seismic shift in our concept of what it is to be alive. This puts us in the driver's seat, free to make conscious choices and willing to accept the consequences. We become aware that the thoughts previously accepted as fact are simply spoon-fed stories, guiding us down a specific thought path of the form A + B = C. This new understanding instantly reveals alternative explanations and paths. Awakening powers of critical evaluation allows us to not only see but also escape a dull life of dogma and compliance.

Emphasising the flow of creation, *subjective thought always precedes objective language*. Therefore, it follows that everything we sense and comprehend outside of ourselves first began as a thought. The more extensive our vocabulary and its comprehension, the more specific and richer will be our objective creation. Association of thought reveals new objective possibilities.

CHAPTER THIRTY

THE EGO ILLUSION

'I' IS NOT A PREDETERMINED, OBJECTIVE PERSONALITY, BOUND BY genetics and ancestry, but an ephemeral ego, a self-constructed illusion masquerading as objective personality. After discovering the ego illusion, I realised that without an understanding of ego formation, self-development is pointless. Because the 'Oak Tree is in the Acorn', all the ingredients for us to bloom fully are within us at conception, part of the flow that happens regardless of how we 'Will' life to fit our agenda through forced action. How much, or how little, effort we put into improving ourselves has no effect on the eventual outcome. Paradoxically, believing that we've been sold short, reveals a lack of faith in our maker, the cause of all our suffering.

Ego development practices devised throughout history, by design or ignorance, conceal our original splendour. Our full potential remains untapped. Development of the ego illusion begins the moment we're given our specific identity, or Christian name. After this, our experiences are interpreted, personalised and unconsciously fused with our name. Because children lack the maturity required to evaluate critically and manage this merging, our name becomes a limiting pronoun, affecting potential. Eventually, through repetition of suggestion (self or external and often negative), stimulus response is automatic (cf autosuggestion), outside conscious control. Now, these unconscious reactions are identified with the objective ego, synonymous with us and our Christian name. An incredibly powerful ally if constructed habits support our progress. While we're born free to choose our destiny, survival requires that this choice is appropriated by our guardians. We follow in their footsteps, cast in the same mould, restricted by their level of consciousness, perpetuating their strengths and weaknesses, while they're blissfully unaware that they're creating the child's potential adult outcomes.

Striving to attain society's dubious ideal, hoping we'll finally feel worthy, is the cause of all anxiety and self-loathing. When we undoubtedly know that we all possess the same potential at conception, confident with who we are and where we are, self-development becomes optional rather than essential. We stop letting others ration our happiness with their self-serving, manipulative suggestions that reinforcing a belief that we're victims of inferior genetics and environment.

The ego illusion results from a mistake in emphasis. It fails to recognise the existence of our duality. The ability to perceive other possibilities is educated out of us as children. Through years of suggestion and questionable feedback, our personal perception becomes habitual, our future a self-fulfilling prophecy, cast in the stone of rigid belief. Upon waking, while staring into the mirror every morning, we appear to be a congruent, objective self. Hypnotised by our own deceptive, unquestioned and apparent solid form, we reinforce our self-construct, confirming that we are indeed separate from our surroundings. This is our core schema or the pattern that repeats until we die, unless through some accidental event we awake to the illusion.

Religion promotes a personified God, having the almighty power to raise us into Heaven or dispatch us to an eternity in Hell. Historically, this objective, supreme embodiment was employed with intent, wielding the ungodly power of fear to control the resource that we are. Personifying God conceals the reality that we are one in God, the universe, source or love—all terms describing life-enabling energy. The self-development/improvement industry perpetuates the illusion that the physical plane is where success is achieved and that we can only reach inner peace after mastering the outer world. This industry is a significant influence within this culture of action where doing is elevated above being, and it has exploded in tandem with the expansion of neoliberalism—considered a natural extension of Darwinism or 'survival of the fittest' (Herbert Spencer)—into the field of economic theory. Unfortunately, this capitalist ethos and the level playing field promised by open market theory failed. In practice, those already enjoying most of the world's wealth, influence and power aren't about to relinquish control without a fight to the death. History shows this is the inevitable result of any man-made (synthetic) economic system, be it socialist or capitalist (Rockefeller 1930s).

The existing system ideologically promises performance-based results but cannot provide the spiritual, foundational education needed as a prerequisite to taking part and benefiting from unconstrained wealth generation, beyond simply being inputs of production. The powerful are aware their elite status is gained by controlling the hearts and minds of the flock, using the same proven methods of suggestion and dogma used by ancient religion. However, now the measure of worth is not religious devotion, but the attainment of extreme material wealth, fame or notoriety—just another form of the same ancient but effective heaven-versus-hell argument, repurposed as the carrot and the stick to herd the masses in the desired direction. Now heaven is not some nirvana aspired to after death, but some advantage vested on us by rising above the minions, securing a merited position, finally free of life's drudgery.

Without accompanying redistribution of wealth in the beginning, a system favouring meritocracy is doomed. Neoliberal dogma causes detachment and division between individuals. Influenced by our cultural training, we struggle and fight against one another, mistakenly believing life is a race for survival, where success depends on surpassing others, being first to the prize. This dysfunctional life approach leaves us suffering in silence, while we push on, striving toward the next essential shiny object, caught on a perpetual treadmill to nowhere while hoping our grasping existence will finally deliver us a sense of worthiness. This is like trying to quench our hunger with refined, complex carbohydrates; we never feel satisfied. It means that the majority remain asleep, captured by their cultural upbringing.

Childhood training convinces us we're able to experience just one go at life as separate, unrelated individuals with potential determined at birth. Death, being the ultimate deadline, motivates us to squeeze every drop out of each day, compelled to experience everything that the world offers, mindful that the clock is ticking toward our death. Doing defines our existence; it's how our culture ranks our value to mankind. We rush about, travelling to this country and to that, learning new cultures in the pretence of respect, inclusion and understanding. More likely, we're annoying the locals, overloading their infrastructure and natural resources, while we tick off a meaningless bucket list inspired by our neighbours, the Joneses! Our legacy is a coffee-table photo album, an objective token reflecting how well we've done against society's benchmark. Hopefully, our efforts will be remembered for eternity, motivating our descendants to achieve even greater things, differentiating them from the masses. The truth is, this convincing evidence that life is an objective experience, in which we can believe only what we can see, is a brief, incomplete snapshot of a dynamic understanding.

CHAPTER THIRTY-ONE

RIGHT HERE, RIGHT NOW

COMPREHEND IT OR NOT, *WE ARE ALL OF IT, RIGHT HERE, RIGHT NOW;* part of everything. We are stardust, each the universe, together forming the embodiment of God. That each of us is God, source, love, light (choose any noun you wish to describe all that is incomprehensible) is lost in complexity, or merely withheld. There never has been and never will be a personal God that would discount the existence of free will and personal responsibility. The enduring portrayal of an omniscient God, with the power and will to wreak havoc at any moment, is a myth devised to control. While the danger of physical harm justifies a fear response in some circumstances, fear of the unknown, missing out, embarrassment, comparing unfavourably, homelessness, physical injury and pain are unjustified, negative manifestations, focusing our mind on scarcity. After all, how effective is fear-based motivation when we know that fear of harm is an empty threat appealing to our vanity, for we are nothing but an ego illusion; even death promises new life. We are alone, there is no personal saviour. There's just us, possessing the power of the universe within the matter that forms us. Each of us manifested through thought given attention until formed to match the creators planned intention creating the objective 'i AM'. It follows, then, that you are worthy at conception, because you are from source or love or God. You are the concept of ideas that flow through the collective universal mind, awaiting intention and attention, forming matter from light. This is our innate human power.

We have free will to use this creative gift of intention and attention to create whatever we choose. Intention, coupled with repetitive attention, focuses the power of the universe on our chosen thoughts, causing action and inevitably creating matter after the thought. Hence, 'think and grow rich', or poor, depending on the thought that is intended and attended to. Form always follows from thought. Love is the key to this creative process of physical manifestation. Our unshakable love of the thought will always bear fruit harmonious with it. If dominated by destructive emotions like fear, hate or jealousy, that's what will dominate our experience. Similarly, dominant thoughts of love, faith, belief and confidence give rise to these conditions in our consciousness. This is the secret that has been in plain sight, having the power to set us free: *We choose our experience by the thoughts we love.*

Knowing and embracing this opens the door to control our destiny forever, as described in Luke 3:5 KJV. 'The crooked shall be made straight, and the rough ways shall be made smooth.' Joy is always in evidence.

Our own use of the thought-to-things process is so random that we fail to recognise it follows a pattern. The serial killer is a graphic example. It clearly illustrates the role of definiteness of purpose held until it becomes an obsessive habit, which inevitably leads to action, manifesting the thought in physical reality. Through distorted thinking, a disturbed person, blessed with the same power of the universe to create after the thought as you and I, develops an extreme and irrational hatred for those believed to be the cause of their suffering. Their negative interpretation of past events, combined with persistent, repetitive and emotional attention to the original thought, leads to a powerfully physical, destructive response, which triggers them to act on their desire, thus manifesting the evil in reality. Despite whether society considers the outcome positive or negative, the process is equally creative.

Their love of the thought—reflected by them constantly attending to the intention, believing it will soothe their suffering—ends in creating the conditions they seek, the eradication of their victims from their conscious experience. This is the love of anger and revenge, manifested as destructive physical action. It's a perfect expression of manifesting in the physical world from the world of thought waves, creating an objective experience from a subjective one. This is an extreme example illustrating the formidable power of manifestation when we use our inborn creative process effectively. A serial killer motivated by a single-minded purpose, albeit subconsciously, is using the process with a high degree of skill. Destructive manifestations of the creative force like this are less likely if we've learned the habit of faith, which emphasises the positive emotions and makes us grateful for everything that happens to us, whether or not we like it.

In childhood resistance to events we consider bad sows the seed of bitterness that if nurtured in thought, bears fruit after the seed, ensuring a harvest that reflects negative emotions of fear, greed and envy. Negative emotions corrupt the child-mind while they're forming their objective worldview and their place within it, and they mature into an attitude of 'you have, and I want'. Sometimes, because of repetitive, extreme negative emotion caused by an external influence, a child's development can be completely arrested. For example, a trusted guardian who, in reality, turns out to be a predatory monster who attacks without warning from beneath the bed, inducing graphic daydreams and petrifying night terrors. This leaves the defenceless, innocent child with a distorted view of reality in which they expect the worst from every situation. The rational interpretation of their situation leaves them with the core belief that they have no control over their personal safety, and this manifests as a self-image that is reckless, withdrawn, submissive, worthless and potentially suicidal.

Because these children immerse themselves in their imagination to escape the horror of their situation, they are skilled at using the creative process and capable of experiencing extremes of emotion in normal situations. This makes them prone to extreme anxiety, imagining the worst is about to happen. No matter whether we are consciously or unconsciously applying this innate power, we will always reap the fruits of our most loved thoughts. Which means that even the fallen among us can change their world by becoming a conscious creator, aware that they hold the key to escape their victim status.

Buying a car follows this *thought-to-things* superpower process. The buying cycle involves researching and refining a list of preferred vehicles until we choose a winner. Notice that after finalising our choice, we encounter the exact make, model and colour of car everywhere. Self-development authors call this 'the law of attraction', which is a myth perpetuating the idea that things come from out there. We don't attract a thing, we notice it, after attending to a thought resonating with an existing possibility. This is the process of the inner world before the outer, we only see what we already believe. Until then it's beyond our level of consciousness, energy beyond our comprehension. When we discover the exact car visualised in our mind is parked in the dealer's showroom, we've aligned our thoughts to match the objective possibility. When we buy that car, we can rightfully claim our thought created it at that very moment. If we've been visualising the car we want, but it's not yet parked in our driveway, then we don't love the thought enough; we're not attending to it with the belief that it's already ours. That's not a fault; at that moment it's simply our choice, one that reflects that a new car isn't a priority within our current value system. Remember though, things can only manifest in objective reality 'now', so the emotion of disappointment reflects the wanting of the ego mind, a sure path to suffering. If you don't have it, it's because on some level you don't want it. Disappointment is blame undercover.

Buying a car off the showroom falls into the effortless category of personal creation because the physical equivalent of our desired thought already exists. A definite decision to purchase is all that's needed for the car to fill our garage. That specific car was always within our reach. We just had to conceive it with belief; otherwise it remains in the showroom out of consciousness. Although the information received by our senses is always complete, we're unaware of data on which our mind is not focused—it's extraneous. While there's no thought intention given to purchase a car, the sensory feedback data related to cars washes over us. Our disinterest means we remain unconscious to its existence. Compare this with the phrase 'you have painted on ears', referring to selective hearing. The moment we have the thought that a new car would be great, it was love and believe it by formulating an intention accompanied by regular attention, suddenly the car in our mind, created right within our objective field of view. We create the exact item desired the moment we settle on it, while keeping it in consciousness.

Étienne Lenoir applied this process in 1858 when he revealed the first practical internal-combustion engine. He had a thought pass into consciousness about an explosion in an enclosed space that caused a reaction that may drive a wheel. Piece by piece, he saw that the possibility of what he first imagined already existed. He acted on the thought with belief that whatever the mind of man can conceive, he can achieve through love. This formula applies to all that you desire. The product-development process used by the manufacturer in the initial concept and design phase uses the same method from idea to conception, although at a higher level that requires more thought energy, money or manpower, and ultimately many decisions and courses of action. I call this iterative process a 'hierarchy of objective creation'.

Physical creation through thought is real magic, a fun game indeed. Imagine what other thoughts can be materialised by the process of belief and imagination. Remain mindful of what you decide to love, as it will consume you until you become it. While you run captivated down your rabbit hole of choice, motivated by the love of the thought, every other possibility remains invisible to you—love, after all, is blind. Through love a rocket scientist becomes the rocket, a mechanic becomes the car, a gardener becomes the garden. It's their consciousness. Meanwhile, where once the baby cried and was attended to because of love, it now goes unattended while its parents pursue and attend to the thoughts they've been taught to love more—like smart phones and day care. Whether the thoughts are chosen consciously through self-suggestion or unconsciously through the suggestion of another, whether they're adaptive or maladaptive, while the thought receives love and attention a harvest congruent with the thought is inevitable.

CHAPTER THIRTY-TWO

THE KEY TO YOUR HAPPINESS

EVERYTHING PHYSICAL BEGAN AS A THOUGHT, INCLUDING YOU, conceived from the creator's thought by love. Because we are also innate creators, as determined by the singular source of our seed (the universal creator), it follows that we are the power and the glory in the creator's image. The oak tree is in the acorn, and the chicken is in the egg. Therefore, emotions that weaken our infinite creative power, e.g., jealousy, are illusions generated in childhood from environmental feedback which we interpreted as adverse experiences, and they cause inappropriate adult emotional responses when we're stressed. For example, a child blames themselves for their parents arguing and eventual divorce, even concluding that it's a punishment for not doing as they're told. When triggered as an adult—for example, when their partner is angry with them—they revert to habit, yielding for fear of being abandoned again. Others would simply shrug it off. The natural ability to see this moment with strength, courage and a capacity to overcome, regardless of the outcome, is filtered through suboptimal childhood interpretations made in a distressed state. They view their world through a lens distorted by layers of misunderstanding.

Our interpretation that events are personal, reflecting our innate badness, reduces the otherwise unconstrained present moment to a limited set of outcomes designed in childhood. This results from the wrong application of the subconscious. It's expert at managing objective processes within the physical world, but was never designed to participate in creating matter from abstract thought. The physical world concerns what can be seen, what already exists; while the inner world is about what is yet to be understood but can be perceived. By being mindful, repeatedly coming back to consciousness, to remain awake and in charge is the only way we can discover and weed out false, negative, maladaptive childhood dogma that masks ever-present hope and happiness.

The process of conscious, objective manifestation has always existed, but somehow it remained a secret, latent in all but a few. Understanding that we are creators, able to access all resources of the universe freely, gives us the ability to select a subjective thought, then, driven by its possibility to improve life, focus energy to transform it into objective matter. Despite resistance, an intention given frequent attention must manifest in reality. Conviction that we can reveal a mere possibility in three-dimensional space makes it so. With single-minded focus, persistence and patience (even long-suffering) the thought materialises, composed from the finite chemical elements (periodic table) that make up our objective universe.

The thought objectified, although commonly described as an invention, is more correctly described as a 'discovery'. Once manifested into general consciousness, inventions are often patented, limiting compensation to an exclusive group of benefactors. Yet the thought of the thing is equally accessible to everyone, belonging to us all, potentially enhancing all lives. Until someone gives enough attention or love to the thought, it remains hidden from consciousness. Does the discovery warrant compensating the discoverer for loving the thought into our consciousness? The one source provided the possibility to benefit all; it was just waiting to be revealed to our senses through the faith/love of believing before seeing. Compensation adds necessary motivation to improve the physical life of everyone, in the same way that a Bitcoin miner is compensated for their time and energy in verifying the next chain block, causing a rush of innovation.

In the 70s cars were made globally affordable by a booming Japanese automobile industry that copied and improved European and American motorcar technology. This raised global standards of living, while fierce competition for market share sped up innovation and advances in vehicle safety. Patents reward individuals with extended exclusivity and generates super profits for an elite minority, but they prevent others from applying their own creative ideas that may reveal even better solutions and further advance the beneficial progress of humanity. No one owns or has an exclusive right to any invention; this idea is merely an economic construct enriching a few. It assumes that the 'invention' was only possible because of the inventor's unique intelligence and that that is justification enough for them and their heirs to receive exclusive royalties in perpetuity.

This compensation system fails to recognise that the periodic table comprises a finite number of elements that can be recombined to form a range of possible objective outcomes. This means that nothing is invented; it's uncovered, as if in a celestial treasure hunt planned by the source. A person's unique attributes have little to do with the process. If anything, it's a random event of opportunity and preparedness, of having an open, childlike mind and being in the right place at the right time. The periodic table confirms that everything that is and can be is waiting to be revealed through this process of objective conception of thought waves. Everything that will be already exists in possibility, we just can't sense the objective manifestation yet, because no one has had enough love for the thought to believe it into objective reality. In other words, creation is merely the process of revealing what is and always has been into our collective consciousness. We're not inventing, which is defined as 'create or design (something that has not existed before), be the originator of'. The originator was the source energy that created the possibility of everything.

We must be convinced that everything physical is first conceived mentally. We don't recognise this because we're too busy attending to the urgent cultural-success essentials. For example, most days we use a safety razor without giving a thought to its pedigree; we confidently draw it across our body, leaving it smooth and hairless. Through the creative input and cooperation of many, it's been modified and refined from a dangerous instrument to being practically fail-safe. Potentially lethal in the wrong hands, the first iteration was made from shell or flint. Yet, even then, its current safe iteration was possible. Back in the days of the 'cutthroat' razor, the modern safety razor was a legitimate design, but no one had conceived it in imagination. Once the first razor was objectified, others introduced improvements, building on the discovery and enhancing the previous design. An intention to improve the original thought, accompanied by consistent attention, lead to today's safety razor. We haven't had to take part in this stream of creative events to benefit from a product now taken for granted. Look around, use the same analytical process to think about how, through cooperative thought and imagination, everything in our consciousness reaches this advanced state and what it might develop in to next.

A life model in which the world exists separate from us, and in which we must conform, has passed its use by date. In this model, society bestows worthiness through progressive assessment of competency, achieved through memorising current knowledge and values. The greater our faith in this model, where the world is seen solely as an objective realm, the less likely we are to achieve our natural potential. In this model, when we look into the mirror each day, rather than seeing the universe personified, we see our limited selves. Our learned filters govern our view of personal possibilities, making us a spectator of life, rather than an active participant. Participants know that today's objective truth manifests from past thought, which is then consumed until replaced by a new, better version, conceived by someone familiar with the objective creation process. Everything outside of us arose from past thoughts, brought into consciousness through repetition of action. Its future is either obsolescence and replacement, or refinement through additional thought, cooperative interpersonal reflection and objective adjustment. This creation process was undeniably around from the beginning, yet we continue to be mere spectators. This will only change when we see ourselves as subjective creators who are able to manifest the physical world from the thoughts we consciously choose to focus on.

Our life goal is to strengthen and develop our unique ability to create from subjective thought, thus fulfilling our needs in the present and transforming our world into a massive playground or sandpit. This ultimate construction project is made possible by our unlimited creative possibility. Realising that we're not bound by any past moment, we can build and destroy today and start from scratch on something else tomorrow, all for the fun of it. We have the choice to reinvent ourselves anytime we like.

CHAPTER THIRTY-THREE

REINVENTING YOURSELF

L IVING AS THOUGH WE'RE BOUND TO AN EVER-EXPANDING PAST within our allotted timeline is an illusion of wrong thought. It keeps us trapped within a virtual world of past and future, mostly asleep to real life; asleep to now. This world view condemns us to living as victims of circumstance, subconsciously—through destructive self-suggestion or the suggestion of society—captured by love of the thoughts to which we choose to attend.

This is what we understand as consciousness, yet our loved ones and close associates already know our reaction if they push certain emotional buttons. Our children have been observing our response model for years, making them expert mood manipulators who can control our emotional response with words and gestures. Similarly, age groups are a reliable predictor of response to certain beliefs because they're a snapshot of the educational era. Politicians and the media use this information when they want to trigger a predictable response across entire demographics. The degree to which we awake, becoming conscious of our dominant thoughts, determines whether we're facilitating our own heaven or hell on earth.

Sadly, our family has endured our lectures so often that they've stopped listening, like a sermon so familiar they could recite it word for word. We've become like a computer operating system, a static unconscious loop, with the same stimulus returning the same predictable response. When we're tuned out by those closest to us who have heard it all before, lends truth to the phrase, 'You can never be a prophet in your own land'. Desensitised to our stale message, they're now preoccupied with their own story. Hypnotised by their own thought habits, consumed in an illusion, they relive the past or invent their idea of the future, blind to the reality surrounding them. Bound by their child ego, they live their life the way we taught them, as a random fantasy with few choices. It takes a rude intrusion from the real environment to bring them back into the reality of the present moment. A click of the fingers, a stubbed toe or even an act of God, like an earthquake, or two.

Against the odds, some lift the veil and discover their choice of self-renewal with every 'now' moment. Unconstrained by their past decisions or future dreams, they expand naturally, one with the universe, and form and sustain a happy life by accepting the moment as it is.

We're all aware of those elderly, who even after enduring a lifetime of suffering, remain vibrant and active to their last days, living for now and wisely choosing to only occasionally dwell on their good memories to sustain and multiply their joy. They're not bound by limiting memories and regrets anchored in a bygone era, nor continuously captured in the hollow promise of a fantasy yet to happen. That would only diminish the abundance available to them now. Unfortunately for many, the only programme upgrade they get occurs in the moment before death. Free of pretence, resigned to their fate, for the first time they understand the meaning of consciousness. If only they had realised their choice to remain awake to every moment while still in their prime, enjoying the life gifted them by our maker as it was intended, as a glorious game. As shocking as this discovery is, there is a surprise making it all worthwhile.

The exponentially accelerating process of uncovering possibilities through technology emphasises this error of living within an ego illusion. The gulf between generations and even within generations is widening as relatively recent innovations become redundant, replaced by seemingly daily discovery. Thankfully, AI has the potential to look after the menial and keep score, while all around us ceaselessly changes. Technological redundancy is happening at such a pace that soon it will be impossible to deny there is only one moment we can be 100% effective, that's right now. The rate of change will seem like an endless slap in the face, forcing us out of our old familiar-but-irrelevant stories, until we wake up to the truth that change is, and always has been, normal.

Now more than ever we must question the old ways, revising them in light of what is in front of us. Although actions have consequences, we're infinitely free to choose new paths, making different choices, renewed at the moment we consciously shift our awareness. We need only awake to our own consciousness and become aware of our habitual thought patterns, like a foreigner eventually becomes aware of their own accent, to reveal that we are the universe embodied, conceived into an objective world of infinite possibility. Our innate ability to harness creative thought means we always possess the means to discover the solution to overcoming any obstacle in our way. This realisation is the beginning of creative, continuous review of our operating programme using a critical, fresh approach to thought.

Each moment is a rebirth untarnished by perceived past sins. Even punishment is powerless to dent the conscious soul; it's merely an act of revenge by a fearful or controlling ego, seeking to maintain the model of objective existence. Our value is not determined by another, or by a society operating under compromise to the agreed, era-appropriate, greater good. However, the education system is founded on the concept that our value is proportional to our utility to society, rather than by our nature. Similarly, self-punishment from feelings of regret or failure arises from a belief in scarcity. This reflects an ego mind that believes time is real and consumes our life like a pie, piece by diminishing piece, until it's all gone. Collective blindness to our individual, perpetual creative abundance leaves us scrambling over each other in a race to get our share and more before the hourglass is turned for another.

Believe all things are possible for he/she who has faith, and know that we are conceived with the innate ability to overcome all our obstacles and thrive. Know in your heart that God, source, love, starlight exists in you and you in it. You are of its essence, known to us objectively as the universe. Our ego may deny this, deliberately setting traps to recapture us in memorised webs of past limiting thoughts. The moment we make an excuse or apportion blame for our situation, we're denying our life force, choosing to operate in a state of self-doubt and limitation. Yet we arrive into life equally worthy members of humanity.

The proof surrounds us, undeniable evidence of our personal power to overcome all suffering, no matter our objective situation. If we know that all things are possible, then no one, no matter their malicious intent, can convince us our worth is derived only from achievement. Our birth brings worth; we need not seek it. Conception implies success. With this as our true-north attitude, our purpose becomes only about refining our innate skill at cooperatively playing the game of creation with those we encounter during this journey of discovery. The aim is to have fun exploring our abilities, refining them until we've reached the level of excellence we choose, not someone else.

CHAPTER THIRTY-FOUR

THE OAK TREE IS IN THE ACORN

ALL OF US ARE CREATORS, EQUALLY ENDOWED WITH ALL THAT IS God; this is the truth that sets us free. Never again do we fear that dark shadows threaten to descend on us. At conception, we are the embodiment of the entire universe, able to overcome any seemingly insurmountable problem with an abundance of free resources that are ours to use. Our primary definite purpose is to have fun creating physical matter from subjective thoughts that we choose and objectify as we desire. Our body, the only finite thing about us, constantly changing, has no connection to the infant we once were. Every cell dies only to be reborn in a continuous process of renewal.

Know that the thought or 'i AM That, i AM', that who we really are, will live on through ever-expanding eternity, while the ego that is 'I am that I am' will die. It's an illusion, having life only because of our Christian name made up of memories across our objective timeline. This is a sad, lonely revelation but also a powerful creative release, revealing we are an infinite and connected experience. We're all brothers and sisters under the illusion that we are in some way separate and competing, full of anxiety and fear, attempting to draw to ourselves as much as the finite pie as we can. After all, if we don't, someone else will claim our share, ensuring they will experience more than we do, guaranteeing we perpetuate the pain caused by our comparative feelings of failure.

We live in a universe of abundance where, with cooperation, everything we need is freely available. We are here to uncover the infinite beauty that is us and all that we sense in perfect harmony. It's a game, not a battle. A game that returns us to full health every time we hit the reset button, just by saying 'next'. Any story of lack only exists to enslave us as a perpetual victim searching for the missing link to complete us, a link that is no more than a castle in the sand. Fortunately, every moment is a gift, unspoiled by past efforts, that offers a new moment to lift our eyes to discover the next truth.

Years of immersion within a standards-based education system convinced us that creative ability is a genetic trait, leaving us with the limiting thought error that some are born more creative than others. Yet I'm sure that, at some point, we've all had the thought, 'Please release me from this merciless tirade of tiring mind chatter.' This request suggests that thoughts are unexclusive, involuntarily, continuously bubbling up within our mind. Thoughts flow in each of us regardless of genetics; they are the source of our infinite creative power and salvation, our very own 'golden goose'. To be human is to be tuned into this vast cache of the one mind, a gift from God available to all that enables each of us to create a life experience with our own unique twist. Because we're taught to view ourselves as separate and distinct from all others, we believe that these thoughts must be exclusively arising from within us, as if we're their source. But we are merely innocent observers, watching as this continuous stream of abundant thoughts flows past, having no power or meaning outside of what we attach to them through bias or desire. That disturbing idea appearing in our thought stream isn't personal; it just is. It doesn't define us unless we choose, consciously or otherwise.

It's only when we claim a thought that it gains substance, the potential to manifest in our reality. This personalisation of thoughts governs our attitude and our altitude. If we claim ownership of random thoughts of evil, as if we're their source, we're left under the illusion that we're born evil, and we become frightened of what harm we appear capable of wreaking on humanity. Fear of our darkest thoughts being revealed leads to self-consciousness and withdrawal. Convinced that we're unworthy, we sink further under the control of our poor self-construct. We fail to realise that all thoughts, even our darkest, are harmless, unless we choose to focus on them, giving them power. In reality a thought passes by harmlessly, powerless, until for whatever reason, we decide to shine a light on it. Our continued attention energises it. By this law, the stronger our resistance to unwanted conditions, the more energised they become.

While we remain ignorant of the creative process, blind to the choices available to us, looking outward for answers to improve our life gives frustrating, unpredictable results. The longer we remain asleep, the more animal-instinct-like our responses become. Revealed to others through us, as if we are the pure reflection of these dominant thoughts. As adults, the 'ego us', through no fault of our own, confines us to these worn-out paths of unconscious habit, ensuring we get what we've always got. Meanwhile, society moves on until eventually our operating model, constructed so long ago with the help of so many, struggles to make sense of things and is unable to navigate the increasingly alien environment. We become victims of our past. Habits formed from association and education cease to serve us in our daily life.

Awareness of our innate ability to mould and reshape ourselves at will is the key to our kingdom of limitless habit creation and recreation—a genie at our command. This knowledge gives us access to the source of humanity's power to choose and set in stone enduring, empowering habits, while simultaneously remaining as adaptable to change as flowing water. With this key in hand, we remain relevant and young of mind, able to adapt and morph quickly, staying congruent within an unceasingly, changing world until our body eventually fails.

Death is an integral part of universal renewal. The thought called birth is infinitely refreshed so life can continue to perfect the adventure through cyclical conception. The 'ego I' of before has gone. It was merely an illusion of emotion, connected memories and family history, a tool to achieve cooperation through the idea of unconditional love. Potentially we carry memories and experience through repeated lifetimes via the DNA and RNA of past manifestations, so we're not sentenced to live the same painful lessons in an endless repeating loop. This way we become more enlightened with each new reincarnation.

A life of suffering caused by the wrong application of our thought process is not unique or accidental. Across the centuries, both religious and sovereign leaders (often linked) deceived us by deliberately distorting civilisations' wisdom, thus controlling the collective mind through thought manipulation. 'Do this and go to Heaven; ignore us and an eternity in Hell awaits,' they said, rather than teaching that heaven or hell is a decision under our control. Their approach may have been beneficial to the survival of ancient civilisations, but perpetuating this ignorance no longer serves us. Governments and corporations have since replaced religion as society's moral teachers; 'financial wealth' is now the proxy for heaven and 'poverty' for hell. Influencing the values and beliefs of many minds was the fast track for these entities to achieve global power and wealth, one yielding exponential economic growth. Now, however, economies of scale are increasingly provided through development of AI and robotics, making control of large groups of people unnecessary and administratively unattractive.

For centuries the bible has been misrepresented by leaders pursuing selfish desires and goals. Still it remains the primary, enduring guidebook that offers the keys to a life filled with love and wisdom. Within its many enlightening parables are a precise blueprint for a successful life we are free to choose 'as we will'. Life is an adventure through which we discover that our separate physical dimension is integral to a larger expanding one called the universe. We can experience endless fun, providing we're prepared to accept the consequences of 'as we will.' Resisting the impact of our choices, and blaming others for our situation, guarantees a lifetime of suffering. Understanding this opens a hidden door to infinite possibility and forgiveness. There is no negative consequence, only the revelation that however congruent or broken our self-construct, its life is brief, while i AM is timeless. We're conceived of light to grow, create, then die. Then with a clean schema, we're again conceived of light, we grow, we create ... all because of the love-force singularity.

CHAPTER THIRTY-FIVE

SEMANTICS CAN REVEAL THE REAL YOU

T HROUGHOUT THIS BOOK, I HAVE OUTLINED EXAMPLES OF MY OWN maladaptive response to events, and how these revealed a solution to end the seemingly endless suffering accompanying our lives. The solution relies on our relationship to the words we use and their meaning or semantics. Wikipedia defines semantics as:

'Semantics (from Ancient Greek: σημαντικός sēmantikos, 'significant')[1][2] is the linguistic and philosophical study of meaning, in language, programming languages, formal logics, and semiotics. It is concerned with the relationship between signifiers—like words, phrases, signs, and symbols—and what they stand for, their denotation.'

We are merely a model of semantics, of words interpreted by our senses based on our understanding of the meaning of all those items collectively known as our language. Naturally, we form our initial understanding of what is happening to and around us when we're least equipped to understand our environment. In fact we have a minimal impact on our ego formulation. It's laid down unconsciously, layer upon layer by our closest influencers. Unable to engage meaningfully in critical thinking, we're left no choice but to accept their objective version of what is predominantly a subjective environment. The nature of habit force[28] means these mostly unintentionally flawed interpretations of meaning that explain our particular life experience remain unquestioned

---

[28] Napoleon Hill, *The Master Key to Riches*, #17 of the 17 Key Success Principles, Sound Wisdom, 2019.

and unchallenged. They become our subconscious core beliefs, which influence all future decisions by filtering our interpretations, reinforcing what we already believe. This confirmation bias means that no matter how much thought we put into a decision, we end up with the same result we've always got.

No matter how hard we try to change things by thinking about them, even making practical changes at the surface level, our life remains a frustrating merry-go-round of our past mistakes caused by our habitual, ego-driven, decision-making process. It's a case of garbage in, garbage out (GIGO)—a computer-science acronym describing how false logic and input data guarantees consistently wrong output. Our influencers have unwittingly passed their limitations onto us via what can be compared to the data delivered at the tail end of a 'Chinese whisper' experiment, making us a true victim. Of course, our own misguided interpretations add subtle errors of thought to the limited range of situational responses on which we rely.

This suboptimal childhood programming can lead to us approaching life with an attitude of fear, impeding the development of our full potential. It manifests as a poor view of ourselves relative to others, often because our point of reference is unrealistic. Television series like *Homes of the Rich and Famous* may motivate those fortunate enough to be nurtured in an environment that assists the development of a healthy, positive mental attitude, but for most, the opposite is true. They strive to match the ideal they're confronted with in the popular media, but their self-programming means that unless they develop a new, better view of their ability, they're unlikely to attain it. Failing to achieve anything like a comparable result leaves us disappointed and upset. Unfortunately, petulant behaviour is suffering's closest companion.

Comparison is a useful impersonal measure to establish a point of reference that reflects our progress toward mastery, but we've learned to use it as a form of personal punishment. We make emotional judgements, comparing ourselves against others, and thinking we're good or bad, right or wrong, a success or failure.

Because we're our own harshest critic, we typically compare our worst with another's best. This distorts reality, making it a worthless benchmark, while causing varying degrees of performance anxiety and a tendency to procrastinate for fear of more failure, pain and suffering. If not consciously controlled, this thought pattern manifests as a lack of trust in our abilities. This further embeds self-destructive habits and maladaptive behaviours such as alcoholism, illicit drug taking and self-harm, which are undertaken in an attempt to escape anxiety and depression. If it persists, it may lead to the desire to kill the wounded beast, ending our suffering once and for all.

Expecting failure guarantees failure, because that is the creative mind's focus. Intentional or accidental emotionally charged feedback response to childhood failure can lead to us believing it's an absolute indicator of our ability. As with all misunderstood repeated experiences, fear of failure or specifically, fear of the accompanying emotional pain, becomes a habitual thought error. When believed, this thought error manifests as logical excuses, absolving us of responsibility when we quit or don't even attempt to have a go. Instead of persisting toward our goal, utilising feedback from previous failures to iterate us toward success, we personalise failure, blaming our circumstances or others for the conditions we're experiencing. Such excuses are made up of elaborate, believable stories, formulated by the mind to protect our suffering ego. For example, I'll never be successful because I'm too short, too fat, big boned, inferior DNA, wrong parents, sex, country, or time or just plain unlucky.

There's always some condition we can blame to justify our role as an unconscious victim, but this paralyses affirmative action, leaving us in a state of regret—a disempowering word that arouses the avoidable self-inflicted pain on which we like to dwell. A mind awake to itself knows that accepting any limitation as a cause of failure is the choice of a mind set that believes in lack rather than abundance. With proper attention to and application of empowering thoughts, each failure becomes a steppingstone to self-determined excellence. All failures have happened; all thought energy in the universe can't change that. Their impact only endures, however, if we continue to attend to their memory. But where is the sense in that? Things can be no other way, no matter our desire for them to be otherwise. Everything is just right and as it should be right now. Accept that the world is abundant in every way and that everything we create is in perfect harmony with our original plan. When we know our true origin as creators of our own experience, it no longer makes sense to treat ourselves or others with anything but a foundational belief of love and kindness in an effective process of self-care.

The ability to achieve our potential is merely about using semantics to consciously create a better view of who and what we are. Happenstance has left us with the belief that we're powerless victims of our genetics and environment. However, when we understand the process leading to this belief, it's our responsibility as a thinking, creative adult to break free of this view. When we realise that we're the interpreter of what we give our attention to and what's happening to us, we cease to be victims. All it takes to remove the self-imposed pressure to measure up against some unattainable ideal is to change the reference point from the external to the internal world, based on the experience we're having right now, not yesterday or tomorrow. Once we embrace the unlimited creative energy gifted us at conception, we can pursue what's important to us and create everything we experience starting from within. This removes the need to apportion blame or for childish excuses anchored in fear. What we get won't always be what we expect, but we'll always have access to all the resources needed to meet and conquer any obstacles encountered along the way. The universe did not set out to defeat itself but to express itself with confidence, and we are the universe, all that was, is and ever will be.

With our new concept of success, life becomes about using our unlimited power to make the most of what's in front of us, whether that's as easy as getting out of bed, solving a resource problem or learning a new skill. There's no enduring failure. Everything we do is a success, every new moment a blank page to start over and move toward achieving mastery over what's important to us. When we hold the thought of our desire in our mind with the attitude that we're innately worthy, we will achieve it. In the absence of excuses, living involves pure acceptance of the moment. Our choice of words interprets the moment, creating our emotional experience. We are the words we think with, the continuous stream flowing through our mind; words are the only experience. The greater our word power, the more sophisticated and nuanced the language we use, the more we're able to control the results we manifest in the objective world. Improving our vocabulary and comprehension significantly expands our creative possibilities, mixing and matching different concepts and focusing our understanding of words, phrases, symbols, etc.

CHAPTER THIRTY-SIX

A FEW EXAMPLES EXPLAINING 'i AM' SEMANTICS

L OVE IS THE PERFECT WORD TO ILLUSTRATE THE SEMANTICS OF I AM and how this simple understanding of our consciousness instantly changes our view of life and its apparent inseparable link to suffering.

Wikipedia describes love as: 'Ancient Greek philosophers identified four forms of love: essentially, familial love (in Greek, *storge*), friendly love (*philia*), romantic love (*eros*), and divine love (*agape*). Modern authors have distinguished further varieties of love: infatuated love, self-love, and courtly love. Non-Western traditions also have distinguished variants or symbioses of these states.[4][5] Love has additional religious or spiritual meaning. This diversity of uses and meanings combined with the complexity of the feelings involved makes love unusually difficult to define, compared to other emotional states consistently.'

Love is a broad, deep rabbit hole around which we could devote an entire life of study. Imagine a walking manifestation of love, an objective identity inseparable from the person's ego, identifying as love and able to claim rightfully i AM love. If this manifestation was by choice, through intention and conscious attention, then the lover has achieved their bliss in consciousness. The same process used to reveal a car formed from imagination into the physical is used to discover a companion matching our desire for romantic love. The match already exists, all we need to do is attend to the thought i AM love to discover them through focused awareness. Then it's i AM love manifesting as the pure feeling of love.

In contrast, 'I am Joe and in love' (where Joe is my Christian name) is contaminated. For the semantics of i AM to work, 'I am Joe and in love' must be 'i AM love'. Removing Joe from the semantic meaning of love leaves us with the pure creation, the bright and focused mirror that is our true perfect self, the i AM that, i am. I am all consumed by the semantics; I am it, the embodiment of love. I am not Joe and it; I am it! So feel consumed by it, feel yourself manifested as the meaning of love, and you will feel it. Otherwise expect disappointment because no one can meet the standards set by our narcissistic ego.

The pure meaning of a word is skewed by self-image and ego. Meaning or semantics of words we take for granted, like for example love, is different for different people. Those with an accurate view of themselves are a closer reflection of their pure, unlimited reality. Their feelings and language are congruent. They work from inner confidence, believing they're worthy, which empowers their actions to achieve their intention, thus they discover the precise vision of their romantic partner. While those with a low opinion of themselves (poor ego) may define romantic love as 'anyone prepared to speak to me'. The meaning of love changes, accurately mirroring ego expectation, in this case leading to poor outcomes.

We are all made of the same stuff, but individual experience mirrors our self-imposed limitations, the truth we've chosen to represent our experience. Our poor understanding of romantic love means we feel like we're being constantly rejected by those placing a higher value on themselves, when it's actually our erroneous beliefs selling us short. Rejection reinforces our low self-image, confirming the belief that we're unworthy and further entrenching our poor self-image.

Our ego model determines whether we reach our potential. Clearly, the meaning we attribute to our life experiences is filtered through our own unique semantic translator. We can't create more than we expect when we're the only creator of our experience. The pure semantics of love is distorted by an array of inaccurate interpretations that translate into personal suffering. Perceived rejection leads to a belief that romantic love is an illusion, that it's not for us, because we're different or undeserving—'different' being the conclusion and the excuse. Our ego acts as a compound modifier to the true meaning of the word.

In the same way, a person who studies to become a surgeon spends thousands of hours investing attention on their desire to become the focus of their intention. Once they've manifested their intention, they are a surgeon along with all that means. The surgeon, like the lover, can claim 'I am a surgeon'. Let's say the surgeon's name is Jane Doe, then we have two I Ams: 'I am a surgeon,' and, 'I am Jane.' Jane is the mostly unconscious, dominant I am, while the surgeon is a subset of, 'I am Jane'. Now Jane is the thing she thought about most, whether that's by conscious choice or her unconscious action on ideas arising from the suggestion of others. This is the danger of unconscious activity, but it's the truth for most of us, and it leads us down the path to feeling unfulfilled because the choices we live were not made by us, but for us.

Jane didn't want to be a surgeon; her caregivers sowed that seed. By accident, she devoted her attention to satisfy the dream of another. Eventually, after years of study, Jane identifies as a surgeon, and at some point, she may wonder why. At this moment, Jane needs to understand the power of the semantics of i AM. She's not a surgeon, she is the universe, who decided to give attention to the intention of being a surgeon, merely a subset of her potential choices. In every moment, Jane can lift her thoughts out of the surgeon rabbit hole, by making a conscious decision to focus on objectifying another thought until she is the thought—let's say an electrician or a priest, or any multitude of nouns, all at once. She may decide to go narrow, rather than deep, down the rabbit hole, becoming many things, or even being content just being and observing in the knowledge that, through the gift of conscious thought, she owes nothing to anyone. Her conception is validation enough that she is worthy. She is the master of her fate and the captain of her soul. The same applies to the 'I am' that is Jane. Jane can decide to drop the Jane that has become her avatar. Her ego, acting as an unconscious filter analogous to a pre-programmed heads-up display (HUD), limits her options on what began as a transparent window to infinite potential and replaces it with a new understanding, unencumbered by the HUD of her past interpretation. She can cast her focus subjectively at the leaf and become as a leaf, or the sky, becoming one with the sky, or the light, becoming connected to the light—after all, we are light manifested as matter. In this way, she casts off her learned limitation of her objective form, much like a small dog doesn't know it's a small dog. (Obviously, we have an essential objective reality that has specific limitations, but it is the existential, subjective reality that is the missing link to understanding).

So how can the semantics of i AM help us thrive? As a first step, we must accept the proof of our creation from thought. We're conceived of the universe, representing all its infinite possibilities. This is the only path to congruent happiness, an awareness immediately revealing the cloak of limitation we've woven since given our name. Unfortunately, the cloak is the dominant player in our life, even up to our last breath. There is a vast chasm between our true nature and the experience we create. This duality is outside our awareness and is the source of our feelings of fear and anxiety. Past interpretations form an opaque filter that distorts our view, reducing, and even preventing, our power to create. Our mind eventually becomes fossilised, set from decisions of the past that now no longer serve us.

When we drop our model or ego, the filter vanishes, revealing infinite possibility and awakening to perpetual renewal with pure semantic meaning. 'i Am That' becomes our true avatar, unencumbered by the compound modifier with our given name, in my case, 'I am Geoff'. The need to read books, take courses, attend seminars to become a better me instantly disappears. How do you perfect what is already perfect? We're no longer pressured to seek validation by doing, instead we realise that we already are; we just need to let it be. All things come to us naturally. We don't need to feel compelled to chase that one missing link that will fix what must be fixed. We can give up the incessant search for the magic snake oil peddled by self-help gurus professing to have the secret guaranteeing our transformation from clueless frog to Prince Charming. We are freed of our obsessional need to meditate, affirm, chant or any other prerequisite technique on our path to achieving perfection.

There's value in these activities. They can help, but only when we understand that we already possess everything we need to thrive, and we always have. Techniques are fun resources assisting us to achieve optional, consciously predetermined, worthwhile goals that are not always linked with the narrow definition of success. We may reach our nirvana or bliss by simply sitting quietly and pondering the beauty surrounding us and within us.

We're taught that in return for the gift of life we owe society, a debt committing us to 'do', to earn our keep. After awakening, we realise we owe nothing to anybody. We're satisfied by being—not being a lazy derelict, but alive, having an unrestricted view of who we really are. We're transformed. With a confident sense of knowing, we become a conduit to others. We alert them to their birth right, their own inexhaustible creative power, naturally worthy, entitled to their share of an abundant universe. We realise that the life society had planned out for us, and the economic wealth we've been chasing, are part of a game of compromise and power, manipulated to advantage those who are desperate to maintain the control they've had for centuries.

The more of us who awake to this truth, the faster we will change and improve the experience of our collective, objective existence. Realising that we are seeds of the all-powerful universe, nodes possessing equal access to the connected network of thought, we can begin creating using pure meaning or semantics. We can confidently create what we seek from thought, knowing that whatsoever we conceive and believe in the subjective world, with intention and attention, will be achieved in the objective world.

CHAPTER THIRTY-SEVEN

ALL BLACK IS A COMPOUND MODIFIER AND SO ARE YOU

B EING THAT I AM A NATIVE OF NZ, WHERE THE NATIONAL GAME IS rugby, using this sport as an analogy to reinforce the 'I am that, I am' seems appropriate. Rugby has been at the centre of my country's greatest sporting moments—the national men's team (All Blacks) exploits are woven into its cultural identity. Senior All Blacks describe their tenure as part of this exceptional rugby team as a fleeting moment in time; while the All Black team forever (or at least for as long as the nation gives the thought love) captivates the imagination of the population across generations. This enduring team is objectified by the distinctive black jersey bearing the famous silver fern. Like the flightless kiwi, it's an icon of New Zealand, representing the spirit of all New Zealanders. The man becomes the jersey, transcending the individual player's ego. Players come and go, briefly experiencing all that the black jersey embodies—the eternal spirit of what it is to be an All Black.

Zinzan Brooke (All Black 1987-97) was quoted in the NZ Dominion newspaper as saying: 'I feel outsiders still underestimate the power that the black shirt holds for New Zealanders, of course, every player from Georgia to Uruguay is incredibly proud to pull on their national shirt and represent their country, but with Kiwis, it is something more, something almost spiritual. Every year people who wear that shirt create history and leave a benchmark for the next generation to aspire to ... it is about submitting yourself to an ideal far bigger than your individual ambitions. The shirt demands that you leave the ego at the door.'[29]

This realisation that the ego is secondary to the thread of eternal thought that manifests in the objective world as the All Blacks explains the huge success this team has experienced. Despite it being such a small nation at the bottom of the world, its achievements are recognised globally. The team has been nominated for the Laureus World Sports Award Team of the Year many times. They took home the top prize in 2016 after becoming the first team to win the Rugby Union World Cup three times and the first to win consecutive tournaments.

Richie McCaw, a man of great mana in New Zealand and around the World, led the All Blacks to their cup wins at both the 2011 and 2015 Rugby World Cups, the only captain to achieve the feat. When he wore the All-Black jersey, he became one with it, becoming what he understood to be the pure semantics of the jersey, unequivocal in its meaning. A legacy forged across All Black generations by the cooperation of many minds holding the same intention, giving attention to and focusing on what mattered most to the expanding success of the jersey. This persistent application of intention and attention to the original subjective thought eventually created the greatest rugby team of all time. In 1999 as a sixteen-year-old and with help from his uncle in a McDonalds fast-food outlet, McCaw formulated his own complimentary goal.[30] On a Macca's paper napkin, he wrote that he'd become not just any All Black, but a great all black. His thought, loved until objectified in the form of the iconic black Adidas jersey, became irrefutably 'i AM All Black' and in McCaw's case, arguably the greatest All Black of all time. This one phrase, 'All Black' has its own semantics, distilled across many decades, that embodies many powerful concepts including i AM power, i AM loyal, i AM love, i AM concentration, i AM courage and i AM strength etc. 'All Black' is the compound modifier of the pure thoughts. Just as our own Christian name should be.

i AM Geoff Keall is the compound of the pure thoughts I held of

---

[29] NZ Stuff, 12/9/2015, *Former All Blacks No 8 Zinzan Brooke says power of black jersey keeps team strong.*

[30] Justin Pemberton and Michelle Walshe, *Chasing Great: The Richie McCaw Story*; Prime Video, 2016.

myself in childhood. Unfortunately the compounded thoughts didn't add up to 'All Black', just 'dark and self-defeating'. This ability to compound from thought, creating an objective being with extraordinary intrinsic power, has always been ours, lying dormant only because of ignorance. Until now our 'i AM' has developed randomly, built unconsciously. To be part of the game, we must first accept we are as worthy as the mythical gods to which our ancient ancestors submitted, then choose the i AM statements resonating with our vision of bliss. Just like the phrase 'All Black' conjures up feelings and emotions within players and fans, stirring images of power and respect, we can use the same process, generating the same power and respect for ourselves, honouring the reality of our source. This is the correct way to build a regenerating, obedient ego servant and reveal our consciously planned and built unique i AM to the world. Blessed with free will, we can choose to be a powerfully evil creator or a powerful creator of all that is right, pure, patient, uplifting and beautiful—every choice is valid, and each has its own consequences. If all we want to do is sit on a hilltop watching the sun rise and set, while pondering the meaning of life, do it. Armed with our new understanding, we can effortlessly build a new i AM, a new consciously chosen me.

We're born with nothing, indebted to no one, and we'll die with nothing. At birth, we're given the keys to the entire kingdom to make of ourselves what we will. We arrive into this world of particles with every right to plant our feet firmly anywhere and rest our head wherever it falls for however long we live. No one may withhold these simple rights. If the system says otherwise, then the system is wrong, and we must change it through conscious application of love, the essence of all that's collectively recognised as our universe. Through conscious thought and the understanding of the 'i AM that, I Am' we can all create a fairer world, providing equality for all. Not my version or your version, though. Our free will doesn't extend to imposing my choices or beliefs on another. That is a deception that perpetuates human suffering.

If we choose our thoughts consciously, we're no longer bound to our ego and are able to change our i AM any time. The thoughts we love, identified by intention and attention, is what we create, an irrefutable law of the sower (Matthew 13:3-8 KJV). We can easily change who we were a moment ago by a decision to integrate and love a new thought, thus shedding our old skin. There is no pressure here; we're never wrong. The die is not cast forever by past decisions, leaving us suffering a life filled with regret. Notice this and you'll understand that meditation is only capturing yourself in the past or the future—both unreal, ego-driven states. Whether or not we know it, or even accept it, this is happening to us in every second of every day. An uncontrolled ego is like leaving a child with unrestricted control of your life. It's guaranteed to end in anarchy.

Love the thought 'butterfly', and at the moment you become the butterfly (or your understanding of what it is to be the butterfly), you become what you interpret to be the meaning of those words—just as if you love the thought 'fear' or the thought 'lack'. With constant unconscious attention, 'you' create your understanding of lack and fear, sowing and nurturing the thought, eventually reaping the thing. Know this and realise that excuses are justifications used to hypnotise ourselves into accepting why our lives are less than we think they should be. Notice these judgments of less than are all from our own interpretation of feedback and mostly wrong.

Knowing we choose the 'that' in the 'i AM that' means we are no longer the victim, but the invigorated creator. Because we are what we are thinking, the change is immediate. Just like water, we move freely with the flow, with faith, without the need to resist or force a path to fit our will. All the problems in our life have already been answered, we just have to stay soft and awake for the solutions to surface. There is always another option, another path open to us because we get to create it. Every moment we're free to decide what we want to be, because while we're born once into the objective world, we're born infinitely in the subjective world. Just like the All-Black team is eternal but the player's ego is ephemeral, our body dies, but we are an endless universe. Yes, we are alone, but we are also, simultaneously, everything, inextricably bound forever.

CHAPTER THIRTY-EIGHT

LIVING CONSCIOUSLY WITH 'i AM'

ECAUSE THEY'RE WORLD CLASS AND STRIVE FOR EXCELLENCE IN ALL
they do, I'll use team All Black to illustrate i Am consciousness
again. Naturally, the players' identities or egos are associated
strongly with their profession, specifically with the team bringing their
fame and fortune, however humble they may be. They build their ego
foundation around a strongly differentiated idea for achieving, at all
costs, a narrow set of well-defined objectives, which is why they often
cannot live up to the public's view of them as role models. Broader
social goals, while a nice addition, are unnecessary to achieve game-day
success.

The All Black captain Richie McCaw recently retired after a long,
celebrated career. He's replaced rugby with flying, piloting commercial
helicopters for a living, a role even the most confident would hesitate to
attempt as a second career. Even as an All Black, he found time for his
leisure-time passion of flying gliders in the alpine area of NZ's rugged
and beautiful South Island. He had already developed skills and a strong
i AM relationship with flying, so it was a logical post-sport career choice
which allowed him to transition seamlessly from i AM an All Black to i
AM a pilot. He took on a new and relevant i AM that is congruent with
his abilities and skills, giving him a sense of value and achievement.
Since retiring, he has married and had a child, taking on the i AM
married and i AM dad roles. He didn't just wake up one day surprised
to find he was a helicopter pilot with a wife and a child; he thought this
into his reality.

These three new rabbit holes will consume him for as long as he remains in love with the objective concept that I am a pilot, I am married and I'm a dad. They will stay steadfast in his objective life while he continues to feed these thoughts by giving them his dominant attention. What started as a mental thought, invisible to the outside world, through conscious desire and repetition of the thought is now woven into an unbreakable steel cable. This is the only way to develop the neurons that build the objective world called our reality. For most of us, it happens through the unconscious programming, developing a network of primary pathways, giving us an adaptive or maladaptive start to our life as creators. Through repetition of the thought, these first plastic pathways or neuron bundles become roadways then motorways, becoming part of our unconscious autonomic nervous system, becoming second nature or our habits. At this point we are a prisoner to our unconscious past and makes changing these habits seem all but impossible.

The term 'reborn' is an appropriate description of that moment when, through a flash of inspiration, we recognise the cable binding us to our response to the moment. Like the cable binding the circus elephant, it can be instantly severed. All it takes is a persistent return to conscious thought. My personal and enduring 'that i am' (identity) established in childhood died the moment I recognised that our essential nature is only a small part of what it is to be human. Like all objective life, survival of the species is reliant on strong gene selection. But unlike other life, at birth humans are a blank canvas that must be taught essential survival skills or perish. This training fails to teach us that the same process used to fill us with essential skills is the key to unlocking the door to our full potential. Our lack of pre-programmed, guiding instincts is the clue to the existence of our infinitely programmable ability to create—the human equivalent of the 80% of the iceberg, hidden beneath the water's surface.

We begin life believing our body defines us—two sticks for arms, two more for legs and a head—then after experiencing self-inflicted suffering, we become seekers, who after much reflection and self-assessment are opened up to another world. A world where we realise that we are not our bodies; they are simply convenient containers for focusing, through love, thoughts of the universe into objective reality. We create whatever we desire using an endless supply of plasticine in every moment within the abundant, loving universe that is us. We are whatever our attention falls and dwells on, because i Am THAT, i AM. *Where 'THAT' is the object of your attention and will be manifested in direct correlation to your understanding of THAT. In other words, it's all semantics.*

God is the source; the source rewards us; i AM the source. How do I travel? As a breathing beam of light.

'I Am' AFFIRMATIONS

I N 2011 I WAS CONCERNED I'D LOST MY MIND AFTER A REVELATION or 'light-bulb moment' in which I realised that I was living a second-hand life. Suddenly the thinking part of me seemed to be separate from my body. I could cast my mind anywhere all at once, free of the idea that I was Geoff, and all that conjured up, exposing a grand lie. I'd discovered that my limited mind was a subset of a super mind. Turned out the mind I was concerned at losing was my ego or limited mind, the small 'i' known as Geoff. Geoff is like the muddy water in a battered rock pool, a limited subset until it wears away the rock walls, allowing the captive water to re-join the superset or ocean. It's unlikely I'm the only one to have experienced this revelation. I would accept that I'd lost my grip on reality if there were no other documented instances of my experience. That wouldn't be surprising since plenty had tested me over the last fifteen years.

Fortunately, today we can literally search the entire knowledge base of man's history. I discovered many teachers spreading this philosophy of duality and ego construct. If I'd lost my marbles, at least I was in good company! Teachers included well-known psychologist Carl Jung, philosopher Guy Finley, spiritual author Byron Katie, and psychologist the late Dr Wayne Dyer. These teachers confirmed my new understanding. It became clear to me that suffering was a path to the greatest gift of all, the truth that we are everything and everything is us, that we are the disease and the cure. If there is a meaning to be found from life's challenges, then it's in the discovery that we are the answer to our suffering. We bring it on ourselves through the application of wrong thought when we suppose that events are loaded with personal meaning.

Although it was new to me, I doubted the semantics of i AM was a new concept. In the past, others must have described it and its relationship to objective creation. Through the Gutenberg project I discovered that Milton Scott wrote the book *I Am* in 1913. His book of i AM affirmations captures the semantics involved in creating a life that is a pure reflection of the thoughts we love. Scott presents the concept of I am that, i AM in the form of affirmation meditations. Since creation starts then flows within with every thought you decide to love and attend to until we objectify it in reality, reading affirmations can help unlock the door, so you can escape your own self-imposed prison. A copy of Milton Scotts book 'I AM' affirmations is available for download from my website https://www.soiamthat.com

I wrote this book for those who have lost hope and desperately need to find a way to awaken to the misinterpretations causing their suffering. We are never broken, defective or beyond hope. This is my best attempt to explain how we're conceived from the same stuff as the universe. We're born with all we need to prosper, eternally connected to the ether or God Mind, with access to all the knowledge and power that will ever be that will help us eventually, with persistence, conquer any challenge. By universal law, we all grow from our acorn into an oak tree, despite our interfering and doubting self-ego. We have no choice.

You are deluding yourself if any analysis, self or otherwise, concludes that you were somehow born defective or less than others. Faith will keep you safely on the path but knowing that whatever the mind can conceive and believe, it can achieve will deliver a life at peace with yourself and full of grace.

Believe! You are a self-designed, adaptable experience flowing from the universe, source, light or God in a buffet of choices made possible through the gift of free will. This dimension individually and collectively enables the whole beautiful, rich, eternal experience that is humanity.